THE GAY AND LESBIAN
LIBERATION
MOVEMENT

■ ■ ■

Revolutionary Thought/ Radical Movements

A book series edited by Roger S. Gottlieb

Other books in the series:

Marxism 1844–1990: Origins, Betrayal, Rebirth
Roger S. Gottlieb

Radical Ecology: The Search for a Livable World
Carolyn Merchant

Women in Movement: Feminism and Social Action
Sheila Rowbotham

THE GAY AND LESBIAN
LIBERATION
MOVEMENT
■ ■ ■
MARGARET CRUIKSHANK

Revolutionary thought/
Radical movements
Series Editor: Roger S. Gottlieb

First published in 1992 by

Routledge
an imprint of
Routledge, Chapman & Hall, Inc.
29 West 35 Street
New York, NY 10001

Published in Great Britain by

Routledge
11 New Fetter Lane
London EC4P 4EE

©1992 by Routledge, Chapman & Hall, Inc.

Printed in the United States of America on acid free paper.

Library of Congress Cataloging in Publication Data

Cruikshank, Margaret.
    The gay and lesbian liberation movement / by Margaret Cruikshank.
       p.   cm.—(Revolutionary thought/radical movements)
    Includes bibliographical references and index.
    ISBN 0-415-90647-4   ISBN 0-415-90648-2 (pbk.)
    1. Gay liberation movement—United States.   I. Title.
    II. Series.
    HQ76.8.U5C78   1992
    305.9'0664—dc20   92-8622
                                            CIP

British Library Cataloguing in Publication Data also available.

for Barbara

CONTENTS

SERIES EDITOR'S PREFACE

This book, like its companions in the *Revolutionary Thought/Radical Movements* series, challenges contemporary society and civilization.

Perhaps the heart of this challenge is a deeply felt anguish and outrage over the sheer magnitude of human suffering—along with the terrible frustration of knowing that much of this suffering could be avoided. Radicals refuse to blame homelessness and starvation, the rape of women and abuse of children, the theft of labor and land, hope and self-respect on divine Providence or unchangeable human nature. Rather, they believe that much of it comes from injustice, exploitation, violence, and organized cruelty that can be eradicated. If we drastically alter our social arrangements in the direction of equality, justice, and human fulfillment, the brutal realities of the present can give way to vastly increased material security, social harmony, and self-realization.

Philanthropists and political reformers share radicals' concern for human suffering. But unlike reformers and philanthropists, radicals and revolutionaries address whole *systems* of injustice. In these systems, particular groups are humiliated, denied rights, subject to unjust control. The few become rich while the many suffer from poverty or economic insecurity. The select get privileges while millions learn submission or humiliation. We are conditioned to false needs for endless consumption while nature is poisoned. The powers-that-be profit from these systems, "common sense" enshrines them as necessary, and ideological mystification obscures their origin and nature by blaming the victims. Responses to people's pain, if they are to be truly and lastingly effective, must be aimed *at the system:* at capitalism, sexism, racism, imperialism, homophobia, the bureaucratic state, and the domination of nature.

Governments and economies, families and culture, science and individual psychology—all are shaped by these systems of domination and exclusion. That is why the radical ideal goes beyond piecemeal improvements to a Utopian vision; and tries to realize that vision in everyday struggles for a fair distribution of power, human dignity, and a livable environment. Revolutionaries have argued that a modern economy can be democratically controlled and oriented to human needs rather than profit; can do without vast differences of wealth and power; and can preserve rather than destroy the earth. Radicals claim that in a true 'democracy' ordinary men and women would help shape the basic conditions which affect their lives: not just by an occasional trip to the ballot box, but by active involvement in decisions about political and economic life.

How will these sweeping changes take place? Revolutionaries have offered many answers—from large political parties to angry uprisings, from decentralized groups based in consciousness-raising to international organizations. In any case, however, the conception of radicalism which informs the series stipulates that authentic revolutionary change requires the self-action of sizable groups of people, not the self-promotion of a self-proclaimed revolutionary "elite." The only way to prevent the betrayal of the revolution by a privileged bureaucracy is to base radical politics on free discussion, mutual respect, and collective empowerment *from the beginning*. This is one of the clearest and most painful lessons from the history of communism.

Of course much of this sounds good on paper. Yet it may be—as many have claimed—that radical visions are really unrealistic fantasies. However, if we abandon these visions we also abandon human life to its current misery, with little to hope for but token reforms. Radicals reject this essentially cynical "realism," opting for a continuing faith in the human capacity for a fundamentally different and profoundly liberating form of life.

In fact, people have always dreamed of a better world. Yet it is only since the late eighteenth century that organized groups developed a systematic theoretical critique of social life; and tried to embody that critique in mass political movements designed to overthrow the existing order of economic ownership and political control. American revolutionaries claimed that "All men are endowed with certain inalienable rights." The French revolution demanded "liberty, equality, fraternity."

Since then Marxist, socialist, feminist, national liberation, civil rights, gay and lesbian liberation, and ecology movements have been born. Each movement utilized some of the accomplishments of its predecessors, criticized the past for its limitations, and broke new ground. *Revolutionary Thought/Radical Movements* will focus on the theory and practice, successes and failures, of these movements.

While the series' authors are part of the radical tradition, we are painfully aware that this tradition has committed grave errors and at times failed completely. The communism of the Eastern bloc, while maintaining certain valuable social welfare programs, combined economic inefficiency, brutal tyranny, and ecological devastation. Many of us who took to the streets in the 1960s joined arrogance with idealism, self-indulgence with utopian hopes. Much of contemporary radical or socialist feminism fails to reach beyond a circle of the already converted.

These and other failures of radicalism are certainly apparent today. Daily headlines trumpet the collapse of the Eastern bloc, the US victory in the Cold War, the eternal superiority of capitalism and free markets, and the transformation of yesterday's radicals into today's yuppies. Governments of countries that had called themselves "socialist" or "communist" (however much they were distorting the meaning of these terms) trip over each other rushing west for foreign corporate investment and economic advice.

But there are also *successes,* ways in which radicals have changed social life for the better. Though these achievements have been partial reforms rather than sweeping revolutions, many of the basic freedoms, rights, and material advantages of modern life were fought for by people called radicals, dangerous revolutionaries, or anti-American:

- restrictions on the exploitation of workers, from the eight-hour day to the right to unionize;
- resistance to cultural imperialism and racial discrimination;
- a host of government programs, from unemployment insurance to social security, from the Environmental Protection Agency to fair housing laws;
- restrictions on opportunistic and destructive American foreign policy in Vietnam, El Salvador, Nicaragua, and other nations.

While radicals have not been alone in seeking these goals, they have often led the fight. Perhaps more important, they have offered a theoretical analysis which shows the *connections* between problems which may appear to be separate. They have argued that the sexist treatment of women and ecological devastation may have the same root. They have shown the links between the private control of wealth and an expansionist foreign policy. They have analyzed the family, the factory, the army, and the government as parts of the same system of domination.

Along with both the concrete successes and the global vision, radicals have—sadly—too often reproduced the ideas and relationships they sought to destroy. Marxists demanded an end to unjust society— yet formed authoritarian organizations where dissent was repressed. Radical feminists proclaimed "sisterhood is powerful," but often ignored Black women or poor women. At times ecologists, in trying to save nature, have been disrespectful if human beings.

Some of the worst failures came, in short, not from being radical, but from *not being radical enough:* not inclusive enough, not honest enough, not willing to examine how radical political programs and group behavior reproduced an oppressive, unjust society. Awareness of these failures reminds us that revolutionary thought cannot limit itself to critique of the larger society, but also requires self-criticism. While this process can degenerate into petty sectarian hostilities, it also shows that authentic radicalism is not a dead graven image, but a living quest to learn from the past and change the future. In the attempt to create solidarity and community among the oppressed, for instance, radicals have recently spent much effort trying to address and appreciate fundamental differences in social experience—between black and

white workers, men and women, temporarily able-bodied and disabled, gay/lesbian and straight. In this effort, radicals have wrestled
with the paradox that persons may simultaneously be victims of one
system of domination and agents of another one.

The books in this series are part of this radical quest for revolutionary change and continued self-examination. In an era of the sudden fall
of totalitarian communism and the frightening rise in the federal deficit,
of the possibility of a peace dividend and the specter of the death of
nature—these discussions of revolutionary thought and radical movements are needed more than ever before.★

Roger S. Gottlieb

★Thanks for editorial suggestions to Bland Addison, Mario Moussa,
Miriam Greenspan, Tom Shannon and John Trimbur.

PREFACE

This book is not primarily a history of the gay and lesbian liberation movement, although it contains historical sketches and examples. Rather, it is a personal interpretation of the movement by a writer who has participated in it since 1974. My view of gay and lesbian liberation is naturally shaped by who I am—a white, middle-class woman who has spent most of her working life as an academic. Since 1978, I have observed the movement from San Francisco, which many regard as its center in the United States. I learned a great deal about gay people and organizations by working as resources director for a short-lived grassroots project, the Gay National Educational Switchboard, which provided a toll-free information line. I bring a feminist perspective to the study of gay and lesbian liberation. The movement I describe may be viewed quite differently by gay men, by gay people of color, by the old, by young activists, by people with AIDS. No single account of a complex movement can do justice to it. My aim in this book has been to make gay and lesbian liberation understandable to students who have no previous knowledge of it. I hope many of them will finish this book wanting to know more about one of the major movements of the 1990s.

ACKNOWLEDGEMENTS

I thank Firebrand Books for permission to reprint several stanzas from Pat Parker's poem "Where Will You Be" from her collection *Movement in Black,* published by Diana Press in 1978 and reissued by Firebrand Books in 1990.

I thank all of the writers whose books and articles I cite in the following pages.

Devoted friends of many years, Mary Harlow Segal and Barbara Gherty Moore, cheered me on. My sister Cathy Cruikshank shared with me her astute observations about lesbian culture. Writing exchanges with Nancy Manahan and Mab Maher influenced my work.

For helping me revise several passages and loaning me the reader she prepared for her course "Anthropology of Homosexualities" at Sonoma State, I thank Mildred Dickemann. Don Allen of Grey Fox Press, publisher of two of my lesbian anthologies, has taught me much about gay editing. My colleagues at City College, Jack Collins, head of the gay and lesbian studies department, has long supported my work with warmth and wit. My dear friend Matile Rothschild tracked down articles for me, found materials in her files, read parts of the manuscript, and discussed many issues with me as we walked around Stow Lake in Golden Gate Park. Above all, I thank my partner, Barbara Giles, for editorial suggestions and for hours of word processing. Her constant encouragement and loving regard sustained me while I wrote this book.

1

INTRODUCTION

When a formerly taboo subject becomes so openly discussed that a college text can be written about it, some great change in attitudes has evidently occurred. The existence of this book is a sign of social change. A decade ago, most college students would not have been assigned a text on homosexuality, nor would the subject have come up in their classes. They would not have seen the relevance of homosexuality to anything else they were learning. Homosexuality was either shrouded in silence or mentioned briefly as a perversion, an illness, a threat to society, or simply as an embarrassment; reading books or articles about the subject would have made most students uncomfortable. Perhaps they had never spoken to an openly gay person or come across any representation of homosexuality in art, literature, or film. Certainly none of their high school or college teachers would have mentioned that they were gay. Today, because of the growth of gay liberation and because of AIDS, students are more likely than their counterparts a decade ago to understand that gay rights is a major social and political movement and some of them will expect to read about it in college courses.

Students who have studied radical movements such as Marxism and feminism or read about environmentalism and animal rights may wonder how gay and lesbian liberation can be considered a political movement. Can the claim to a sexual identity be the basis of a liberation movement? Isn't sex a private matter, outside the sphere of politics? Why would anyone want to be known as queer? Wouldn't gay people be better off if they stayed in the closet (concealed their identities)? Since radical social change means "from the roots" or foundations of society and since gay liberation demands a fundamental rethinking of sex, sexuality, sex roles, gender, the regulation of sex, and the constitutional guarantee of the right to "life, liberty, and the pursuit of happiness," gay and lesbian liberation is a radical social movement, even though it may sometimes present itself as reformist.

Sexual practices clearly are a private matter; they become politicized when groups or institutions try to stamp them out. If gay people claimed only the right to perform certain sexual acts, however, they would not have been able to create a movement. Their claim rests on sexual identity, which is a sufficient basis for a movement because: (1) the sexual identity in question is a minority identity, condemned or discouraged by the dominant heterosexual majority; and (2) great numbers of individuals are involved in the process of coming out, which means declaring their homosexuality to themselves, first of all, to their family, friends, and co-workers; and finally, when they march and demonstrate, to everyone who sees them.

People did not want to be identified as homosexual before the 1970s because of the severe punishments attendant upon self-disclosure. Many gay people today hide their sexual orientation to avoid being penalized for it, but many others are able to reveal who they are because they are no longer alone. Group solidarity lets them risk being different from the majority. Closeted gays pay a psychological price for passing (pretending to be heterosexual), a price that has become too high for hundreds of thousands of gay men and lesbians in the 1990s. To be fully human, fully themselves, they need to declare themselves to family and friends in order to become full participants in American life.

"Queer" was always a label of scorn and contempt until lesbians and gay men reclaimed it, like Black people reappropriating "nigger" for use among themselves. When a despised minority becomes strong enough to bend language to its own uses, some of the stigma formerly attached to it falls away. Rather than accept the designation "homosexual," with its old, negative connotations, the minority chose their own term, "gay." When did homosexuals become gay? This book attempts to explain the process from several different angles. Briefly, homosexuals became gay when they rejected the notion that they were sick or sinful, claimed equality with heterosexuals, banded together to protest second-class citizenship, created a subculture, and came out in large numbers. Pride followed visibility: for lesbians and gay men, shame and invisibility are inseparable.

Although revolutionary movements do not usually have a single spark, most gays believe that June 27, 1969 is the date marking their passage from homosexual to gay. When police raided a Greenwich village bar, the Stonewall Inn, bar patrons responded with a riot lasting through the weekend. Stonewall unleashed the fury of those no longer willing to be victims. Soon afterwards, New York City lesbians and gay men founded the Gay Liberation Front, and the idea quickly spread to other cities. "Gay Power" was born. Stonewall would not have had such an electrifying effect, however, if pioneering advocates of equal rights for homosexuals had not worked from 1950 to 1969 to lay the groundwork for a broader movement.

In this book, "gay" is used to signify homosexuals and homosexual life after Stonewall; it is a political term. "Homosexual" is a broad descriptive term for feelings and behavior and for people who are attracted to their own sex. Even though it is sometimes used interchangeably with gay, the meanings are distinct. The description "gay" applies to either women or men but most female homosexuals prefer to call themselves lesbians. "Gays" as a plural term includes both sexes. Because popular usage of "gay" sometimes conflates the term with "gay man," I often choose "gay *and* lesbian" to emphasize the co-sexual nature of this liberation movement. Sometimes, though, for brevity I simply say "gay" to designate both sexes.

The ambiguities of language here reflect an important fact about the gay and lesbian liberation movement: it has been male-dominated. Lesbians have participated since the beginnings but they have often had the secondary role that characterizes their position in mainstream society. This imbalance has deep cultural and historical roots and it points to the dilemma lesbians face when they identify with gay and lesbian liberation. Some lesbians in fact believe that lesbianism cannot be understood alongside of male homosexuality because the two are entirely different phenomena, partly because women are oppressed and men are part of the dominant culture. Thus the very notion of gay and lesbian liberation can be challenged. On the other hand, excluding women from an analysis of gay liberation would create a false impression of the movement. Though sometimes uneasily aligned, lesbians and gay men share common goals and interests as well as common enemies. Because lesbian liberation is rooted in both the women's movement and the gay movement, lesbian issues must be examined from both perspectives. Ideally, a student who wishes to understand lesbianism would study both the women's movement and the gay rights movement. While this text considers only the latter, the significance of women's liberation is implied throughout and sometimes explicitly stated.

Homosexuality has an ancient history, extending back to the earliest historical records and including most cultures for which we have information. The fragments of Sappho's songs from Greece in the sixth century B.C., for example, describe sexual love between women, and sex between men is depicted on Grecian urns. Plato's *Symposium* discusses homosexual love, a theme that appears also in ancient Chinese literature. If the behavior has been well established for centuries, however, the meaning of the behavior is less certain. The categories of homosexual and heterosexual, first appearing in the late nineteenth century, are a modern interpretation. These two concepts would not have been meaningful to Sappho or Plato because, for them, particular sexual practices did not place a person into a special category. Acts were homosexual; people were not.

Thus homosexual identity, or the condition of being homosexual, is distinct from the phenomenon of same-sex behavior. In an atmosphere such as a prison, a boarding school, or a military barracks where sexes are segregated, people may engage in homosexual acts, but the practice does not necessarily give them a homosexual identity. That comes from an emotional history of deep, powerful attractions to people of the same sex and from a sense that the feelings set them apart.

The term "homosexual," first coined in 1869 by K. M. Kertbeny, a translator who opposed German sodomy laws, but not popularized until the 1880s, was adopted by people who wanted to make sense of their own experiences, which were not adequately explained by labeling them unnatural or immoral. A spirit of scientific inquiry motivated those who practiced "Greek love" to define feelings and acts which were not understood. Just as scientists challenged religion on the origins of life and the age of the earth, lovers of their own sex countered the idea that they were sinful or criminal. Soon people who had only a scientific and not a personal interest in the subject began to publish articles about it. Early sexologists believed, for example, that homosexuals could be considered members of a third sex, an intermediate sex. Another explanation was that men who desired men had women's souls inside their male bodies, and women who desired women had men's souls within their female bodies. They were called "inverts," which literally means inside out or upside down or to turn inward. These ideas seem bizarre to modern lesbians and gay men because their sexual orientation seems natural to them, not a condition requiring an explanation. It simply is.

A third late nineteenth-century way of accounting for homosexuality was to say that everyone has both masculine and feminine traits and people in whom masculine and feminine combine, that is, androgynous people, are often homosexual. This idea is congenial to many gay men and lesbians today: the men consider themselves thoroughly manly and at the same time value the sensitivity and emotional life stereotypically associated with women, while the lesbians affirm their womanhood as they take on some of the characteristics and roles traditionally reserved for men, such as physical strength, power, and autonomy. From the viewpoint of the 1990s, sexual desire for a person of the same sex is unrelated to one's physical appearance or feelings of masculinity or femininity. It is a variant form of sexual expression, as characteristically human as left-handedness.

The evolution of Victorian understanding of homosexuality can be traced through the work of Richard von Krafft-Ebing, a German psychiatrist; Havelock Ellis, an English sexologist; and Edward Carpenter, an English socialist, vegetarian, and supporter of women's rights. In 1876, Krafft-Ebing defined homosexuality as "an absence of normal sexual feeling, with compensatory attraction to members of the same sex." Although he considered it abnormal, he did not believe it should be punished by the state. Ellis took a bolder stance. His book, *Sexual Inversion,* published in 1897, was "the first book in English to treat homosexuality as neither a disease nor a crime." Ellis considered it inborn and unmodifiable. His view of lesbianism was very negative, however. Because his plea for tolerance was shocking at the time, his bookseller was prosecuted. Carpenter, who lived openly as a homosexual, went one step further by imagining a positive identity for homosexual men. The gentle male who experienced "homogenic love" was an intermediate type between man and woman. Carpenter believed that homosexuals would be in the vanguard of a movement to transform society "by substituting the bond of personal affection and compassion for the monetary, legal and other external ties which now control and confine society."[1]

The step from Carpenter to gay liberation is a short one. The Victorian roots of this movement may surprise students who associate the period only with sexual repression and prudery. It was also a time when many modern ideas like feminism and animal rights first appeared. One of the ways Victorian women who won the freedom to become educated and work outside the home expressed their psychological freedom was to form passionate emotional and sexual bonds with other women, but this aspect of women's history was not known until feminist scholars began reinterpreting the Victorian period in the 1970s and 1980s.[2]

More influential than either Ellis or Carpenter was the founder of psychoanalysis, Sigmund Freud. He speculated that homosexuality involved a narcissistic search for a love that symbolizes the self, a castration fear for men and penis envy for women. He did not regard it as a sickness, however, or as a condition that could be changed, and thus he opposed criminal punishments for homosexuality. Freud believed that the natural sexual feelings of children are both homosexual and heterosexual and that social conditioning usefully represses both bisexuality and homosexuality. Thus a homosexual person is arrested in his or her development. Followers of Freud, especially in the United States, interpreted this to mean that homosexuals are perpetually adolescents, immature, blocked in some way, incapable of leading normal lives. Abandoning Freud's tolerant views, his disciples advocated treatment for homosexuality. Their influence caused much harm to homosexuals in the twentieth century by encouraging a popular belief that homosexuality is an illness. On the other hand, gay rights activists found in the idea of children's undifferentiated sexual drives some evidence for their belief that heterosexuality is socially rather than biologically determined. In addition, the central importance Freud gave to sex aided later reformers, whether their cause was women's liberation, gay and lesbian rights, contraception, or sex education.

The late nineteenth-century sexologists' interpretations of homosexuality and the theory of arrested development, misguided though they now seem, at least succeeded in taking homosexuality out of the realm of moral judgment. Whatever the origins of their condition, homosexuals clearly could not be held responsible for it and thus condemnations of them as sinful or immoral were pointless.

As doctors and psychiatrists took on much of the power to tell right from wrong formerly reserved for religious leaders, the status of homosexuals changed from sinful to sick. When regarded as sinners, they were selectively persecuted by churches. As allegedly sick, they were subject to more scrutiny and social control, and they were still viewed as lesser beings. Thus the decline of religion and the rise of modern science, progressive developments in general, were not beneficial to homosexuals, because one bias replaced another. The sickness theory required an assumption that the number of people who are exclusively homosexual is very small, an assumption that was emphatically contradicted in the 1970s. Furthermore, the psychiatric concept of homosexuality does not rest upon scientific studies but ultimately derives from Christian ascetism (*Encyclopedia of Homosexuality* 1990: 793). It is likely that if homosexuality had not been criminalized, as a result of Christian influences upon law, psychiatrists would have had no reason to focus on it.

Fortunately, some homosexuals were not much influenced by psychiatric dogmas, even before they began to think of themselves as belonging to a minority group. At a time when Blacks were considered promiscuous, mentally inferior figures of fun, Blacks knew better. And some women never accepted sexist stereotypes of themselves, in the days before either word became common. So, too, some homosexuals escaped self-loathing and a desire to convert to heterosexuality. They were able to do this even though the few images they found in literature portrayed them as doomed or damned—D. H. Lawrence's novellas *The Fox* and *The Prussian Officer,* for example. Their own experience told them that they were neither sick nor stopped in their development. They found others who agreed with them; they lived quietly. For the first six decades of the twentieth century, many American families had a son, daughter, aunt, uncle or cousin who never married, who moved to a distant city, about whose life little was known. These thousands of émigrés were homosexuals. Because they believed in their right to love as they wished, they were the forerunners of gay liberation.

Thus the small band of 1960s' rebels who first chanted "gay power" and wrote those slogans on walls and on banners represented far more than a new offshoot of leftist activism; they represented a constituency that had been building for a long time.

Even though some homosexuals did not regard themselves as radicals, they agreed with the demands of gay and lesbian liberation, which were:

(1) an end to all forms of social control of homosexuals;
(2) civil rights legislation to prevent housing and job discrimination;
(3) repeal of sodomy laws;
(4) acceptance of lesbian and gay relationships;
(5) accurate portrayal in the mass media.

For some women and men who took on the name "gay" in the 1970s, the right to be left alone was sufficient. For many others, radical social change was a precondition to freedom and self-expression. Tolerance was a first step, but tolerance was not enough. Lesbians and gay men wanted to be recognized as equal to heterosexuals in their sexuality, creativity, and social usefulness.

Why was a political agenda necessary? Persecution of homosexuals in the McCarthy era of the early 1950s showed how vulnerable they were to attack, and the political movements of the sixties provided models of organized protest. Many homosexuals who were later to identify as gay played active roles in civil rights, the anti-war movement, and women's liberation before they took up the cause of gay rights. In the other movements, they had usually felt compelled to conceal their identities. This was expedient and prudent when no alternative could be imagined, but it kept the heterosexual majority ignorant of the extent of homosexuality and helped perpetuate myths of its sinfulness and sickness. Homosexuality among the Greeks could be admitted because it happened too long ago to be threatening. If Shakespeare's love sonnets were written to a man, scholars could bend the evidence to protect his reputation. If King James I of England kept his male lovers at court, that could be overlooked and he could be remembered for the King James Bible. Leonardo da Vinci and Michelangelo? They were too famous and too long dead for their reputations to be assailed by rumors of homosexual liaisons. Tchaikovsky and Leonard Bernstein? Thoreau and Melville? W. H. Auden and Dag Hammarskjöld? None of these figures became publicly identified with homosexuality, in the way Oscar Wilde had been in the 1890s. Even though Walt Whitman wrote explicitly erotic love poetry about men, especially in his 'Calamus' poems, in which the calamus plant is a phallic symbol, his homosexuality was ignored. Virginia Woolf's passionate love for women was alluded to but neither understood nor explained by her nephew and biographer Quentin Bell.

A political agenda was also necessary because of homophobia. Gay people coined that term to mean the irrational dread or hatred of homosexuals or homosexuality. Like racism, homophobia pervades American life. Because it is widespread, deeply rooted, and apparently ineradicable, gay and lesbian liberation must be a radical ("going to the roots") force to counteract it. The movement is radical not only negatively, in response to opposition, but positively as well, for it challenges heterosexual domination.

Why are lesbians and gay men hated? They speculate that the reasons include:

- sexual anxiety in puritanical America
- a need for scapegoats in times of rapid social change
- fear of the unknown
- new visibility and perceived power of homosexuals
- perceived threat to the nuclear family
- AIDS

Recognizing homophobia is crucial to understanding gay liberation. Like racism, it is more damaging as a disease of institutions than as an individual's failing. Three institutions characterized by homophobia are the military, fundamentalist religion and Roman Catholicism.

The relationship between the military and homosexuality is an ancient one. Athens and Sparta had a tradition of warrior-lovers, as did the samurai of Japan. The bond between the medieval knight and his squire was sometimes a sexual one. Paul Fussell describes the homoerotic feelings of British soldiers who fought in World War I in his book *The Great War and Modern Memory*, and a more recently published study, Allan Berube's *Coming out under Fire* records the lives of American lesbians and gay men who served in World War II. Needed for the war effort, they were later thrown out of the military with discharges that often kept them from obtaining good civilian jobs. Before the war, the policy of the military had been to sentence men to five to twelve years of hard labor for a single act of sodomy. But during the war, psychiatrists, who considered homosexuals sick but not deserving of punishment, argued for discharge instead of imprisonment. The effect of this apparently humane shift in policy, however, was to give the military a new apparatus for persecuting homosexuals, the discharge system.[3]

Today, military policy is still based on homophobia. According to the Defense Department, "the presence in the military of persons who engage in homosexual conduct seriously impairs the accomplishment of the military mission" (*New York Times,* 19 February 1990: A8). A *San Francisco Examiner* editorial rejecting this view as outmoded asked the Supreme Court to challenge the Pentagon (5 February 1991: A12).

Oddly, the same form of love thought to strengthen armies in the past is now condemned as weakening them, at least by the military in the United States. Although based on prejudice rather than reason, the military interdiction has a certain logic, if one considers that homosexual lovers might be less easily bent to military discipline than men and women who are emotionally more distant from one another and that male homosexuals might be unwilling to kill other men in combat. This was the attitude of Christopher Isherwood in World War II. Having lived in Berlin before the war with a male lover who was German, he did not wish to kill any German soldiers.

Nevertheless, the military ban on homosexuals is blatant discrimination, as a 1988 Pentagon report, "Nonconforming Sexual Orientations and Military Suitability," by University of California Santa Cruz criminology professor Theodore Sarbin, tacitly admits. The fear that homosexuals pose a security risk is unjustifiable, according to a 1957 Pentagon study cited by Sarbin, and no new data since then have challenged this conclusion (*Bay Area Reporter,* 2 November 1989). Thus, official military policy has been discredited for more than thirty years, a fact which has not restrained its anti-gay harassment.

In 1988, after the Marine Corps investigated lesbians at Parris Island in South Carolina, three women were court-martialed and fourteen received administrative discharges. In 1989, the Navy discharged a number of lesbians stationed on ships. In 1990, an extensive investigation of homosexuality was conducted at Carswell Airforce base in Fort Worth. The strategy of the military, according to gay activist Frank Kameny, was to threaten service members with harsh treatment if they refused to name other gays (*Washington Blade,* 5 January 1990). The military became even more zealously homophobic in the spring of 1990 when it began trying to force expelled service people to pay for the cost of their training, even those who would have stayed in the service if they had been allowed to do so. This policy forces victims of discrimination to pay the group that discriminates against them.

The Parris Island investigation was a virtual witch hunt. In 1988, 10 percent of the 120 women drill instructors there were discharged or imprisoned for homosexual behavior. Many were hounded and threatened. One was interrogated in the presence of her estranged husband and threatened with the loss of her 6-month-old child if she did not name lesbian Marines. The case of Corporal Barbara Baum was much worse. She was sentenced to a year in jail for sexual acts with another woman Marine. After five months she was released, but her discharge stripped her of her rank. Military attorneys acknowledged that she did not get a fair trial because a judge made anti-gay remarks in public (*Washington Blade,* 5 January 1990).

Statistics about members persecuted and length of prison stays cannot adequately convey an impression of the cruelty and injustice perpetrated by the military. The author of a memoir titled "Coming out in the Navy" describes harrowing experiences. Barracks sweeps were common. A suspected lesbian would have to allow the Naval Investigative Service to search her belongings for photos, letters, and poems. If she refused to talk she was put under protective custody while the military took a long time assigning her legal counsel. She would be grilled by two officers in a small room:

> *The offending sailor would be asked to name the other lesbians in her barracks. If she refused, the investigating officers would threaten to call her family and inform them that their daughter was a lesbian. This was illegal, but frightened eighteen-year-old women do not have a good grasp of military law. Finally the men would threaten dishonorable discharge if their charge refused to sign a confessional form—in triplicate, of course. This also was underhanded: Military law required the statements of two or more witnesses who had seen the person*

interacting sexually with a partner, and this meant genitally. Any woman could explain hand-holding or kissing. So with no feet to stand on but their ability to put the fear of god and family into young dykes, NIS agents were powerful operatives. They followed us to bars where they took pictures of us dancing and drinking. Going into a gay bar was not evidence enough to bust a woman, but it meant her name would be entered on the official list of possible lesbians.[4]

In another respect as well, the present military policy is worthy of a totalitarian state: lesbians and gay men are punished not only for sexual acts but simply for *saying* they are gay. Thus the military attacks their being. In 1976, the Army discharged Miriam Ben-Shalom when her gay rights work in Milwaukee was discovered. Her thirteen-year legal battle with the Army ended in February 1990 when the Supreme Court refused to hear her case. Her First Amendment rights were clearly violated, as a federal court ruled in 1980. Although she acknowledges that many Jews claim homosexuality is an abomination, she believes that her gay rights activism is part of the Jewish tradition of seeking social justice (*Northern California Jewish Bulletin,* 2 June 1989: 2).

Aside from the political and moral issues in these discrimination cases, there is an economic issue—the great waste of taxpayers' money by the military. Citizens who worry about $750 screwdrivers and $250 ashtrays should also worry about the cost of spying, interrogation, court-martials, and protracted litigation. Expelled Midshipman Joseph Steffan's Navy training cost $110,000. He estimates that the cost of discharging several thousand gay people a year from the military, 2,500 in the Navy alone, runs into hundreds of millions of dollars (*New York Times,* 9 September 1988). According to the National Gay and Lesbian Task Force, between 1986 and 1988 ten times as many women as men were accused of homosexuality and discharged, an example of sexism compounding homophobia.

The absurdity of the military threat of homosexuals was succinctly expressed by Leonard Matlovich, a Vietnam veteran who said "They gave me a Purple Heart for killing two men and a dishonorable discharge for loving one." Eventually the military will be forced to end its discrimination against homosexuals, just as it was forced to end racial segregation. The question is, how many more lives will be damaged and careers disrupted by its current repressive policies.

The common link between military and religious persecution of homosexuals is authoritarianism. The military requires blind obedience to fashion efficient armies, and unquestioning obedience to authority is also expected of fundamentalists and Catholics. The military and the anti-gay religions base their objections to homosexuality on their *authority* to condemn, not upon evidence. That is why their condemnations persisted long after psychiatrists abandoned their belief that homosexuals are abnormal. Although the mental health profession has not become entirely free of oppressive attitudes towards gays in the years since 1974, when the pejorative label "disorder" was dropped, psychiatrists and psychologists at least examined the available evidence and changed their minds.

Anti-gay sentiment among American fundamentalists and Roman Catholics in the 1990s rises from a centuries-old tradition of persecution and intolerance. After Christianity became the state religion of the Roman empire, homosexual acts were punished by death by the sword (*Encyclopedia of Homosexuality* 1990: 197). In the eleventh century, Sappho's poetry was officially condemned and burned. During the Inquisition the punishments were torture, banishment or imprisonment for life, hanging, and burning (*Encyclopedia of Homosexuality*: 602–5). Later the punishment was strangling. Men were victims more often than women, although some women executed for witchcraft were undoubtedly lesbians. A justification for capital punishment, popular in the Middle Ages, was that homosexual acts were murder because they threatened human survival (*Encyclopedia of Homosexuality*: 197). Sexual pleasure was not separated from procreation.

Today, lesbians and gay men have become a convenient target for fundamentalists at a time when their traditional enemies have lost their value as scapegoats. Catholics and Jews are more assimilated into mainstream American life than they were fifty years ago, and even communists are not very threatening any more. Women who had abortions were once condemned, but now most Americans favor legalized abortion. Fundamentalists need enemies whom they can convert to mythic figures of evil. Before Jerry Falwell's Moral Majority crusade ended in 1989, his radio broadcasts to millions of people denounced homosexuals as "brute beasts." It is unlikely that Falwell or his followers could seriously have maintained this view in the presence of real people who are gay. In this case, the myth was far more important than the reality. "Brute beasts" are not ordinary citizens who go to work or school, pay their taxes, visit friends, take vacations, or raise children. The notion that "gay is good" threatens the world view of fundamentalists, and they respond by attributing great powers of evil to those who seem to embody sexual pleasure. It is possible that preachers who denounce gays as "brute beasts" do not believe such inflammatory slogans themselves but use them to frighten followers into sending money to build their power base. Certainly the sex scandals at the end of the 1980s involving Jim Bakker and Jimmy Swaggert revealed a large gap between preaching and practice.

The Traditional Values Coalition of fundamentalist minister Lou Sheldon has a three-fold strategy: (1) deny that lesbians and gay men make up 10 or 15 percent of the population; say that they are only 1 percent; (2) tell them to stay in the closet or be cured; (3) promote Exodus International. This group uses "reparation therapy," a form of brainwashing, to "convert" homosexuals to heterosexuals (*Bay Area Reporter,* 22 February 1990). The co-founders of Exodus International have admitted that techniques such as isolation, indoctrination and guilt tripping cannot alter sexual orientation and that "reparation therapy" is a fraud, but it will probably continue to appeal to fundamentalists. If homosexuals really were only 1 percent of the population they could be safely ignored. The fervor of anti-gay fundamentalists belies the 1 percent claim.

Anita Bryant used fundamentalist church networks to organize an anti-gay crusade in Dade County, Florida, in 1977. Called "Save Our Children," Bryant's campaign forced repeal of an ordinance prohibiting discrimination based on sexual orientation. Similar actions caused repeal of gay rights in St. Paul and Eugene, but Seattle voters kept a comparable ordinance. The Oklahoma legislature, however, passed a law requiring the dismissal of lesbian and gay school teachers. Bryant and her followers successfully persuaded voters to equate anti-discrimination laws with child molesting, gay "recruiting," prostitution, threats to the family, and a national gay conspiracy (Adam 1987: 104). For fundamentalists as for Nazis, homosexuality symbolically represents "the modernity, the sexual freedom, and the dissolving underpinnings of traditional domesticity." Thus fundamentalists "displace their fear and anger of modern society upon lesbians and gay men" (Adam 1987: 111).

This analysis explains the fury of fundamentalists at homosexuals. In addition, anti-gay prejudice is fueled by threats to religious authority. As with abortion, homosexuality represents a symbolic struggle for the right to impose moral judgments on a secular society. If fundamentalist religion loses the battle against abortion and homosexuality, it will lose power and influence, just as it did in the nineteenth century when its version of creation, based on a literal interpretation of the Bible, was proven false by scientists. In the late twentieth century, religious notions of homosexuality are significant only because of the alliance between fundamentalists and right-wing politicians, an alliance which has the potential to transform bigotry into public policy. Fundamentalists and the elected officials who carry forward their agenda fear that if gay rights legislation is passed, eventually the law will not distinguish between traditional marriages and homosexual unions. The religious objections to homosexuality made by right-wing politicians such as Senator Jesse Helms and southern California Congressmen Robert Dornan and William Dannemeyer assume that Protestantism has the force of a state religion in America. In theory it does not, but in practice it does, if lesbians and gay men are discriminated against for essentially religious reasons.

Anti-gay prejudice is also common among Protestants who are not fundamentalists. In July 1990 two San Francisco congregations were suspended for five years from the Evangelical Lutheran Church in America for ordaining a gay man and a lesbian couple as assistant pastors. When Methodist minister Rosemary Denman was subjected to an ecclesiastical trial for her lesbianism in 1987, her counsel pointed out that gay men and lesbians are not allowed to marry. "I have blessed cats, dogs, and mobile homes," he said. "But I am not allowed to bless two Christians who love each other."[5]

The sheer irrationality of anti-gay condemnation is well expressed by this protest. To lesbians and gay men themselves, their condition is not more unusual or remarkable than the condition of being left-handed, an analogy mentioned above. In the 1940s and earlier, left-handed school children were forced to write with their right hands, and some homosexuals were given frontal lobotomies. The stigma against left-handedness was lifted more completely than the stigma against homosexuality. As normal human variant behaviors the two are parallel. But the left-handed analogy is flawed because a complex emotional and psychological phenomenon cannot adequately be compared to a physical trait. The meaning of left-handedness is probably much the same for a spear thrower in a simple society and a Wall Street stockbroker. The use of the left hand is automatic. But the meaning of homosexuality is entirely different for these men. For the hunter, it may be a ritual activity having no meaning outside of a group and having no power to set him apart from others. For the stockbroker, on the other hand, it may entail pressure from his family to get married or difficulty getting promoted. Homosexuality definitely sets the stockbroker apart from his co-workers, whether or not they are aware of his sexual preference. Meanings vary within a culture as well. The significance of lesbianism for two war widows in the 1940s who became life partners and lived almost exactly as they had before is different from the significance of lesbianism for a woman living on a lesbian land collective today or a lesbian who heads a gay community center. These distinctions are lost sight of when anti-gay prejudice lumps all homosexuals into a single category of sinner.

The need to condemn others often originates in self-condemnation, and an obvious parallel between fundamentalists and Catholics is that their religions encourage self-condemnation. Body loathing in general and fear of sexual expression in particular have been part of the Christian tradition. Thus the celebration of sex often associated with homosexuality or simply the approval of hedonism makes fundamentalists and many Catholics uneasy. Sexual exuberance looks like promiscuity to them and the idea that sexuality can be expressed in diverse ways seems threatening to the social order. People who are inventing their own lives, as gay people today must do because their coming out is a recent development, resist rules about how to live.

Some believe that the term "promiscuity" is simply a slur word to discredit whatever the speaker dislikes, while others, especially lesbian feminists, believe that, even though the charge of "promiscuity" typifies anti-gay rhetoric, the concept itself remains viable. In either case, in deciding what, if any, curbs on sexual expression are appropriate, gay men and lesbians look to themselves for answers rather than to authority figures.

At the time when heretics were burned at the stake, heresy and sodomy were linked; both threatened clerical domination. But Christianity has not always oppressed homosexuals. Exceptions are described in John Boswell's book *Christianity, Social Tolerance, and Homosexuality* (1980). Even though Christians no longer murder homosexuals, the spirit of intolerance remains strong. The homophobia of the Roman Catholic church is one of the best examples.

Catholics have been instrumental in defeating gay rights bills in many cities. In 1989, after the San Francisco Board of Supervisors passed domestic partners legislation, granting symbolic recognition of lesbian/gay relationships, the controversial measure was put on the ballot, and the Catholic Archdiocese hired a political consultant to defeat it (*San Francisco Chronicle*, 6 September 1989: A10). The old Christian idea that homosexuals deserve to die is perpetuated by the anti-condoms policy of the Church: condoms prevent the spread of AIDS. Because the Catholic Church in New York receives state funds for its AIDS hospitals but refuses to follow state guidelines on AIDS education (which stress the importance of condoms), it is being sued by the American Civil Liberties Union. The New York cardinal's attack on condoms has provoked dramatic demonstrations in front of St Patrick's Cathedral by hundreds of lesbians and gay men. Members of ACT UP (AIDS Coalition to Unleash Power) have disrupted services; others have stood during Mass in silent protest against the anti-gay politics of the Church. Polls have shown, however, that as many as 85 percent of American Catholics believe that condoms should be used to stop the spread of AIDS.

Nuns and priests who dissent from the official view that homosexuality is immoral are the modern-day heretics of the Church. After the publication of his book *The Church and the Homosexual* in 1976,[6] John

McNeill was forbidden to speak publicly about homosexuality. In 1985 he was expelled from the Jesuit order for refusing to obey an order to stop his ministry to gay people. Bill Dorn was fired from his job as a Newman chaplain at St Cloud State University in Minnesota after writing a column in the local Catholic paper in which he said that homosexuality is a healthy, normal life choice. He was later defrocked and excommunicated. Dorn believes the Catholic Church finds gay male sexuality threatening because it implies an abdication of male control over women (Miller 1989: 231). The same is true of abortion. Pat O'Donnell, a Dominican nun, was fired from her job at a Catholic retreat house after her autobiographical article appeared in *Lesbian Nuns: Breaking Silence.*[7]

So vigorously challenged had the Church position become by 1986 that the Vatican issued a formal attack on homosexuality, "Doctrinal Congregation's Letter to Bishops: The Pastoral Care of Homosexual Persons." Pastoral condemnation would have been a more accurate title because the document calls homosexuality "intrinsically disordered" and attacks civil rights legislation for gays. "No one has any conceivable right to protection for homosexual behavior," the Vatican letter asserts, adding that if gays press for their rights they should not be surprised if "irrational and violent reactions occur." Religious leaders who believe in the moral power of their teaching do not threaten violence to enforce it. Disregarded by many Catholics as obviously contradictory to the spirit of the gospel, the Vatican letter ended tolerance for the Catholic gay group Dignity, founded in 1972. It was no longer allowed to conduct Masses in Catholic churches. Dignity incurred the wrath of Rome by challenging the official Catholic teaching that homosexuals must remain celibate. This teaching is the moral equivalent of castration for men and clitoridectomy for women: it tells a class of people that they have no right to sexual pleasure. St Augustine's notion that the body is evil is a fifth-century superstition which lives on in Catholic doctrine, to the detriment not only of practicing Catholics but of all citizens whose freedoms are threatened or curtailed by the power of the Church.

The homophobia of Roman Catholicism is worse than the homophobia of fundamentalists because, in attacking lesbians and gay men, the Church is attacking its own people—many priests and nuns who have devoted their lives to its service. Because many heterosexual priests left the priesthood in the 1960s and 1970s to marry, the remaining priest population contains a large number of homosexuals. Estimates range from 20 to 40 percent, and in some seminaries and monasteries the number is probably closer to 60 percent, according to men who have left. The Vatican could expel all homosexual priests and lesbian nuns in the United States, but the dwindling supply of priests would make expulsion too risky.[8] Church officials have good reasons for covering up the deaths of priests and monks from AIDS: first, honesty about these deaths would call attention to homosexuality in the priesthood; second, honest reporting would reveal to Catholic congregations that not all priests are faithful to their vows of celibacy; and finally, if the true number of AIDS deaths among priests were known, the hypocrisy of the Church's condemnation of gay people would be more obvious.[9]

Homophobia can be harmful even when it is not the official policy of an institution such as the military, fundamentalist churches, or the Catholic Church. Many young Americans first encounter homophobia at school. Boys who are called sissies get beaten up more often than girls who are tomboys, but the epithet "dyke" hurled at an adolescent or pre-adolescent can be just as wounding as the label "faggot" or "queer." In fact, the last two terms are the most popular insults on school playgrounds all over America. Sometimes teens are taunted at school before they are aware of their own sexual orientation and some targets of abuse are girls and boys who grow up to be heterosexual. The pressure to conform, so strong in middle school and high school, can be intolerable for those who know or suspect they are different from their classmates. The suicide attempt rate is an estimated 30–40 percent among gay boys and 20 percent among young lesbians.[10] A federal report stating that 30 percent or more of *all* youth suicides in the United States are gay was denounced by right-wing congressmen and disavowed by Health and Human Services secretary Louis Sullivan (*San Francisco Sentinel*, 2 November 1989). As with the 1957 Department of Defense report concluding that homosexuals are fit for military service, the suicide report of 1989 is attacked because government officials cannot tolerate objective views of homosexuality, even when they come from inside the government itself.

Homophobia also characterizes the courts. A Dallas judge who presided over a murder case in which two men were gunned down by an 18 year old said, for example, that the murderer deserved a lighter sentence for killing homosexuals, a statement that implied that gays are fair game and that violent attacks upon them are at least "partially excusable" (*New York Times,* 29 December 1989: A15).

Hatred of gay people exists outside of the United States as well. They are subjected to shock treatment in China, for example. On New Year's Day, 1990, three men accused of homosexuality were beheaded in a city square in Nahavand, Iran, and two women accused of lesbianism were stoned to death in Langrood (Jack Anderson, *San Francisco Chronicle,* 22 January 1990). In the same month in Queensland, Australia, a state librarian shredded two books of erotic photographs by Robert Mapplethorpe, an artist who died of AIDS. A Turkish gay leader was jailed after calling a press conference to protest police brutality. The human rights group Amnesty International refuses to defend lesbians and gay men who are imprisoned or tortured for their sexual preference (see Epilogue).

The AIDS epidemic has made homophobia more acceptable than it used to be. It is important to distinguish between HIV and AIDS. The Human Immunodeficiency Virus is thought to be the cause of Acquired Immune Deficiency Syndrome. People who test positive for HIV may be symptom free for a long time and thus able to continue working. Both those infected by HIV and those who have the disease of AIDS have been targets of homophobia. Blamed for getting sick, gay men with AIDS have been evicted from their homes, fired from their jobs, denied medical services or given inferior care, denied life-saving drugs, cheated by insurance companies, and rejected by their families. And surviving partners of people who died of AIDS sometimes have joint property taken away by families. After a congressman died of AIDS, leaving his male partner a share of his estate, his widow went to court to get the entire estate. For the impact of AIDS see Chapter 7 and for AIDS discrimination cases see Chapter 4.

In the twentieth century, the worst example of irrational hatred of homosexuals was the attempt by the Nazis to exterminate them, along with Jews. The exact number killed is unknown but was probably many thousands. The fate of homosexuals, who were forced to wear pink triangles in the concentration camps, was not mentioned by historians until recently. Despite efforts by the Green Party in Germany, homosexuals have not yet been recognized as a specific group of Nazi victims and have received no reparations, even though their internment is well documented. The Austrian government, on the other hand, recently decided to compensate homosexual victims of the Holocaust.

Like American Jews who do not fear concentration camps here but have very sharp antennae for the kind of anti-Semitism that leads to violence, lesbians and gay men are forced to be aware of violent attacks upon them. In 1988, more than 7,000 physical attacks on gays or people perceived to be gay were reported to the National Gay and Lesbian Task Force, including seventy murders in thirty-eight states. These statistics probably record fewer than a third of the actual number of crimes. A San Francisco organization, Community United Against Violence, reported in 1989 that attacks on lesbians and gay men had increased 67 percent. According to the Justice Department, the most frequent victims of hate crimes in America today are homosexuals, who are targeted more often than Blacks, Hispanics, Southeast Asians, and Jews (*New Directions for Women,* April 1989: 6).

Some of the most violent anti-gay attacks have been directed at Metropolitan Community Church, a gay church founded in 1968 by Protestant minister Troy Perry. MCC ministers have been shot at and murdered. In New Orleans many members died when the church was set on fire. In Kansas City, two choir members were shot during choir practice. In Springfield, Missouri, church equipment was destroyed and the pastor threatened with death. The San Francisco MCC church was burned several years ago, and services are sometimes disrupted by anti-gay demonstrations (letter by John Wahl, *Bay Area Reporter,* January 1990: 8). The freedom to worship as one chooses is a fundamental human right. Assaults on lesbians and gay men in their places of worship violate the Constitution. If America is a pluralistic society, homosexual citizens are as entitled as anyone to free speech and freedom of assembly.

Every minority group in America has its enemies but, for the most part, the enemies of Blacks, Hispanics, Asians, and Jews are not very influential figures; often they are uneducated. The Klu Klux Klan, for example, is powerful in some places but its bigoted views would not appear on the editorial page of a major newspaper. Synagogues are bombed but no congressman or congresswoman tells Jews to become Gentiles. Hispanics and Asians are resented as newcomers but they are not mocked by television comics. A dilemma of lesbians and gay men is that their enemies are very powerful: doctors, priests, ministers, military leaders, judges, politicians, federal government officials, and publishers. Any group so opposed by the people who control the major institutions of American life needs a movement to protect its right to exist.

Newsweek's cover story "Gays in America" (12 March 1990) shows the clasped hands of two men, with the phrase "testing the limits of tolerance" placed over the hands. Aside from the gross distortion of picturing the gay and lesbian movement as one of men only, this cover is objectionable because it implies that only the tolerance of heterosexuals matters. Gay people are marginalized in the U.S. In the minds of *Newsweek* editors, they are an irritant. If they go too far, they will be pushed back, as the phrase "testing the limits of tolerance" implies.

This cover illustrates the inadequacy of mainstream news treatment of gay issues. Lesbians and gay men cannot even tell who among them has been murdered by reading mainstream newspapers unless the victim is prominent. For that information and for all issues concerning them, they rely on their own national periodicals and newspapers such as *The Advocate* and *Gay Community News* and newspapers in major cities such as the *Bay Area Reporter* and the *Washington Blade*. In general, the most accurate portrayal of gay life comes from writers of novels, plays, poetry, and autobiography.

One of the first questions students ask about homosexuality is, why make an issue of it? Why can't the sexual partner one chooses be a private matter? Homosexuality is more than a sexual preference, as later chapters explain; it is an identity. Just as a single, divorced, widowed, or celibate heterosexual person remains heterosexual despite the temporary or permanent absence of a sexual partner, so, too, a homosexual person maintains that identity no matter what his or her relationship status. Heterosexuals who think about homosexuals naturally think of sexual practices because that is what distinguishes homosexuality in their eyes. But the sexual acts of people in the dominant group are not equivalent to the sexual acts of people who deviate from the norm (here "deviance" has no negative connotations but simply recognizes that heterosexuals are the majority) because one sexual identity is encouraged and the other is condemned. As long as this is the case, homosexual acts will carry a political as well as a private meaning. However much they may wish to make their sex lives *only* private, lesbians and gay men do not currently have that option. Of course, their lives may be secret and invisible to others, but the very choice to hide has a political meaning. Gay people do not make an issue of their lives: the dominant culture makes an issue of homosexuality by opposing it. If and when lesbians and gay men are completely free to express themselves, then their sexual choices may truly be a private matter. At that time, their sexual orientation will be seen as only one facet of their lives, as is now the case with heterosexuals.

Homophobia stands in the way of that social revolution. The following chapters tell how lesbians and gay men respond to homophobia:

(1) by creating a political movement based on the idea of sexual freedom;
(2) by developing their own culture;
(3) by influencing the world of books and ideas.

2

GAY AND LESBIAN LIBERATION AS A SEXUAL FREEDOM MOVEMENT

Is homosexuality innate or acquired? Is it an essence, a core self, or is it the product of social forces? Did homosexuals exist before sexologists gave them a label, or were homosexuals an invention of sexologists? These questions have been debated by lesbian and gay writers and theorists. Some believe that homosexuals have always existed, while others think they have existed only since the nineteenth century. Before then, of course, same-sex acts were known, but they did not lead the people who engaged in them to place themselves into a separate sexual category.

This chapter discusses ways of conceiving homosexual identity, preconditions for its development, influences on it, sex-related issues, coming out, attacks on gay sex, the justifications for it, and visual images of lesbian and gay male sex.

HOMOSEXUAL IDENTITY

The causes of homosexuality, like the causes of heterosexuality, are unknown. So far no evidence of biological determination has been discovered, although a few studies have reported that identical twins are more likely to share the same sexual orientation than fraternal twins, and that close relatives of homosexuals have higher incidences of homosexuality than the general population.[1] Despite these hints of genetic influence, it seems likely that homosexuality has complex social origins. No particular family structure is known to favor its development, however, and homosexuals are as diverse as heterosexuals in their personality types.

Whatever its cause, homosexuality is regarded by many lesbians and gay men as an essence, a fixed and unchanging aspect of their identities. For many others, sexuality is much more fluid. It results not from nature but from social conditioning. These contrasting views are known as essentialism and social construction.[2] For essentialists, the category "homosexual" is universal and transhistorical. Some are genetic determinists, believing they were born homosexual. Others simply believe that homosexuals have existed always and everywhere. Essentialism stresses the sameness among people throughout history who have loved their own sex and social construction emphasizes the differences. Essentialism sharply differentiates homosexuals from heterosexuals, while social construction de-emphasizes the differences. Those who reject essentialism argue that even though "there may well be a timeless homosexual desire, it has been—and still is—variously channeled in diverse social organizations" (Murray 1984: 2).

In the Middle Ages, for example, when sodomy was equated with heresy, homosexual acts had a different meaning from the meaning they have today for residents of gay neighborhoods in large American cities. The flourishing medieval tradition of sex between monks who were influenced by classical literature, described by John Boswell in *Christianity, Social Tolerance, and Homosexuality* (1980), bears little resemblance to the lives of modern monks who have lost lovers and friends to AIDS. Social clubs for men who sought sex and friendship with other men are described in Alan Bray's book *Homosexuality in Renaissance England.*[3] Patterns of homosexual behavior among soldiers and sailors differ from patterns of those who meet at work, at school, or at church. Jonathan Katz and other American historians have discovered evidence of homosexual relations among cowboys. Women who cross-dressed to fight in the War of 1812 and the Civil War had little in common with upper-middle-class women of the nineteenth century who spent long periods in Rome, Paris, and Florence, where they socialized with expatriate writers and artists. Some of the women who drove ambulances in France in World War I discovered their lesbianism by socializing with other ambulance drivers, and the same was true of war nurses. For some of them, lesbianism was a war-time interlude; for some it was a continuation of pre-war sexual and emotional patterns; and for some it was the beginning of a different way of life, made possible in part by the new sense of freedom and autonomy they gained from doing dangerous work. With any of these groups, the question is whether to emphasize "timeless homosexual desire" or the impact of social forces, particularly the legal and medical notions of homosexuality.

The late nineteenth-century laws against homosexuality and the writings of the early sexologists helped to create a new class of people, homosexuals. As they reacted to attempts to regulate their behavior, their identities became more sharply defined. In attempting to label a form of deviant behavior, doctors and lawmakers called more attention to it. Thus the development of homosexual consciousness, of the awareness of being different in a fundamental way, depends to some degree on organized opposition to homosexual behavior. That is why some scholars say that social forces not only shaped attitudes towards homosexuality but actually constructed it (Weeks 1981: 97).

The idea that the homosexual person appears only in the late

Victorian period can be challenged, however: many medieval writers viewed homosexuality as the special mark of certain individuals and linked it to personality (Boswell in Duberman *et al.* 1989: 28). Another challenge to social construction is that it tends to see "the sexual actor as object, a mere passive recipient of definitions imposed on him or her from the top of the social pyramid,"[4] a view uncongenial to writers, artists, and other individualists.

The theme of homosexuals as a people with a long history rather than a Victorian construct pervades Judy Grahn's popular book *Another Mother Tongue*.[5] This theme is connected to self-esteem. The homosexual scholars of Oxford and Cambridge from the late Victorian period through the 1960s looked to the Greeks to assure themselves that they belonged to an honorable tradition. Likeness to the Greeks was the important point. Lesbians took great pride in the sixth-century poet Sappho. In the early days of gay liberation, the use of the past for self-justification was a necessary psychological and political act. To be part of a group going back centuries was better than belonging to a tiny splinter group. Essentialism can be interpreted as a validation of gay people, in the sense that a fixed and permanent identity is a desirable counterweight to arguments that homosexuals are just "going through a phase."[6] On the other hand, the more recent emphasis on cultural difference by social constructionists means that, for example, the homosexuality of ancient Greece can be understood on its own terms. It was considered natural and laws did not forbid it; its chief form was a relationship between a man and a youth; and their love fit Athenian notions of honor.[7]

Some believe that the debate between those who emphasize the recent appearance of the homosexual as a distinct type of person and those who believe in a core homosexual self is a fruitless rehashing of the old nature versus nurture question. Are we shaped more by biology or by culture? Others think the debate between social construction and essentialism can be transcended (Epstein 1987; Roscoe 1988). In any case, lively discussions over the origins and meanings of homosexuality mark an intellectual advance because scholars until recently were prevented by prejudice from openly discussing homosexuality.

PRE-CONDITIONS FOR THE DEVELOPMENT OF GAY SEX

Although homosexual behavior occurs cross-culturally (in New Guinea and among Australian aborigines, for example) and throughout history, certain conditions favor its appearance. Several trends in the past one hundred years which have greatly influenced the ways most Americans live are also significant for their impact on homosexual life: (1) the change from a rural to an urban society; (2) the decline of the traditional family; (3) changing views of sex; (4) the emancipation of women; and (5) the growth of capitalism.

When most people lived on farms and grew up knowing they would farm for a living, they came into contact with a relatively small number of people, who were much like themselves. Thus it was fairly easy to live as their parents had lived and difficult to imagine alternatives. When the hero of Willa Cather's novel *One of Ours* goes to France to fight in World War I, he discovers an exciting new world of variety, expansiveness, and emotion which he had never dreamed of while living as a farmer. He becomes deeply dissatisfied with his former life, including his marriage. Throughout the twentieth century, the young who moved from the country to the city met people different from themselves, including homosexuals, and experienced a new sense of freedom. In farming towns and villages their lives could easily be scrutinized by those around them, while city life offered anonymity and privacy, conditions conducive to finding sexual partners and friends.

Although Willa Cather could not write openly about homosexuals, she invented subtly disguised homosexual characters who escape from small towns to live in New York, for example the men in her short story "The Sculptor's Funeral." Cather herself could not have lived comfortably as a lesbian in Red Cloud, Nebraska, but needed New York for artistic stimulation and companionship. As large cities grew, their hidden homosexual populations grew as well, and this growth was a necessary precondition to the development of homosexual life in the second half of the twentieth century.

29

The city not only offered more possibilities for meeting potential sexual partners and a wider social life in general, it also created possibilities for living permanently outside of the traditional family structure. While the extended or nuclear family pattern was nearly universal, few people could break away. In rural families, young people played an important economic role because their labor was needed to sustain the family farm or small business. As cities grew and people had job opportunities away from their birthplaces, family control over them declined. The invention of the car increased the mobility of young people and provided a place away from home for sexual experimentation. Cities became more accessible. Young people new to cities saw that not everyone lived in a male-female couple, and many remained single. Friendship groups took on some of the functions of the family for homosexuals who settled in cities.

The religious right, which attacks lesbians and gay men for allegedly destroying the family, misses the irony that the importance of the family had to diminish considerably before homosexuality could become a salient feature of American life. Widespread homosexuality is one of the results of a weakened family structure, not a cause. Where young people are influenced by their peers and the media as much as by their families, they have the freedom to make life choices different from those of their parents. No longer the employer of young people, the family can no longer be the sole arbiter of behavior. Under these conditions, homosexuality is a possible life choice for those aware of same-sex attractions. When families were more dominant, homosexuality could only be aberrant behavior except for a few unusually strong, autonomous, or rich individuals who could make it a way of life.

Since the 1960s, cohabitation, divorce, birth control, and abortion have greatly altered families, but decades before then the forces weakening the family were already beginning to create conditions favorable to the formation of homosexual identity. In the 1860s, Walt Whitman's 'Calamus' poems shocked readers by their explicit references to male homosexuality, but they were equally radical for their vision of male comrades forming their own society. To complement the love between women and men, which the poet called "amative," he proposed "adhesiveness," or erotic love between men. Whitman was probably one of the first Americans to realize that large numbers of men could thrive outside of the family system, singly, in pairs, and in groups. By representing adhesiveness as a desirable life pattern equivalent to heterosexual love, he implicitly challenged the central position of the family. Adhesiveness was not subversive, however. On the contrary, Whitman believed it would strengthen American democracy by providing a spiritual and emotional foundation for a country in danger of becoming excessively materialistic as it rapidly expanded.

Obviously, Whitman's vision of manly love taking a place of honor beside heterosexual love has not yet been realized, but Whitman understood that the traditional family could not encompass all of the forms of modern emotional and sexual life. Whitman was one of the first American poets to write of sexual pleasure and fulfillment. All bodily sensations were holy to him. Sexuality existed to be celebrated rather than suppressed. In their book *Intimate Matters: a History of Sexuality in America* (1988), John D'Emilio and Estelle Freedman trace the development of the related idea that sexuality is one of our most basic forms of expression, and that sexual pleasure is an end in itself. In the past, traditional religions considered sex permissible only as the means of procreation. Homosexual men may father children and lesbians may bear them—they have the same reproductive capacity as heterosexuals—but the fact that homosexual acts themselves are non-procreative has led to the judgment that they are unnatural and sinful. A precondition for accepting homosexuality is the rejection of this traditional view in favor of the modern idea that sexual expression is intrinsically good.

Changing views of sex paralleled and interconnected with changing views of women. The traditional view of sex as acceptable only for procreation often accompanied a view that women are subordinate to men. In the late nineteenth century the social purity movement challenged these views, especially the latter, by advocating a single standard for sexual morality. Its supporters wanted an end to prostitution, for example, and they successfully petitioned state legislatures to raise the age at which women could legally consent to sex. Because of its emphasis on the sanctity of the family and control of sexuality, the social purity movement did not foreshadow lesbianism, but its attack on the double standard, which justified greater sexual freedom for men, encouraged the emancipation of women.

Surpassing the Love of Men: Romantic Love and Friendship Between Women from the Renaissance to the Present, a study by Lillian Faderman (1981), shows that passionate attachments between women in the nineteenth and early twentieth century were tolerated as long as the status of women was clearly inferior to that of men. As soon as social and economic changes in the 1920s brought more women into the workforce and made them more independent, intense female attachments became a threat. The "new woman" who could vote was acceptable as long as she deferred to men. If she wanted a life apart from men she was called unnatural. The primacy of heterosexual love and marriage was never really threatened, either in the early days of feminism or after its revival in the late 1960s, but the new possibility that large numbers of women would resist marriage and focus their lives on other women was certainly radical. College-educated women were the most independent. Some found female lovers and life partners while attending college; others learned to accept erotic love between women as natural, whatever their own sexual preference. The idea that women could be fulfilled only by heterosexual marriage remained virtually unassailable until the late 1960s, however, because of Freud's influence and because economic pressures forced most women to marry. Nevertheless, the belief that women are inherently equal to men had as a corollary the belief that some women appropriately choose other women as emotional and sexual partners. Not everyone who believed in women's emancipation went that far, of course, but the groundwork was laid for future extensions of the notion of women's equality.

The idea that custom rather than biology subordinates women held importance for homosexual men as well. One of their first champions, Edward Carpenter, advocated feminism in the late Victorian period. A critique of the social arrangements for women made it possible to see the constraints placed on men who did not fit into the traditional masculine role in appearance or interests or who simply did not want to play the conventional part of breadwinner.

The growth of capitalism has helped to create both the economic and the psychological conditions which encourage homosexuality (Altman 1982: 93). The decline of the family as a producer of goods and the concentration of goods and services in large urban centers brought about a population shift favorable to the formation of homosexual communities. With its emphasis on an ever-growing need for new products, capitalism tends to make sex itself a commodity, now that it is no longer an activity wholly controlled by the family or by religious precepts. A great deal of attention is focused on sex, compared to the nineteenth century, for example, through the use of sex to sell products. These economic forces have influenced our psychology as well: as traditional sources of meaning such as family, religion, and community life become less important in defining who we are, sex becomes more important. Urban, often isolated people need meaning from sex more than their grandparents in small villages and farming communities needed it. Thus the quest for sexual satisfaction is likely to be far more significant for us than for our grandparents, and for some this quest will inevitably lead to homosexuality, not as a transitory experience, as it may have been in the nineteenth century, but as a life choice. Encouraged by capitalism to see ourselves as consumers with an infinite variety of choices, we do not stay in unhappy relationships as some of our grandparents did, but readily move on to new ones. Consequently, today we have more opportunity to discover whether or not we are homosexual. And we know that, if marriage does not suit us, we have an option besides remaining single.

INFLUENCES ON GAY SEX

One of the most important modern influences on gay sex was World War II. The war "temporarily weakened the patterns of daily life that channeled men and women towards heterosexuality and inhibited homosexual expression" (D'Emilio 1983b: 31). In his book *Coming out under Fire,* Allen Berube tells how war-time conditions increased access to gay sex: thousands of young lesbians and gay men, many from small towns and rural areas, met large numbers of other homosexuals for the first time on military bases, in nearby bars, or in hotels where service people congregated. In this milieu, a growing number of "displaced young men and women learned to think of themselves as gay" (Berube 1990: 117). Before the war, homosexual *acts* were punished by court-martial and imprisonment, but during the war the condition of being homosexual itself became undesirable and a new class of persons came under surveillance. Thus the military greatly extended its control over homosexuals because far more of them could be discharged than could be imprisoned (p. 147). At the same time, under the extreme conditions of combat, homosexual feelings and behavior tended to be accepted as normal, both by heterosexual soldiers, who formed more intense friendships with men than would have been usual in peace time, and by homosexual soldiers, who felt validated as they observed the powerful bonds existing between men who faced death together daily. Psychiatrists who worked on the bases discovered that, despite extreme disapproval, harassment, and even confinement in government mental hospitals, homosexuals in the military had no desire to change their orientation (p. 203). Thus the fixed quality of homosexual identity became more apparent than it had been earlier when psychiatrists, seeing only a few homosexual patients, one by one, instead of the large numbers they saw in the service, could not distinguish illness from homosexuality.

Another significant influence was the publication of Alfred Kinsey's best-selling books *Sexual Behavior in the Human Male* (1948) and *Sexual Behavior in the Human Female* (1953). Based on case histories of 18,000 Americans, they revealed that one-half of the men felt erotic attractions for other men and more than one-third as adults had a homosexual experience that resulted in orgasm. Twenty eight percent of the women surveyed had erotic feelings for their own sex and 13 percent had experienced orgasm with another woman. Kinsey concluded that homosexuals could be found throughout the population. Thus, a form of behavior that had once seemed unusual, existing only on the fringes of society, "now seemed to permeate American life" (D'Emilio and Freedman 1988: 292). Kinsey's findings so dramatically contradicted the common view of sex that their implications could not readily be grasped by most Americans, particularly when Senator Joseph McCarthy was stirring up hatred of homosexuals by linking them to communists. The revelation that homosexual behavior is fairly common ought logically to have undercut the prejudice that it is unnatural, but as long as people who practiced it felt compelled to be silent and to pass for heterosexual, the Kinsey numbers were mere abstractions. Nevertheless, his reports were useful later as scientific evidence of the high incidence of homosexuality, and they showed that the subject could be discussed rationally, outside a context of religious beliefs.

The most important influence on lesbian sex in the past two decades has been the women's movement. Earlier in this chapter the phrase "emancipation of women" referred to women's rights as an historical movement; here "women's movement" means the current one beginning in the late 1960s. The movement freed women to be sexual. They rebelled against sexual repression and the stereotyped views of themselves as virgins or whores. They said they would no longer subordinate their sexual needs to those of men. This position was compatible with the position that some women could be fulfilled in emotional/sexual relationships with other women. Even though a majority of feminists were heterosexual, the new openness about sex and the defiant rejection of traditional notions of sexual morality led many women to question the condemnation of homosexuality. This questioning not only affected their private lives but influenced all of society because it challenged "the whole range of coercive morality" (Altman 1983: 92). If women were entitled to sexual pleasure on their own terms, then people in general were entitled to define "normal" sexual behavior for themselves.

In the 1980s the popularity of women-centered spirituality and of recovery groups such as AA, Al Anon, and Adult Children of Alcoholics influenced the sexual lives of many lesbian feminists. Feminist witchcraft, goddess worship, solstice rituals, and various formal and informal celebrations of women's life-giving powers held at conferences, retreats, and parties inspired a new reverence for the female body and an appreciation of lesbian sex. Visual images of ancient goddesses became popular among lesbian feminists. The important place given to recovery groups in the lesbian community is not surprising because alcoholism has been a serious problem. Of the many benefits resulting from participation in these groups, none is more important than increased acceptance of one's sexuality. To reach this point, some lesbians have had to grapple with long-buried memories of childhood sexual abuse and other past family traumas that interfere with their intimate relationships in the present.

Recovery groups were also popular among gay men, and for some the group Radical Faeries provided a spiritual community comparable to the feminist spirituality circles.

In the 1970s, feminism profoundly influenced gay men because it questioned sex roles and the function of the family, encouraged the emotional development of men, and fostered a spirit of equality in male-female friendships. Under the influence of feminist thinking, the passive partner in gay male sex, the receiver of the penis, who had been stigmatized as womanly, became respected. The distinction between top and bottom grew less important as men wanted to exchange roles. Not all gay men identified with women's liberation, however. Some were hostile to it and others indifferent. Some wanted lesbians to align with gay liberation instead of women's liberation. Some gay men created a cult of masculinity which was harmful to them, according to Charles Silverstein, author of *Man to Man: Gay Male Couples in America,* because it involved phallus worship, public displays of masculinity, "the confusion between sexual pleasure and aggression, competition with lovers and fear of intimacy, and the need to control another man sexually."[8] Like heterosexual men, gay men are programmed to talk more comfortably about sex than about love. Psychologist Rik Isensee, author of *Love Between Men,* believes that, since anger is the only emotion men are encouraged to express as they grow up, anger of adult males masks hurt, sadness, and fear.[9] In other words, gay men do not escape their socialization as males. Many influenced by feminism enter into equal partnerships, however.

It is widely believed in the gay community that gay men have more sexual contacts than lesbians, that their long-term relationships are much more likely to be "open," that is, non-monogamous, and that lesbians are more likely to have sex in the context of an emotionally close relationship. Apparently true, this generalization could only be proven by studies of thousands of lesbians and gay men, preferably more ambitious studies than those based on a single questionnaire or interview. Another popular belief is that the HIV has prompted gay men to focus more on relationships than on casual sex, but many gay men made that choice long before HIV appeared, and some lesbians have always preferred affairs or multiple sexual partners to long-term commitments. Perhaps gay men are not as different from women sexually as social conditioning makes them appear to be.

Gay men had no movement comparable to women's liberation to affiliate with because they belonged to the dominant sex, but many were strongly influenced by the hippie movement, which was, in part, a sharp attack on the 1950s' concept of manhood. The males among the "flower children" were self-consciously anti-macho because the traditional male image connoted war and killing as well as subservience to an economic system that trapped them in 9 to 5 jobs. The sexual freedom and the anti-authoritarian spirit of the hippies were adopted by many men who did not take on their dress or their communal living style. Protests against the Viet Nam war intensified this spirit. The hippie movement introduced many men who would later come out as gay to the idea of androgyny. Unisex dress styles at the huge anti-war demonstrations and on campuses softened the old lines of demarcation between the sexes. And fear of being killed in Viet Nam opened up men emotionally, prompting them to question all they had been taught to believe in, including the importance of suppressing feelings.

SEX-RELATED ISSUES

Gay sex is just sex. One of the challenges of gay and lesbian liberation is to gain acceptance for this view. Surveys show that anti-gay prejudice is inversely proportional to personal association with gay people. Therefore, as time passes, and more heterosexuals have the opportunity to meet lesbians and gay men at school, or work, or in their neighborhoods, the perception that gay sex is evil or unnatural may gradually disappear. On the other hand, fear of difference is deeply ingrained and, when fear of sex is added to it, the result is a powerful impulse to repress or deny one's own difference and to attack it in others.

By now the view that lesbian and gay sex is just sex might have become widely accepted if the AIDS epidemic had not appeared in the second decade of gay liberation. AIDS and HIV created a fear that gay sex is not only bad but equals death, a fear exacerbated by media treatment of the disease. People with AIDS have been stereotyped as promiscuous and treated like lepers. The association of gay sex with fatal illness had an extremely negative effect on gay liberation as a sexual freedom movement.

The very free, open, exuberant, and celebratory attitudes towards gay sex in the 1970s changed in the 1980s as gay men, especially those in large cities, struggled against sex-negative attitudes in themselves and in the often hostile heterosexual world. To reaffirm the dignity and value of their sexual lives as their friends and lovers died all around them took great courage, an aspect of the epidemic ignored by the media. After a decade of fighting illness and facing death in their midst, gay men knew that an adequate response to AIDS from federal, state, and local governments would have saved lives. Right-wing bigots and some doctors whose loathing of homosexuality led them to say it was God's punishment for AIDS expected gay men to recoil from sex. Reagan's inaction reinforced the folk belief that there was something wrong with gay sex. If there had been any rational or scientific basis for this belief, it could have been amply demonstrated during World War II, when Army and Navy psychiatrists had the opportunity to study thousands of homosexuals from diverse backgrounds.

Even though AIDS and HIV encouraged a negative view of gay sex, the educational efforts to combat the disease, inadequate as they were, helped to demystify gay sex and, as a result, public awareness of homosexuality is much greater now than it was before AIDS was first identified in 1981.

One of the patterns noted by the authors of *Intimate Matters* is that purity campaigns in American history have linked sex to many evils. "Sex appeared as an uncontrollable force that spawned social chaos when its power was let loose" (D'Emilio and Freedman 1988: 284). Thus one of the impulses behind attempts to suppress homosexuality is simply the fear of any kind of uninhibited sexual expression. Homosexuality was especially threatening in the past because it was secret.

The stereotype of the homosexual as child molester results from "a social need to protect the appearance of the family as innocent and sex as simple, manageable and useful, rather than awesome, ecstatic, and risky" (Mohr 1983: 127).[10] Homosexuals are a convenient scapegoat for the disintegration of the nuclear family. Although their lives are not necessarily characterized by awesome and ecstatic sex, lesbians and gay men symbolize sexual freedom simply by existing.

Some heterosexuals displace their sexual anxieties by projecting onto gay people so exaggerated a sexual life that gay equals sex. This process is parallel to the one by which Black men were once mythologized as highly sexed. Those in a feared category lose their humanity, their roundness, when they become sex symbols. No other facets of their lives are of interest. The myth of the sex-obsessed faggot or dyke sharply separates heterosexuals from those they perceive as different and at the same time blurs the identity of the minority person. This has happened with women and the old as well as with Blacks and homosexuals. It may be that the search for sexual pleasure and a heightened sense of sexual needs are more characteristic of lesbians and gay men than of heterosexuals because gay sex has been outlawed and therefore has the lure of forbidden fruit; because many gays have no family responsibilities; and because the conditions of gay life may encourage a philosophy of *carpe diem* (seize the day: enjoy life in the present moment). But this philosophy probably characterizes urban people in general. In addition, some gay people may focus great attention on sex because they have been denied sexual outlets for long periods of their lives or have been unfulfilled in heterosexual marriages.

Because women and men are socialized differently and because gender differences are so basic to a sense of who we are, male homosexuals and lesbians must be seen as two distinct types, even though obviously they have a great deal in common. Gay male sexual life tends to be more visible and more public. Boston in the 1950s, for example, had two dozen gay male bars but only one lesbian bar (D'Emilio and Freedman 1988: 291). More recently, the disco has become a place where gay people can express erotic feelings. Casual sex with strangers was fairly common among gay men until AIDS; the freedom to be gay was directly linked to the freedom to have many sexual partners. Writing of gay men before AIDS, Dennis Altman interpreted their willingness to have sex with strangers, for example at gay baths, as a desire to experience "a type of brotherhood far removed from the male bonding of rank, hierarchy, and competition" of the outside world, and he acknowledged that the baths have their own hierarchy, for the young and the good-looking are especially prized (1983: 79–80).

Lesbians generally do not see each other as sex objects, a requirement for cruising. A few lesbians enjoy cruising in women's bars, but the art of picking up strangers for sex is usually not a part of their lives. Even though they tend to have longer courtships than gay men and less public forms of sexual expression, lesbians are very interested in sex, as the popularity of Celeste West's *Lesbian Love Advisor* shows.[11]

Sex seems more central to gay men's identity and self-presentation, however. Most of the subjects interviewed in *Quiet Fire, Memoirs of Older Gay Men,* delight in recounting their sexual conquests and experiences, while the women interviewed in *Long Time Passing,* a book about older lesbians, mention sex much less frequently.[12] The study *American Couples* by Pepper Schwarz and Philip Blumstein found that gay male couples are the most sexually active and lesbian couples the least.[13] Broad patterns tell little about an individual's sexual patterns, however, and homosexuals, like heterosexuals, differ greatly in their sexual rhythms and tastes.

A significant difference between gay men and lesbians is that middle-aged and old lesbians are likely to see themselves as sexually attractive and desirable and to be seen that way by other lesbians, whereas gay men value youthful good looks. Some tend to objectify other men, to value size of penis for example or muscular bodies. Gay men over 50 or even over 40 may be dismissed as old. Ageist attitudes appear among lesbians, too, but aging has much more status in the lesbian community. An older gay man who prefers young sex partners (called a chickenhawk) serves as a mentor or father figure for the youth, but this traditional pattern of gay male sex roles seems to be changing, as more young gay men are able to find sexual partners of their own age.

Lesbians also seem not to cross class lines for sexual partners as readily as gay men do. When Auden, Isherwood, and Spender went to Berlin in the 1930s looking for adventure and sex, they were drawn to working-class boys. E. M. Forster fell in love with working-class Englishmen. Notable lesbian couples such as Natalie Barney and Romaine Brooks, Alice B. Toklas and Gertrude Stein, and Una Troubridge and Radclyffe Hall came from the same class.

The tragic spread of AIDS has further differentiated lesbian sex from gay male sex. Although a few lesbians have been infected by HIV through blood transfusions, the Center for Disease Control has found no cases of lesbian sexual HIV transmission. At the very time lesbians are being more experimental and open about sex, gay men need to be cautious. Of course lesbians too must take precautions against HIV. Most have lost friends to AIDS and thus feel aligned with gay men. Some lesbians were married to gay men and it is not unusual today for lesbians to help care for ex-husbands who are dying of AIDS.

Historically a major difference between lesbians and gay men is that men who deviated from the heterosexual norm were much more threatening to the social order and hence were more brutally punished. In this case the higher status of men was disadvantageous to homosexual men. As individuals, women who loved women were condemned as unnatural and sometimes executed (see Bibliography, Crompton) but were generally ignored. Laws against homosexuality in Victorian England did not extend to them, for example. In 1921, when Members of Parliament tried to pass legislation against lesbianism, they were opposed by a former Director of Public Prosecutions who told them, "You are going to tell the whole world that there is such an offense, to bring it to the notice of women who have never even heard of it, never thought of it, never dreamt of it" (Weeks 1981: 105).[14] Similarly, Nazi laws against homosexuals were intended only for men. According to University of Florida historian Geoffrey Giles,[15] the Nazis reasoned that homosexuality was more prevalent among men and thus more likely to set a corrupting example, that lesbians would be harder to identify since women may freely express affection for each other in public, and that lesbians were not dangerous because they played no role in government. Was lesbianism really less prevalent than male homosexuality or was it merely less noticed? Giles has found evidence that the Nazis punished lesbians by sending them to concentration camps to be prostitutes.

Public sex is a gay issue because of police harassment and entrapment. Sometimes men who are arrested in cruising areas or restrooms have their names printed in the local newspaper. Attitudes towards public sex vary in the gay community. For many gay men, it has always been an important and acceptable part of gay life; for many lesbian feminists, it is not acceptable. Some gay men seek public sex when they are first coming out but not later. Others choose it infrequently. A sense of adventure, the excitement of sexual conquest, or simply the desire for sexual release motivate men to perform sex with strangers. Anonymous bathroom sex on a college campus is portrayed very positively in Edmund White's novel *The Beautiful Room is Empty*.[16] The threat of AIDS has made gay men more cautious about anonymous sex and has increased the popularity of jerk-off clubs, where men gather in a relaxed atmosphere. Novelist Bo Huston recalls that, in the early days of gay liberation, anonymous sex seemed to him "the legacy of the closet, a place for keeping secrets, a place without choices." But later he saw that public sex could also be chosen by openly gay men (*San Francisco Bay Times*, December 1989: 23).

Although lesbians have no comparable tradition of public sex, partly because they are raised to seek sex less aggressively than men and often have less mobility, it is likely that some lesbians make anonymous sexual contacts in public places, for example at bath houses on women's night.

Bisexuality is often discussed with homosexuality. Some lesbians and gay men find this linking appropriate, while others prefer that the two phenomena be sharply differentiated. People may go through a bisexual phase before declaring themselves homosexual, but bisexuality is a permanent identification for many others. Bisexuals have occasionally been resented by homosexuals for benefiting from the social acceptability of their opposite sex attraction. On the other hand, in the 1990s the description "lesbian, gay and bisexual" is commonly used in places where "lesbian and gay" would have been the preferred designation earlier, a sign of growing solidarity among people in the three groups. The proposition that all people are potentially bisexual has been controversial in the gay and lesbian community because it has seemed to undercut the claim for a special gay identity, but the idea of

a spectrum of experience is widely accepted; that is, exclusive heterosexuality on one end and exclusive homosexuality on the other, with
many gradations in between.

Lani Kaahumanu, co-editor (with Lorraine Hutchins) of *Bi Any
Other Name: Bisexual People Speak Out,* believes that bisexuality is the
new wave of the sexual freedom movement.[17] Her anthology by writers aged 18–80 includes people of color and people from various wings
of the bisexual population: those who are gay/lesbian identified; those
who have always considered themselves bisexual; and those who are
heterosexually identified. In the beginning of gay liberation, Kaahumanu believes, the term "gay" was an umbrella term. Then gay women
joined the women's liberation movement and adopted the label "lesbian," while bisexuals remained invisible. In the 1980s they began
organizing and at the 1987 gay march on Washington they formed a
separate contingent. Their first national conference was held in San
Francisco in June 1990.

Gender is our awareness of being male or female. Gender and sex
are different concepts. Some homosexual males assume the traits or
dress associated with women, but most do not; some lesbians may
appear masculine, but most do not. Some heterosexual men are effeminate and some heterosexual women mannish. Homosexuality has been
linked to gender nonconformity because the most visible homosexuals
are the effeminate males and the mannish females, the "nellies" or
"sissies" and the "butches" or "bulldaggers." In the past, some young
people being socialized into homosexual life cross-dressed because they
thought they were supposed to. The complex relation between gender
and sex is indicated by two parallel trends in the 1980s: many gay men
took on a macho style of dress, an exaggeratedly masculine appearance,
and lesbians gave up the jeans, workshirt, and boots look of the 1970s.
Some older lesbians have a powerful identification with men and male
power, but this is not as common among young lesbians. Similarly,
drag queens who totally assume a female persona are likely to be older
gay men. As a style, drag appeals to gay men of all ages, however.

The parallel influences of gay liberation and women's liberation
have made androgyny an ideal for many lesbians and gay men; that is,
the blending of masculine and feminine into a single personality. In

general, men who identify themselves as homosexual have more free-dom to express feminine aspects of themselves such as gentleness and sensitivity to others' feelings than do heterosexual males, and lesbians give each other approval and support for adopting behaviors associated with men, displaying physical strength, for example, being competi-tive, and focusing on work as much as on relationships.

It is important to distinguish between homosexuality and transves-tism, which simply means cross-dressing—that is, a man wears wom-en's clothes and a woman wears men's clothes. At present in the United States, where clothing styles are casual and unisex, clothes make only muted gender statements, but the phenomenon of cross-dressing, found in many cultures, can have diverse meanings. Even when dis-guised as women, male transvestites identify themselves as male. They are not transsexuals, that is, men who feel they are women trapped in men's bodies (or women who feel their bodies do not match their sex).

In ancient fertility rites, cross-dressing was associated with growth and rebirth and also with supernatural power. In the nineteenth cen-tury, it was seen as a sign of mental illness, but today it is more commonly viewed as slightly freakish or comical. Cross-dressing by men may be a way of reuniting with the mother or a way of integrating very strong female feelings into an essentially masculine personality, or it may simply reduce tension about sexual roles.[18]

Transvestism is clearly related to the illusion of the theater and to the pleasurable surprise of seeing the usually fixed roles of women and men turned upside down. Men who appear as women on stage may "compensate the males in the audience for the loss or the suppression of their female component."[19] Cross-dressing by males can be viewed as a mockery of women, but the reverse is not true, because the usual motive for female cross-dressing is to gain the status, power, and autonomy conferred by the male role. In the past, cross-dressing al-lowed working-class lesbian couples to live together disguised as hus-band and wife (D'Emilio 1983b: 97). Queen Christina of Sweden was considered a transvestite lesbian (Faderman 1981: 54–5).

The politics of cross-dressing is sometimes called "gender fuck," which means an intentionally shocking, theatrical disturbance of tradi-tional gender distinctions. Calling into question the apparently fixed categories of male and female implicitly challenges the social order. When a bearded man with a hairy chest wears a dress and high heels, for example, he scoffs at the artificiality of social roles.

Although transvestites may be heterosexual, a strong association exists between transvestism and homosexuality in literature. Love of concealment and disguise comes naturally to those who feel a gap between prescribed social behavior and their deepest feelings. One of the best examples for women is Virginia Woolf's elaborate spoof, *Orlando,* a record of her passionate love for Vita Sackville-West who, disguised as Orlando, changes sexes through the centuries. More recently, Patrick White's novel *The Twyborn Affair* portrays a man disguised as a woman.[20]

Although distinct, homosexuality and transvestism are parallel in some ways. Attempts to suppress both have been futile because the behaviors are ancient and universal. In England, transvestites were put into stocks and dragged through the streets, and they were burned to death in France as late as 1760. Both homosexuality and transvestism challenge the authority of the state to regulate private behavior.

An advantage of cross-dressing for lesbians and gay men is that it allows them to signal their homosexuality and thus to be approached by other homosexuals for friendship or sex and at the same time avoid unwanted sexual advances from persons of the opposite sex. Often cross-dressing is a style assumed for fun, as at Halloween, or for parties, or as a way of playing around with one's identity. A lesbian, for example, can compare the responses she gets in a lesbian bar when she is dressed in stereotypically male clothing with the responses she gets when she wears traditionally feminine attire.

Of special interest to gay studies is the berdache, the Native American male who cross-dressed.[21] Common to many tribes (but existing with many variations), berdaches took on the occupation as well as the dress of women. They took care of the sick and the old, for example. The berdache was not necessarily homosexual, according to some anthropologists, but others believe that the significance of the berdache role was that it allowed social recognition of homosexual relationships. Walter Williams, author of *The Spirit and the Flesh: Sexual Diversity in American Indian Culture* reports that in some tribes the marriage of the berdache to a person of the same sex was just as acceptable as heterosexual marriage, and homosexual behavior was not stigmatized.[22] Rather than brand the atypical individual as a threat or a sinner, as is common in mainstream American culture, the Native Americans sanctified the berdaches. They were credited with possessing supernatural powers because they combined both male and female spirits. Will Roscoe's book *The Zuni Man Woman* describes the life of We'wha, born in 1849.[23] Sharon Day, an Ojibway gay activist in Minneapolis, blames the Catholic Church for spreading anti-homosexual attitudes among native people and encouraging the abolition of the berdache role (Miller 1989: 193).

Information about the female berdache, who was apparently less common than the male, is scanty. Williams calls these women who assumed the dress and function of men "amazons." In some tribes, women past child-bearing age assumed some of the functions of the berdache, acting as go-betweens, for example. They were typically women of unusual physical strength and skill. Among Plains tribes, a highly productive worker who was also a wealthy woman was called "manly heart."

Because the berdache began to disappear with the arrival of the white conquerors, it is difficult to know whether same-sex feelings and behavior for the berdache were similar to same-sex feelings and behavior for twentieth-century gay men. Nevertheless, the berdache role in Native American culture clearly has some links to modern-day homosexuality, and informed discussion of this role in schools would perhaps encourage tolerance for both transvestites and gay people.

COMING OUT

Although sex between two men or two women has much in common with heterosexual sex, lesbians and gay men have a unique experience, coming out of the closet, or "coming out," as it is more simply put. Coming out refers to a complex emotional, psychological, and sexual experience of naming oneself lesbian or gay. It is a process of self-acceptance that usually involves sex with another gay person, although lesbians and gay men may also be celibate and come out. Their identity does not depend on genital sex. Celibate lesbians and gay men are just as homosexual as heterosexuals without partners are heterosexual.

Coming out takes different forms for different individuals and often occurs at an earlier age for men than for women. Several stages in the process can be identified. First, the individual becomes aware that he or she is homosexual. This may be a very tentative self-label in the beginning. Then the individual communicates his or her awareness of homosexual feelings to others. At the same time, or later, he or she makes friends with other lesbians or gay men, cautiously in small towns and rural areas, more casually and openly in big cities. As a result of these steps, the individual adapts a positive attitude towards being gay. Finally, in a short time or a long time, depending on his or her circumstances and personality, this recognition of being homosexual is integrated into other aspects of the self.

The term "come out" is sometimes used to mean one's first sexual experience with a same-sex partner, but coming out is better understood as a process rather than a single event. Because of the force of homophobia, coming out fully may take a long time. Twenty years or more after one's first homosexual experience, a step in the coming out process may occur—telling one's parents one is gay, for example, telling co-workers, joining a lesbian or gay organization, or reading books about the process of developing a positive gay identity (for example, *The Lesbian Path* or *The Coming Out Stories*[24]). Sometimes healing experiences after a relationship ends or growth through therapy or recovery groups allow middle-aged lesbians and gay men to accept their homosexuality more fully than was possible earlier in their lives. Sometimes coming out is not possible until a parent dies. Even in old age, lesbians and gay men may still be coming out—when a partner dies, for example, when lifetime habits of secrecy change, or when a practice such as yoga or meditation leads to greater integration of sexual and spiritual lives.

In the 1990s, more than ever before, it is possible for young people to come out relatively easily, because they have both the support of older lesbians and gay men and many sources of information about homosexuality. On the other hand, even today the coming out process for many in their teens and early twenties is complicated by rejection by family and friends, harassment at school, and the resulting feelings of self-doubt.

A common experience for people just beginning to be aware of their gay identity, whatever their age, is to feel some discomfort or even shame and guilt at the thought of sex with another woman or another man, or to feel these emotions after the first couple of sexual encounters, but soon thereafter to accept their feelings completely. The self-disapproval comes from external voices which have been internalized by the person until he or she actually experiences gay or lesbian sex, when overwhelmingly positive feelings take over. The heightened sense of well-being resulting from sexual pleasure is accompanied by a recognition that "this is who I am" or "now I understand the feelings I have always had." When two people experience this transformation simultaneously, their euphoria may be more intense than anything they have ever felt before, and it may lead them to make bold choices they would otherwise not make—to quit jobs or change careers, for example, to leave husbands or wives, to move across the country, to become involved in gay liberation or women's liberation. The sexual experience, powerful in itself, is doubly powerful when it explains for the first time the meaning of one's deepest longings and desires. Gay sex is potent and irrepressible because it brings self-discovery. It is as deeply felt as one's racial identity, nationality, or gender. That is why it cannot be suppressed.

How do people know they are lesbian or gay? By seeing a pattern in their emotional lives—often or always feeling drawn to those of their own sex and feeling little or no sexual interest in the opposite sex. A single experience does not make a person gay, but a single experience may illuminate his or her past emotional history, as usually happens in coming out. Some people grow up knowing they are gay and they remain exclusively gay; others who are not sure try heterosexual experiences before coming out; and still others grow up assuming they are heterosexual, remain for years in heterosexual relationships, and only later have feelings and experiences that reveal their gay identities.

Chris Bates, a member of Black and White Men Together, believes that it is harder for Blacks to come out than for whites: "we don't have a strong economic and social circle to fall back on when our families turn away . . . so there is a greater hesitancy to put our lives on the line" (*Gay in America* 1989: 63).

Many homosexuals are "out of the closet" in some areas of their lives but not in others, either because they have a strong sense of privacy or because they fear negative consequences of revealing their emotional/sexual identity. Some women are out to their friends and co-workers but not to their children, while others may be out at home but not at work. Some gay men and lesbians are out to everyone but their parents. Occasionally a lesbian or gay man goes back into the closet, when changing jobs, for example, or when leaving a big city for a small town. It happens, too, that a politically active lesbian or gay man, one who has been completely out of the closet for a long time, will have an experience that reveals that even she or he has not been totally self-accepting. A gay writer may not want his hometown newspaper to publish the titles of his works, or a lesbian may conceal the sex of her partner when she visits an old school friend.

ATTACKS ON GAY SEXUALITY

The basis for the attack on gay sex is a religious belief that sex exists only for procreation. When large families were economic units and when the United States' population was small, this belief had some justification. Today it is an anachronism, although non-procreative sex has been considered a threat to capitalism, which needs a big labor force to expand (Adam 1987: 34). Attacks on homosexuals for not reproducing mask racist fears that the decline in the fertility of white women threatens white domination. Gradually the attitude that sexual pleasure is the purpose of sexual acts replaced the older view, as more people followed their own instincts and experiences rather than religious pronouncements, but the influence of the traditional view of sex can still be felt. When a group of United Church of Christ members in Minneapolis formed a gay congregation, Spirit of the Lakes Church, they were rebuked by a UCC minister who said that gay sex is addictive, selfish, and adulterous (*Minneapolis Star Tribune,* 23 April 1990: 1A). This is a new variation of the old charge that gay sex is unnatural because it does not lead to procreation. These slurs reveal more about religious prejudice than about the actual day-to-day lives of lesbians and gay men. Individuals among them, like individual heterosexuals, may be selfish or addicted to sex, but to characterize 10–15 percent of the US population with these pejorative labels is grossly unfair. Since gay men and lesbians in long-term monogamous relationships are just as condemned here as gays who have several sexual partners, it is clear that homosexuality itself, the state of being, not just a kind of sex act, provokes the minister's wrath. Furthermore, the adultery charge is absurd: the concept is meaningful only in the context of marriage, and homosexual marriage is presently forbidden by law except in Denmark.

Prejudice against gay sexuality is not limited to the uneducated. In May 1990, when lesbian and gay teachers in San Francisco proposed a modest counseling program for gay students, arguing that they have special needs, the school superintendent opposed the plan, saying that schools must not "entice" students into homosexuality. Young people do not become heterosexual or homosexual because of what they read or hear at school. The point is to help them be comfortable with the identities that are already being formed. It is ludicrous to suppose that heterosexual teens will be drawn to homosexuality simply because they are given unbiased information about it in a classroom or by a counselor. The high suicide rate among gay teens is more than enough justification for school counseling programs. After the San Francisco superintendent's enticement remark was widely quoted in the newspapers and on television, he agreed to a counseling program based on a Los Angeles model, Project 10. The staid *Wall Street Journal* ran a front-page story on the controversy over Project 10 and comparable school programs (12 June 1990), a sign that the open discussion of homosexuality is slowly becoming acceptable. Encouraging it in schools benefits heterosexual students as well as gay students. Until the AIDS epidemic ends, school officials unable to deal with homosexuality will not only perpetuate ignorance and stereotypes, they will also endanger the lives of young people.

The furor in 1989 and 1990 over the photographs of Robert Mapplethorpe, an artist who died of AIDS, showed how anti-gay bigotry and a more general distrust of art can become intertwined. An exhibit of Mapplethorpe's work, some of it portraying explicit gay male sex, was dropped by the Corcoran gallery after members of Congress, notably Senator Helms, called the photography obscene and attacked the National Endowment for the Arts for funding the exhibit. In the same interviews in which Helms said that no art work on homosexual themes should be federally funded, he scorned an Alexander Calder mobile of clouds and mountains in front of the Senate Office Building. The Mapplethorpe exhibit was eventually shown in several cities, including Cincinnati, where museum curator Dennis Barrie was ordered by a judge to face a jury trial on misdemeanor obscenity charges. Standards for judging obscenity are notoriously imprecise, and no workable definition has been agreed upon.

Helms was offended by the depiction of sex acts between men and by photographs which showed Black men in erotic poses with white men. Paradoxically, gay sex is more acceptable now than it has ever been before, but at the same time it is more vehemently attacked. Mapplethorpe's exhibit would not have interested a large non-gay audience ten years ago, nor would it have been funded by the National Endowment for the Arts. But its very visibility led to angry denunciations of gay people. The attack by Helms made Mapplethorpe much better known than he had been before.

DEFENSE OF GAY SEXUALITY

The simplest and most basic justification for the sexual practices of lesbians and gay men is that gay sex is as natural for them as heterosexual expression is for the majority. "Natural" means occurring in the animal world as well as among humans in most societies throughout history. Whether "natural" as applied to gay sex also means innate drives is a more complex question. The idea that gay sex is natural is not a new one; it is a Victorian idea that gained little acceptance until the 1970s. In theory, if a behavior is natural for humans, it is so whether practiced by a few or by millions. In practice, however, the idea that gay sex is natural was not persuasive until thousands of people said it was. As long as homosexuality was thought to be rare, it could be labeled abnormal. Anyone who dared to call the evidence flawed or nonexistent could be ignored or ostracized. Thus the discovery that homosexual behavior is widespread became the most effective rebuttal to the statement that it is unnatural.

A second justification is that lesbians and gay men have the right to privacy when they have consensual sex with other adults. This principle has long been accepted for heterosexuals; its extension to homosexuals remains controversial. In the past, the right to privacy of people thought sick or sinful could easily be ignored, and since public disclosure could carry severe penalties—loss of jobs, loss of child custody, shock treatment, imprisonment, public humiliation— claiming the right to privacy was unthinkable. The majority, whose privacy *was* respected, could see no parallel between their sexuality and homosexuality. Only the willingness of huge numbers of lesbians and gay men to announce their sexual preference in the 1970s and 1980s made the parallel obvious: if heterosexuals have the right to privacy, so, too, do they.[25]

In a free society where people claim the right to self-determination, they decide for themselves what sexual behavior suits them and leads to their full emotional and psychological development. Their habits and choices may not seem reasonable or normal to their neighbors and may even seem dangerous, but, as long as the rights of others are not infringed, the choices should be tolerated. For gay men and lesbians, self-determination means not only the right to privacy but the right to public sexual expression. The Olga Broumas poem "Kissing Against the Light" describes a lesbian couple kissing as they cross the street. Police who arrest gay men cruising in public places attack not just a particular sexual practice but the principle of free sexual expression. Society places many limits on the right of its citizens to self-expression—zoning laws for example, and child abuse laws—but the fundamental unfairness of punishing people for being homosexual is now obvious to most people.

And even if harassing lesbians and gay men could be defended on philosophical or religious grounds, the state has no legitimate reason to control their sexual expression and no interest in creating the machinery it would need to pursue anti-homosexual policies in a thorough and systematic way, or even in a way that would ensure that heterosexuals would not be caught in the machinery. In fact, in America, these policies, although they have done much harm, have never gone beyond capricious and sporadic attempts to suppress behavior, and they have varied greatly from place to place. Thus another reason for tolerating gay sex is that the alternative is unworkable. Furthermore, when police spy on homosexuals, courts prosecute them, and jails house them, a great deal of taxpayers' money is wasted.

The issue is not only whether certain forms of sexual behavior are natural or moral but whether any form of individual behavior not harmful to others should be regulated by the state. In *Bowers* v. *Hardwick* (1986), the Supreme Court upheld the constitutionality of sodomy laws by a vote of 5 to 4. The majority reasoned that private sexual activity between consenting adults is not protected by the Constitution even in a person's own bedroom. Hardwick was arrested in his bedroom by a policeman looking for him because of an unpaid ticket. The minority opinion in this case was that private homosexual conduct should not be condemned because it does not interfere with the rights of others. Although sodomy laws are often ignored, their existence is oppressive and even in the 1990s people are prosecuted under them. In justifying their opinion, the majority in *Bowers* v. *Hardwick* cited proscriptions against homosexuality in the time of Henry VIII. But the 1553 statute that had homosexuality punishable by death was simply a Church law taken over by the state, which accepted the Church rationale that homosexuality was unnatural. The fact that religious prejudice was written into English law in the sixteenth century hardly justifies writing it into American law in 1986. By a one vote margin, lesbians and gay men were relegated to second-class citizenship. If a future Supreme Court takes seriously the principle of the separation of church and state, *Bowers* v. *Hardwick* will be overturned.

The struggle for the acceptance of gay male and lesbian sexuality is part of a much larger struggle between advocates of many forms of sexual freedom and those who favor authoritarian control over private lives. When Margaret Sanger crusaded for birth control early in this century, for example, she was met by the same kind of opposition now venting its fury on gay liberation. Artists and film-makers who wanted to depict sex before the 1960s strove for the same freedom of expression now sought by lesbians and gay men. Inter-racial love affairs or marriage, generally accepted today, were once regarded as unnatural, the same judgment now passed on gay sex. Although widely practiced today, non-monogamy, cohabitation, divorce, and abortion were once condemned.

VISUAL IMAGES

Widespread acceptance of visual images of lesbian or gay male sex is one of the last frontiers of gay liberation. Lesbians and gay men are beginning to be accepted in many roles, as parents, friends, co-workers, teachers, taxpayers. Their sexuality has been grudgingly accepted as long as they kept quiet about it. If they mentioned it they were called "too blatant." Now lesbians and gay men are demanding that they be seen as sexual beings, without being stereotyped as *only* sexual beings. The explicitness of Mapplethorpe's photographs is a step towards liberation because it offers gay men the mirror of their sexual selves that heterosexuals take for granted. Visual images demystify homosexual acts and make them less frightening, except to people who find sex itself frightening. The taboo-breaking Mapplethorpe exhibit encourages freedom of sexual expression in areas besides photography—in books and movies, for example, and in dance, theater, and painting. In the past, homosexuals were isolated when they incurred the wrath of right-wing politicians and community leaders. Now that they and artists have a common enemy, the irrationality of attacks on them is easier to recognize.

Because women artists are not as likely as male artists to get national attention, the paintings and photographs by lesbian artists are not as well known as the works of Mapplethorpe. Since the late 1960s, however, lesbian artists have created many sexually explicit images. Slideshows at lesbian events and at women's bookstores, presentations at women's studies conferences, and exhibitions at women's cultural centers have helped to popularize lesbian images and to educate women about lesbian sex. The film *Desert Hearts,* based on Jane Rule's novel, was the first mainstream film to portray lesbian lovemaking. Several short story collections describe sex between women.[26] In the past, lesbian erotic images were created for men and, like other pornography, degraded women by objectifying them. Women-created images of lesbian sex celebrate it in the context of lesbian lives. This is true of the work published early in the 1980s in *The Blatant Image,* a feminist photography journal. In the 1990s, women who enjoy reading explicit descriptions of sex between women subscribe to the periodicals *On Our Backs* and *Bad Attitude.*

Some lesbians disapprove of these publications, believing that any explicit descriptions of lesbian sex serve only to titillate men, while others claim that the production by lesbians of sexually explicit work properly challenges the monopoly on sexual representation by the heterosexual majority. "Drawing the Line," an exhibit of sexually explicit photographs of lesbians created by a group of Vancouver artists, is accompanied by a blank wall on which viewers write their reactions to what they have seen. The title alludes to the fact that drawing the line between sexually explicit art and pornography is difficult.

The work of Tee Corinne has been especially important in conveying positive sexual images of lesbians. A photographer, artist, art historian, writer, and sex educator, Tee Corinne has introduced many women to the historical aspects of lesbian sexuality through her lectures and slideshows. In one of her slideshows, two rag dolls make love. Her publications include the erotic photo collection *Yantras of Women Love; Dreams of the Woman who Loved Sex;* and *Intricate Passions: a Collection of Erotic Short Fiction.*[27]

CONCLUSION

The topic of gay and lesbian sex deserves a great deal of further study. We have no idea, for example, how many people, past and present, have repressed homosexual feelings. Nor do we know how many today would act upon their homosexual instincts if social conditioning to be heterosexual were not so strong. As more biographies are written about homosexuals, more light will be shed on sexual behavior. Homosexuality turns up as an influence in surprising places. British travel literature of the eighteenth and nineteenth centuries, for example, is to some extent a byproduct of the homosexual drives of its authors: sex with men in distant lands was far safer than it was in England. The Chinese communists regard homosexuality as an example of Western decadence, but research in progress by Louis Crompton reveals a 2500 year tradition of homosexuality in China. A survey could be done of countries that still imprison people for homosexual acts.

Acceptance of gay and lesbian sex has greatly increased since 1949, when *Reader's Guide* used "sex perversion" as a cross-reference for homosexuality. Capital punishment for sodomy in England ended only ninety years before that. The case of Alan Turing dramatically illustrates the revolutionary change in thinking: Turing was a British mathematician whose machine, a forerunner of the computer, broke the German code in World War II. Later discovered by police to be homosexual, Turing was arrested and injected with female hormones for a year because psychiatrists believed they could kill his sexual instincts. The story of this savagery has a tinge of medieval torture to it. Even if they do not approve of homosexuality, most people today do not favor execution, castration, or injections as punishment for it; they say "sexual orientation" instead of "sexual perversion." When the *San Francisco Examiner* ran a front-page picture of two gay teenagers naked from the waist up holding a condom (2 May 1990), it marked a significant shift in the perception of gay sex. Slowly its widespread existence is becoming acknowledged. But the sexual liberation of gay men and lesbians has a long way to go. The attitudes held by Turing's tormentors have not disappeared. Sodomy laws have not been declared unconstitutional. Most middle-school and high-school students who are gay have no gay counseling program at their schools and the streets of America are not as safe for lesbians and gay men as they are for heterosexuals.

3

GAY AND LESBIAN LIBERATION AS A POLITICAL MOVEMENT

Imagine that you are a college student who happens to be left-handed. You encounter the following situations:

* All of the seats in the lecture hall where your American history class meets have a wide arm on the right side for a notebook. The instructor, seeing you turned at an awkward angle to write with your left hand, tells the class that left-handedness is unnatural.
* Curious about this judgment, you go to the library to read a book on left-handedness. You locate only two; the acquisitions librarian finds the topic embarrassing.
* You find an apartment near the campus. The landlord is friendly until

he sees you sign the application with your left hand. Abruptly he tells you that the apartment is taken.

★ You work in one of the science labs on campus. One day the professor who runs lab sees you holding a test tube in your left hand. He fires you saying, "I don't want your kind here."

★ Your friend's application to attend a seminary is rejected because she is left-handed, making her morally flawed in the eyes of the admissions committee.

★ Two married left-handers apply to live in married students' housing. They are rejected because married students' housing is only for the right-handed.

★ After you organize a campus group for left-handers, you try to get office space in the student union. You are refused.

Discrimination against homosexuals is just as arbitrary as discrimination against left-handed people would be. No inference can be made about a person's worth or character, habits, emotional stability, or social usefulness when only his or her sexual preference is known. Yet at a time when discrimination against Blacks, Jews, and women, though prevalent, is no longer officially sanctioned, discrimination against homosexuals is condoned by both church and state.

The parts of this chapter are (1) an overview of gay politics; (2) a brief description of the historical roots of modern-day gay liberation and of the period 1970–90; and (3) a discussion of the political issues facing lesbians and gay men today.

OVERVIEW OF GAY POLITICS

The gay and lesbian liberation movement has many political goals. In 1979, a French gay rights group called for:

★ deletion of homosexuality from the World Health Organization classification of mental illness;

★ compensation for gay victims of Nazism;

★ right of asylum to persons persecuted in other countries because of their homosexuality;

★ international recognition of the problem of anti-gay violence.

In addition to these international goals, the group listed reforms within individual countries:

* an end to housing and job discrimination;
* addition of sexual preference to civil rights laws;
* custody, visitation, and adoption rights;
* recognition of the rights of a same-sex couple;
* destruction of police files on lesbians and gay men (Adam 1987: 123).

These and other gay rights goals, such as an end to stereotypic portrayals in the media and First Amendment protection for art and literature depicting homosexuality, can be encompassed by two objectives:

(1) an end to all laws and practices that discriminate against lesbians and gay men;
(2) complete acceptance of their sexuality.

The first will require reforms difficult to achieve. The second is more radical because it requires a change in consciousness: the dominant group, heterosexuals, would have to see the sexual minority as fully equal to themselves. Although that goal seems nearly as unattainable as it was in 1979, it is an essential part of gay liberation because changes in laws and customs, important as they are, cannot guarantee permanent security to homosexuals. Only when the people around them perceive them as honorable, whole human beings will they be full citizens.

A starting point for gay politics is the assumption that lesbians and gay men are a true minority. They are like an ethnic minority, although ethnic identity differs from sexual identity in that it is conferred at birth and passed on through the family. Also, those who take on a lesbian or a gay identity already have various other identities—ethnic, racial, class, gender, religion—which claim allegiance (Epstein 1987: 35). Furthermore, sexual preference differs from race and sex in that the appearance of a person does not make it obvious. Can a group many of whose members are invisible be a minority? Often the most visible gays are affluent white men to whom minority status seems wrongly applied. Nevertheless, lesbians and gay men constitute a minority because they are discriminated against on the basis of their sexual orientation and because heterosexuality is promoted by the major institutions of society.

On the other hand, some gay people believe that they are not a minority because, except for their sexual preference, they are just like everybody else. It is true that the lives of many lesbians and gay men may be indistinguishable from the lives of their heterosexual friends, co-workers, and neighbors, but their single difference is immensely important. It defines them in the eyes of the majority; it means they have fewer civil rights than heterosexuals; and it labels them criminals in the states that still have sodomy laws. Politically conscious gay people understand that even though they may have a great deal in common with heterosexuals—shared goals and values, for example, or race—they are very different. No matter how assimilated into mainstream life a lesbian or a gay man becomes, he or she will always be perceived as different. This situation may change if all sanctions against homosexuality are lifted. Until then, gay people will be a minority.

By the early 1970s, many people who had been conditioned by prejudice and discrimination to cover up their true identities were able to conclude that "gay is good," but this slogan was not merely a rallying cry: it was a fervent rejection of all arguments from authority about homosexuality, of the position that homosexuality is wrong because some expert says it is. "Gay is good" meant that only empirical evidence would now be valid. Weighing their personal experience gay men and lesbians said, in effect, "we are the experts." The popularity of "gay is good" represented a radical move away from victim or criminal status to the status of a self-defining minority.

Why did this change occur in America and why did it come in the 1970s? Here we have the tradition of interest groups and ethic voting blocs, weak national parties, the idea of liberal individualism, and, "above all, the very American belief that we have the power to invent ourselves from scratch."[1] The last is particularly important because homosexual practices had been condemned for centuries, and thus the claim that "gay is good" required those making it to invent themselves from scratch in order to achieve self-respect. No one grew up preparing for a homosexual adult life.

Gay liberation emerged in the 1970s for several reasons, including pervasive police harassment in the 1950s and 1960s and weakening taboos against frank discussion of homosexuality (D'Emilio and Freedman 1988: 319). Other main causes, discussed in this chapter, are (1) social changes in the 1960s and the example of 1960s' protest movements and (2) groundwork laid by the early homosexual rights movement. A third, the growth of a gay subculture, is described in Chapter 5.

By the late 1960s, the people who would come out in the next decade were either radicalized or deeply influenced by the anti-war movement. Its anti-authoritarian spirit was very significant for homosexuals, especially the young, who questioned the traditional labels applied to them such as sick and sinful. In the 1950s homosexuals felt the heavy weight of medical prejudice, police harassment and church condemnation, but were not able to challenge these authorities with the same confidence that they later felt. Just as the military, the government, and the churches that supported the war in Viet Nam were discredited in the eyes of many, medical figures too lost their aura of infallibility. In 1970, lesbians and gay men disrupted a session on aversion therapy (to discourage homosexuality) at a meeting of the American Psychiatric Association. Neither the homophiles of the 1950s nor the militant homosexual organizers of the early 1960s could have done that because they had no context for rowdy, noisy demonstrations. The anti-war movement provided that context.

At the same time, the hippies symbolized a new spirit of sexual freedom which influenced a great many people who did not actually become hippies. Many kinds of non-conformity flourished in the late sixties, creating a climate in which sexual deviance could be mentioned. Male hippies rebelled against the macho look which symbolized aggression and war. Their inferior status led many women to rethink traditional sex roles and to emphasize sexual pleasure. Since sexual experimentation was encouraged, people who were gay discovered that sooner than they might have in the 1950s. Thoreau's phrase about marching to a different drummer, very popular in the sixties, inspired those who felt different in their sexuality.

Homosexuals could call themselves "gay," that is, assume a political identity, however, only because of the example of other movements, especially civil rights. Without the sixties' protest movements, gay and lesbian liberation would not have emerged in the 1970s. In the early 1960s only a few homosexuals, such as Washington DC activist Frank Kameny, saw the parallel between themselves and Blacks which was obvious to many by the end of the decade.

The sixties' protest movements, especially civil rights and later the women's movement, showed that seemingly entrenched ideas that once seemed absolute—the necessity of war, for example, the inferiority of Blacks or the inferiority of women—could be unmasked as prejudices of a ruling elite rather than as verifiable accounts of reality. The model for mass demonstrations came from the civil rights movement and the anti-war movement, as did the sense of having a righteous cause.

Sexual preference alone could not have produced the moral fervor of the gay activists, however; it was the sense of being persecuted for what was normal that drove them to organize. Sustained protest did not begin until large numbers of homosexuals began to see that the prejudices against them were neither natural nor inevitable but the markers of a particular culture. In addition, the civil rights movement, the anti-war movement, and by 1969 the women's movement attracted large numbers of homosexuals. Nearly always closeted, they nevertheless quietly made contact with other homosexuals in these mass movements. A few knew that respected figures such as writer James Baldwin, civil rights leader Bayard Rustin, and pacifist leader Barbara Deming were homosexual. Paul Goodman, admired by the young for his book *Growing Up Absurd,* later joked that FBI films of anti-war demonstrations must have had many shots of him groping another man. When homosexuals active in these causes began organizing under the name "gay," they had an exhilarating sense of creating a movement of their own, as important as the civil rights movement and the women's movement. In a way it was more difficult because homosexuals were more despised than either Blacks or women. Many heterosexual Americans who supported equal rights for Blacks and for women were not prepared to see homosexuals as their equals. And many homosexuals before 1970 did not regard themselves as victims of oppression. Slowly, by analogy to Blacks and women, they began to see themselves in this light and to feel anger at unjust treatment. But before it could be born the movement required a critical mass of people willing first to come out of the closet and second to identify with everyone else who had come out.

Both gay liberation and women's liberation emerged as powerful forces at the end of the 1960s. Both had Victorian roots. Both focused on the right of sexual self-determination and both claimed equality for people long thought to be inferior. The feminist agenda had obvious parallels in the aims of gay liberation: an end to social control of sexuality, institutionalized prejudice, and sexism. Like gay activists, feminists wanted recognition of new relationships. Because lesbian feminism grew out of the women's movement rather than out of gay liberation, it is discussed in a separate chapter.

Participants in the 1960s' protest movements were generally not despised in the way gay people are despised. In fact, one of the hallmarks of gay liberation is the hatred and opposition it arouses. Certainly Blacks have been hated in the United States but no politician dares to condemn them publicly. The families of Blacks do not reject their children. But homosexuals are still targets of intense loathing. Homophobia, the irrational hatred of homosexuals, is discussed in Chapter 4.

HISTORICAL ROOTS OF THE MODERN GAY AND LESBIAN LIBERATION MOVEMENT

The movement known today as gay and lesbian rights may be divided into three broad periods: (1) the 1890s to World War II—homosexual emancipation; (2) post-war to the Stonewall Riot of 1969—the homophile movement; and (3) gay and lesbian liberation.[2]

Homosexual emancipation refers to a series of related and unrelated attempts to study homosexuality, to bring homosexuals together, and to gain acceptance of their difference. The homosexual periodical *Der Eigene* (The Community of the Special) began publishing in 1896. In the following year, a German doctor, Magnus Hirschfeld, founded the Scientific-Humanitarian Committee, the first organization dedicated to ending discrimination against homosexuals (*Encyclopedia of Homosexuality* 1990: 537; Adam (1987): 17–25). In 1903 the Committee obtained 6,000 names on a petition to repeal paragraph 175 of the German penal code, which made homosexuality illegal. Signers included Albert Einstein, Thomas Mann, Karl Jaspers, Martin Buber, and Hermann Hesse. But it was not until 1921 that Hirschfeld founded the Institute for Sex Research in Berlin, followed two years later by the World League for Sexual Reform on a Scientific Basis, which held several conferences. The recurrence of the word "scientific" is important here because it shows that the German reformers believed science was on their side. From the vantage point of the 1990s, their faith seems both misplaced and well placed, misplaced because medical science and social science did great harm to homosexuals until the 1970s; well placed because, in time, research by the zoologist Alfred Kinsey established that homosexuality was widespread, and the first studies of a representative sample of gay men, published in the 1950s and 1960s by psychologist Evelyn Hooker, established that it was normal, a conclusion homosexuals themselves had reached through their own experience. Hooker concluded that previous research was flawed because it was limited to people who sought psychological counseling (Keen 1989, Part 1: 37).

Why did the movement begin in Germany rather than in France, England or America? France had no sodomy law to protest against. In the nineteenth century, moreover, German scholarship was more advanced than scholarship in England or the United States. Germans were free of the puritan heritage of the latter countries, and their social value of cultivating healthy bodies discouraged prudery and sexual repression. Above all, Germany was the only country in the world where homosexual cafes, bars, clubs, and social groups flourished (*Encyclopedia of Homosexuality* 1990: 538).[3] But the Nazis destroyed the Institute for Sex Research. All of its books and papers, including many artistic and literary works having nothing to do with sex, were publicly burned May 6, 1933. As a Jew and a leftist, Hirschfeld was especially hated by the Nazis. They obliterated the early homosexual rights movement "through systematic extermination and ideological control" from 1933 to 1945 (Adam 1987: 54). Sent to concentration camps, thousands of male homosexuals were forced to wear pink triangles, a symbol appropriated later by gay liberation. Paragraph 175 was not removed from the penal code until the late 1960s.[4]

The trial of Oscar Wilde in 1895 helped the cause that would later be known as gay rights by bringing homosexuality into the open for the first time in England. It had been known before—men were executed for it in the early nineteenth century and in 1885 an amendment to an anti-prostitution bill made male homosexuality a criminal act— but the dramatic, much-publicized trial made it a public issue. The results were disastrous for Wilde—imprisonment, disgrace, and death at 44 a few years after his release from prison. But many men in England and other countries who read about the trial must have come to understand their own sexual feelings through it. When the prosecutor asked Wilde about "the love that dare not speak its name," a line from a poem by Wilde's lover, Lord Alfred Douglas, he replied, "It is beautiful, it is fine, it is the noblest form of affection. There is nothing unnatural about it" (Adam 1987: 35). Vehemently disagreeing, Wilde's enemies sought to repress the subculture he represented. His fate created fear among homosexual Englishmen, some of whom went to France to escape detection.

It was not until 1928 that lesbianism made a similarly sensational appearance in England, with the obscenity trial of *The Well of Loneliness* by Radclyffe Hall. Unlike Wilde, Hall had many defenders and she did not go to jail. The fact that *The Well of Loneliness* described sex between women and directly pleaded for tolerance made it an immensely important book. Until the 1970s it helped thousands of women to acknowledge their sexual feelings for other women. The *Well* is significant even today, according to Esther Newton, because its protagonist Stephen Gordon symbolizes "the stigma of lesbianism (by being mannish) just as the effeminate man is the stigma-bearer for gay men."[5] Without the obscenity trial, the novel might have fallen into obscurity. Another novel by Radclyffe Hall, *The Unlit Lamp* (1924), is a better psychological portrait of lesbians.

Although England had no organized homosexual emancipation movement in the years when Magnus Hirschfeld was leading the one in Germany, the Bloomsbury circle of friends who were among the most influential English artists, writers, and intellectuals from 1905 through the 1920s broke the silence surrounding homosexuality in their private conversations, their letters, and, less frequently, in their published works. They were motivated in part by a rejection of the overbearing authoritarianism of their Victorian fathers and of Victorian sexual morality. They valued frankness about sex. "Manly" qualities in women and "womanly" qualities in men appealed to them.[6] Several testified against censorship at the obscenity trial of *The Well of Loneliness*. In view of the accomplishments of Maynard Keynes in economics, E. M. Forster and Virginia Woolf in fiction, Duncan Grant in painting, and Lytton Strachey in biography, the notion that homosexuals were disordered seemed ludicrous. Although the literary, historical and aesthetic aspects of homosexuality interested the Bloomsbury circle more than legal reform, they exemplified the new spirit of open inquiry into homosexuality which was needed to prepare the ground for later political action.

As noted in Chapter 2, World War II was important for American homosexuals because it brought large numbers of them in contact with each other for the first time. After the war, many chose to live in big cities, knowing their relative anonymity there would make a homosexual life easier. War work was empowering for many lesbians who struck out on their own in the late 1940s, and the war gave many men time to consider alternatives to the husband and breadwinner role they might automatically have assumed in peacetime. Unjust and irrational treatment of homosexuals by the military during World War II, documented in Allan Berube's *Coming out under Fire* (1990), did not lead to an organized resistance movement but it did allow many lesbians and gay men to see themselves as belonging to a group. A postwar novel by John Horne Burns, *The Gallery,* described homosexuals as "a minority that should be left alone" (Berube 1990: 251).

This view, echoing the opinions of progressive Germans in the

1890s and of the Bloomsbury painters and writers of the Edwardian period and later, took root finally in 1950, when a small band of southern California men founded the Mattachine Society, taking the name from medieval masked singers, to indicate that homosexuals were an unknown people (*Encyclopedia of Homosexuality* 1990: 779).[7] As Marxists, Harry Hay and other founders of Mattachine believed that prejudice against them was not a problem individuals could solve because it was deeply ingrained in American institutions. Gradually they came to view homosexuals as an oppressed minority, made up of people who for the most part did not place this interpretation on their private lives. Their goal therefore was to popularize the idea of a homosexual minority, to develop group consciousness. Their discussions allowed participants to feel their self-worth for the first time (D'Emilio 1983b: 64–8). Hay resigned from the Communist Party so that it would not be associated with homosexuals at a time when Senator Joseph McCarthy was attacking both groups. A split developed in Mattachine between the founders, who envisioned a separate homosexual culture, and members who thought this strategy would only increase hostility to them and who preferred to integrate into mainstream society because they felt no different from heterosexuals except in their sexual lives (D'Emilio 1983b: 79). This latter view prevailed, with the result that a philosophy of individualism replaced that of collective, militant action. The founders thought they could validate homosexuality through their own positive experience of it, while the integrationists deferred to experts on sexuality (D'Emilio 1983b: 81).

Another way of describing these divergent viewpoints is to say that, for the leftists, homosexuality was not a problem; the problem lay in institutions. The integrationists saw social rejection as their problem, one which they wanted mainstream professionals to treat sympathetically rather than by condemning them. In the McCarthy era, one of the most repressive periods in American history, being different was dangerous. Even socializing with other homosexuals took great courage. In every state, homosexual acts were illegal, and even the American Civil Liberties Union (ACLU) supported these repressive laws (D'Emilio 1983b: 112). The integrationists' safe position had strong appeal, therefore, to people who were keenly aware of the punishment they could face if their homosexuality became known. At that time, purges of homosexuals were supported by the newspapers, and "medical researchers tinkered with lobotomies, castration, and electric shock" to "rehabilitate" them (Adam 1987: 60).

Members of Mattachine and the pioneer lesbian group Daughters of Bilitis (DOB), named for a woman who was thought to be Sappho's contemporary, described themselves as "the homophile movement," literally "love of same." This was a more positive, broader term than "homosexual," suggesting a philosophy or attitude as much as a sexual practice. De-emphasizing sex was strategic because it was sex acts that called down opprobrium on homosexuals.

In the 1960s the movement grew slowly. By then, gay subcultures were thriving in the United States, and heterosexuals began to be aware of their existence. A few books, mostly negative, were published on the subject of homosexuality. Lawyers began to argue for repeal of sodomy laws. As the topic of homosexuality began to lose some of its shock value, homophiles could be more assertive; but the change had a negative consequence as well because the medical view that homosexuality is a mental illness could be more widely disseminated (D'Emilio 1983b: 147, 162). In 1965, for the first time, small numbers of militant homophiles picketed and paraded for their rights. D'Emilio notes that on the same day in May that 20,000 anti-war protesters gathered at the Washington Monument, seven men and three women marched for homosexual rights in front of the White House (p. 165). Targets of other demonstrations were the Pentagon, the State Department, and Independence Hall in Philadelphia July Fourth (p. 165). Del Martin and Phyllis Lyon, two founders of DOB, recall that, on New Year's Day 1965, a costume ball was held in San Francisco to benefit the newly formed Council on Religion and the Homosexual. Police obstructed the entrance with a paddy wagon, flooded the entrance with lights, and took photos of everyone who entered the hall. Five hundred lesbians and gay men, accompanied by many ministers and their wives, defied police by entering. Several people, including lawyers, were arrested. The next day, seven ministers held a press conference to denounce the police, and the ACLU persuaded the judge to dismiss charges.[8] The importance of this incident is that homosexuals were no longer isolated and cowed into submission. A coalition of homosexuals and progressive heterosexuals vigorously protested gross injustices that would previously have been known only to the victims.

In August 1966, movement groups created the North American Conference of Homophile Organizations, which established a legal fund, sponsored protests against discrimination by the federal government, and encouraged new groups to form. New York Mattachine passed out literature in Greenwich Village and sent many members to appear on radio and television shows and to speak to hundreds of non-gay groups (D'Emilio 1983b: 197, 209). In 1967, the ACLU reversed its earlier position by saying that consensual sex acts between adults were protected by the constitutional right to privacy (p. 213). Despite many other signs of progress, a daunting problem remained: most homosexuals had not taken the step of joining the homophile movement. From 1950 to 1969, the membership of all the groups totalled only about 5,000 (p. 219).

Stonewall was the shot heard round the homosexual world. On that day, patrons of the Stonewall Inn, a Greenwich Village bar popular with Puerto Rican drag queens and lesbians, responded to a police raid by throwing beer cans and bottles because they were angry at police surveillance of their private gathering places. In the ensuing riot, which lasted two nights, a crowd of 2,000 battled 400 policemen. Before, the stigma attached to homosexuality and the resulting fear of exposure had kept homosexuals in line. Stonewall was a symbolic end to victim status. Homosexuals had acquiesced to police brutality; gay people fought back. It was fitting that a new phase of the old struggle for acceptance of homosexuals had its start in a bar, for bars held a central place in gay culture: often they were the only places where people could be open. The first visit to a gay bar was often an initiation rite for a person coming to terms with his or her sexuality or for those who accepted their orientation but had never met another homosexual. Also, bars drew people from different races and classes.

After Stonewall, "gay power" graffiti began to appear in Greenwich Village. The Gay Liberation Front (GLF), a New Left group, and the Gay Activist Alliance (GAA) were formed, and similar groups quickly sprang up in other parts of the country (*Encyclopedia of Homo-*

sexuality 1990: 1349). GLF stood for coalitions with other progressive groups, while the GAA, which took a single-issue stance, became more influential in the movement (Adam 1987: 78–80). Gay liberation could not be subsumed by the left, in the view of long-time activist Barbara Gittings, because of its "sheer chaotic nature" (Keen 1989, Part 4: 27). In addition, gay liberation tends to promote a high degree of individualism because sexual identity politics rises directly from private experiences that lead to feelings of being different from others. Nevertheless, Marxism exerted a strong influence on the movement: inspired by revolutionary rhetoric, activists no longer feared being known as homosexuals (D'Emilio 1983b: 233). Through the lens of Marxism the homophile goal of tolerance for homosexuals could be seen as inadequate; sexual freedom required structural change, not just changes in laws. In the 1970s, academic Marxists began to challenge the assumption that homosexuality is fixed and unchanging by examining the social forces that shape its definitions (*Encyclopedia of Homosexuality* 1990: 773–5).

Some homosexuals have been drawn to Marxism out of a sense of disenfranchisement and alienation, but class privilege and the freedom to express homosexuality have also been closely linked historically. When Marx urged workers to unite, he knew who and where they were; in industrialized nations they were highly visible and their numbers could be estimated. But the Victorian homosexuals who believed their lives were as healthy and as productive as the lives of heterosexuals had no idea how many people this radical notion might directly apply to. Neither did the "silent pioneers," the name given to homophile activists of the 1950s. Only in the 1970s did conditions allow isolated individuals who had been invisible to each other to name their sexual difference, come together, and forge a common bond. Now a cliché, the phrase "the personal is the political" made a great impact on homosexuals who heard it for the first time in the 1970s. Declaring their most private feelings was a radical political act. It called on everyone, not just the sexual minority, to rethink their most basic assumptions about love, sex, marriage, the family, and the legitimate role of the state in controlling private life. It rejected centuries of religious teaching and decades of medical hypothesizing. It said that sexual self-determination was a fundamental human right. Homosexuals could not be driven back into the closet because they had left in large numbers. Coming out made gay liberation possible.

Though it had political meaning, the act of coming out was highly personal as well. Some people achieved self-respect as lesbians and gay men and were accepted by friends and families relatively easily; others needed years to become completely comfortable with their sexual orientation. Some were "out" to only a handful of people; others went on television to promote gay rights. Coming out was a different experience for those who risked being fired than it was for lesbians and gay men in secure jobs. It was riskier for married homosexuals than for singles. Coming out was not the same for women and men. People of color found it an especially complex process because they needed to keep the allegiance of their families for protection in a white-ruled society. Often they remained in their communities of origin. In general, greater economic privilege gave white gays more options when families, friends, or employers rejected them. Activist Billy Jones, a founder of the National Coalition of Black Gay Men and Lesbians, recalls feeling torn between primary allegiance to the gay movement and to Black issues (Keen 1989, Part 4: 25), a dilemma that remains current for many people of color who join gay and lesbian liberation.

The experience of discovering an identity or reassessing a familiar one, shared by thousands of people all over America, quickly united strangers. Like people accustomed to blurred vision who suddenly see sharp images, the lesbians and gay men who came out in the 1970s found pieces of their lives forming a coherent pattern for the first time. The childhood and adolescent feelings for which there was no name, fantasies, marriage resistance or discomfort in marriage, attractions to certain movie stars, all bore meaning. Anyone who cannot remember a time when homosexuality was absolutely unmentionable may not fully understand the high spirits of the gay rights movement in its first decade.

The euphoria of coming out and of joining a new movement was channeled into much hard work, organizing, fund raising, and consciousness raising in the 1970s. Gay and lesbian groups were formed all over the country, especially in big cities. A major focus of the movement was the passage of laws protecting those who had come out from housing and job discrimination. Aside from addressing real problems, these laws had a strong symbolic significance for lesbians and gay men because they equated gays with established, respected minorities. Initial victories sparked a right-wing backlash epitomized by Anita Bryant and her "Save Our Children" campaign, which led to repeal of a gay rights ordinance in Dade County, Florida, and in several cities (Adam 1987: 102–20).

In the 1970s, the movement drew many people who didn't have the option of being closeted, according to veteran activist Eric Rofes. They felt queer, and they tended to have a leftist perspective. The mobilization of gays in response to Anita Bryant's homophobic crusade brought into the movement many who wanted assimilation into American society. They were established in careers and had different values from people radicalized in the 1960s. Echoing Rofes, long-time Los Angeles activist and gerontologist Sharon Raphael says that the movement changed in the late 1970s. Until then, volunteers ran everything; gay liberation was a grassroots movement.[9] Another characteristic of the movement in the 1970s is that it took Stonewall as the beginning of liberation. Naturally lesbians and gay men wanted a total break with the past because the past had been so oppressive. But many in the 1970s knew nothing of the homosexual emancipation movement or the homophile movement that began in 1950; that story had to be recovered by lesbian and gay historians.

The gay community in San Francisco, in California, and across the country experienced a traumatic year in 1978.[10] A huge campaign was needed to defeat the Briggs initiative, Proposition 6, which would have required schools to fire homosexuals or any teacher who mentioned homosexuality positively in a classroom. This was one of the most serious threats gay Americans ever faced, not only because it jeopardized the livelihood of some but also because it declared in the most emphatic way that lesbians and gay men were morally unfit; they could not be trusted with children. Like other homophobic demagogues, Briggs encouraged previously silent bigots to voice their hatred for gay people. In the fall of 1978, lesbians and gay men in San Francisco feared their meeting places and their clubs would be bombed.

There were no bombs that fall in San Francisco but everyone who worked in a downtown office housing the Gay National Educational Switchboard sensed danger. They tried to avoid paranoia but jumped when cars backfired. The outpouring of hatred inspired by Briggs awakened white lesbians and gay men to the ugliness of a society in which difference is condemned. It taught them, too, that the struggle for gay rights would be harder than they had imagined earlier in the decade. A state-wide defense against Briggs led to his overwhelming defeat at the polls in November, a victory not only for gay Californians but for those in other states who knew that similar attacks on teachers would be attempted elsewhere if Proposition 6 passed. But the campaign was exhausting because it often seemed that the struggle for equality was really a struggle for survival.

A far greater trauma, however, was the November 27 assassination of San Francisco supervisor Harvey Milk, the first gay person elected to office in a major city, and liberal mayor George Moscone. The candlelight procession that night from the Castro district to City Hall united the San Francisco gay community more deeply than the political victory a few weeks earlier. Thousands of San Franciscans who were not gay joined marchers from the Castro in a spontaneous ritual of grief. On the steps of City Hall friends and colleagues of Moscone and Milk paid tribute to them and played a tape Milk had made in anticipation of his murder. In campaigning against Briggs, he realized that his high profile made him an inviting target for a violent right-wing extremist. It was an eerie experience hearing Milk say, "Let the bullet that rips my brain open every closet door in America."

City supervisor Dan White, a conservative ex-policeman and ex-fireman who represented a blue-collar district of San Francisco, entered City Hall through a basement on the morning of November 27, 1978, so that he could evade the metal detectors at the main entrance. After shooting the mayor several times in the mayor's office, he reloaded his gun, walked to Milk's office, and shot him repeatedly. Ostensibly, he was angry at the mayor for refusing to reinstate him after he resigned from the board and angry at Milk for supporting the mayor. The real reason the two men were killed is that San Francisco had become too gay. Thousands of new gay and lesbian residents had arrived from all over the country in the 1970s. They were flexing their political muscle, as Milk's election in 1977 demonstrated. Though he alone fired the shots, Dan White represented a collective right-wing attempt to drive gay people back underground. No evidence of a conspiracy was found, but the identity of the man who murdered Milk and Moscone was less significant than the gathering storm of anti-gay hatred waiting to burst. After the police arrested Dan White, they treated him like a hero.

By eradicating a perceived threat to the well-being of many San Franciscans, Dan White escaped identification as a cold-blooded murderer. Gay people and their supporters saw him in that light, of course, but gay people were not powerful enough to be avenged. Before the trial, they were excluded from the jury. Neither the prosecution nor the defense wanted the political trial that would have exposed both White's underlying motive for the killings and the entrenched bigotry of the police department. It was safer for both prosecution and defense to portray the murders as the aberrations of an individual rather than as manifestations of a sick social system. Homophobia could not yet be named a social fact. Psychiatrists said White had overdosed on sugar and thus suffered "diminished capacity." The gay press and the liberal *Bay Guardian* scorned the "Twinkies defense."

Five months later, the verdict was manslaughter, the sentence seven years (of which White served five). California law allowed the death penalty for the murder of public officials. Outraged by this exoneration, 5,000 gay people took to the streets. They marched on City Hall and smashed its front doors. They overturned police cars and set them on fire. Hoards of police who were furious because their chief would not let them fight the City Hall demonstrators invaded the Castro and attacked pedestrians. At the Elephant Walk, a gay bar, they went on a rampage, destroying the bar and beating many men, some of them severely. The night's casualty toll was 100 gay people hospitalized and 61 policemen. Gay San Franciscans, mindful of the bar raids of the past and inured to occasional police brutality, were nevertheless shocked by the violence of the retaliatory attack on the Elephant Walk. Like the assassinations, it was a political act, intended to intimidate and silence them.

The "White Night Riots" left the gay community divided over

the question of the violence of their own members. Some leaders deplored it; others said, "consider the provocation." The barbarity of the verdict took time to absorb: the jury had said that premeditated murders were not serious crimes if the victims were a gay man and a mayor sympathetic to the gay community.

An astute grassroots politician, Harvey Milk embodied both the radical and reform strands of gay liberation. As a former Marine and former stockbroker, he had mainstream credentials. As a much-televised debater against Briggs, he wore a suit and spoke about the American tradition of civil liberty. Nearly everywhere else, Milk wore jeans and a T-shirt. He reached out to every minority in San Francisco. He spoke of a time when ordinary people would be empowered. Like Edward Carpenter, he had a vision extending beyond the gay community. Witty, irreverent, charismatic, and theatrical, Milk was very different from mainstream politicians. He celebrated his gay identity so exuberantly that he became a folk hero to lesbians and gay men.

By 1980, gay people seemed to have securely established themselves as a powerful minority. Even though the goal of changing the minds of an entire society about homosexuality seemed utopian, given the relative newness of the idea that "gay is good," thousands of organizations were created and, even more important, a new pride in being gay was expressed. The popular button "We Are Everywhere" signified this radical change.

Before the gains of the 1970s could be completely consolidated, however, a mysterious virus began killing gay men and, as years passed with a mounting death toll and no cure, the movement was deeply affected in ways that only future historians will be able to assess. Much political work was carried on, but not in the seventies' spirit that gay liberation was unstoppable. The right-wing backlash of the late 1970s intensified in the Reagan years. Anti-gay violence increased. Because of AIDS, homosexuality was linked to disease. Gay men and lesbians once again were forced to defend their right to exist.

Although AIDS took an inestimable toll on the gay community, the movement continued, partly because the AIDS crisis resulted in new political organizations and because other gay and lesbian groups kept springing up. Many people who were not ready to come out in the 1970s were ready in the 1980s, and many young people came out then as well. Gay groups in the 1980s tended to be more specialized than earlier ones: youth groups and senior groups, for example, recovery groups, a political action committee to lobby in Washington, groups for gay men and lesbians of color, the Gay Olympics, and campus gay groups.

In the 1970s gay identity was so novel and compelling that it tended to overshadow one's other identities. The more people saw their lesbian or gay identity as the center of their lives, the more likely they were to become politicized. But in the 1980s many people wanted to be gay *and*—gay and Black, for example, gay and working class, gay and disabled, gay and Democratic, gay and old. Although this proliferation of groups tended to diffuse the energy of gay liberation, the movement became stronger both because it became more institutionalized (paid work and permanent organizations assuming more importance) and because it was too large and diverse to be contained by formal organizations. The gay lobbyists who visited Congressional offices were representing an important tendency in gay liberation, the tendency to carve out a secure niche in American society, but they could hardly speak for gay Native Americans, lesbian separatists, working-class lesbian mothers, drag queens, gay teenagers, or all the homosexuals who still remained in the closet.

The old radical impulse in gay liberation, which appeared at the beginning of Mattachine in the early 1950s and again in the Gay Liberation Front after Stonewall, sparked the creation of AIDS Coalition to Unleash Power (ACT UP). In three years it had branches in sixty cities. ACT UP came to life because going through official channels was not saving the lives of gay men. Confrontation and civil disobedience seemed the only alternative. ACT UP members unfurled safe sex banners at baseball games, disrupted many meetings, sat in at the Food and Drug Administration, chained themselves to a balcony in the New York Stock Exchange, covered buildings with red tape to symbolize government delays in helping those with AIDS, and spray-painted outlines of bodies on Castro Street in San Francisco to represent those who had died. These attention-getting tactics were reminiscent of the feminist and gay liberation zaps of the early 1970s when both concepts were still shocking (zaps were disruptions of meetings or events by protestors, often using satirical humor to publicize their cause). The direct action tactics of ACT UP are forcing drug companies and the medical bureaucracy to consider radical changes in drug research and regulation (David Tuller, *San Francisco Chronicle*, 19 June 1990: A8).

A low point for gay liberation in the 1980s was the 1986 Supreme Court decision upholding the constitutionality of sodomy laws (see Chapter 2). Another setback was the May 1988 passage of Clause 28 by the British government, saying that a local authority shall not "intentionally promote homosexuality or publish material with the intention of promoting homosexuality" or "promote the teaching in any maintained school of the acceptability of homosexuality as a pretended family relationship." This repressive measure does not distinguish between mentioning homosexuality in a neutral spirit—acknowledging, for example, the existence of a gay and lesbian rights movement—and "promoting." The bias of the phrase "pretended family relationships" is obvious, for they are not pretended to those who enter into them. In the year following the passage of Clause 28, many lesbian mothers lost custody of their children, attacks on lesbians and gay men rose by 11 percent, and the suicide rate among gay youth went up 20 percent (*Connexions* 29, 1989: 7).

The high point for the movement was the October 1987 March on Washington, which drew 600,000 people. Assuming that each marcher had five friends or acquaintances at home, the gay and lesbian movement is 3 million strong. It may be much larger, however, because the US gay population is estimated to be 22 million (*Gay in America* 1989: 47).

CURRENT ISSUES

Current political issues for gay men and lesbians may be summarized as follows: at the federal level, discrimination in the military and in security clearances; at the state level, discrimination in jobs, housing, and public accommodations and sodomy laws; discrimination in areas of family law such as marriage, custody cases, foster care and adoption; police harassment; violent crimes; and AIDS-related discrimination.[11]

Until recently, gay people from other countries could not enter the US or become citizens: restrictive immigration policies dated back to the McCarran Walters Act of 1952 and to the 1967 Supreme Court ruling that barred homosexuals as sexual deviants. The law, impossible to enforce because lesbians and gay men usually cannot be identified by their appearance, became especially oppressive when persons testing positive for HIV were denied entry into the country. Congress ended these restrictions in October 1990.

Anti-gay military policy, like the immigration policy, assumes that homosexuals are inferior to heterosexuals. In November 1989, the Harvard faculty voted to ban the Reserve Officers' Training Corps (ROTC) because it violates the campus non-discrimination policy, and the following month the University of Wisconsin faculty voted to ask regents to sever ties with ROTC by 1993.

Discrimination by the military was particularly oppressive in the case of Perry Watkins, a Black soldier. In filling out the Army's pre-induction forms he answered "yes" to the question about homosexual tendencies. He was judged qualified for admission, however, and served fourteen years. Then in 1981 new Army regulations disqualified all homosexuals, no matter how long or how ably they had performed in the service, and Watkins was discharged. He sued the Army and won, but the legal battle lasted ten years.

Presently at the federal level, gay men and lesbians are routinely denied security clearances by the FBI, the CIA, and the National Security Agency. Men who join ROTC, for example, are expelled for being gay. Frank Buttino, a gay man who had an outstanding record with the FBI for twenty-five years, was abruptly fired when his homosexuality became known. One lawyer has defended more than 100 gay people denied security clearances. Julie Dubbs, a technical illustrator who is suing the CIA for denying her a security clearance because she is a lesbian, persuaded the US Ninth District Court of Appeals that the CIA automatically denies security clearances to homosexuals (*San Francisco Examiner,* 25 June 1990: A4). In none of these cases was the individual judged on his or her job performance. The government cannot cite a single case of a civil servant, member of the armed forces, or spy successfully blackmailed for being gay (Mohr 1988: 198).

When passed, the federal Gay and Lesbian Civil Rights Bill, first introduced in 1974 by former New York Congresswoman Bella Abzug, will prohibit discrimination based on sexual orientation in employment, housing, public accommodations, and federally assisted programs. Essentially it extends to gay people the protections of the 1964 Civil Rights Act. The bill now has ten sponsors in the Senate and eighty in the House. Whatever its practical effect, the passing of this bill will be an important symbolic victory comparable to the school desegregation decision of the Supreme Court in 1954 because it will acknowledge that a climate of discrimination exists.

In the absence of federal legislation protecting gay citizens, state and city laws take on special significance. Fundamentalists and others have denounced the few existing laws as special treatment for homosexuals; in fact, special treatment is the status quo, special *discriminatory* treatment. State and city gay rights laws simply treat gay men and lesbians like other citizens. They may not be fired from jobs or evicted from housing simply because they are gay. Discrimination in public accommodations occurs when gay groups are not allowed to rent space for their meetings. The laws of course do not insure fair treatment; they merely give victims of discrimination the right to sue. Massachusetts and Wisconsin are the only states which have passed gay rights laws. The Massachusetts law was passed in 1989 after a seventeen-year struggle. A few cities enacted similar laws, for example, San Francisco, Los Angeles, Portland, Seattle, and Washington DC. Opposition by the Catholic Church repeatedly delayed passage of New York City's law, but it was finally enacted in 1986.

Although the huge gay population of California is unprotected by a state gay rights law, the California Supreme Court ruled in 1979 that coming out at work is protected speech. "The court recognized, for the first time in U.S. legal history, the special political plight of gays as an invisible minority. It acknowledged that if gays are to have political rights, they must be free to be open about who they are" (Mohr 1988: 173). An implication of this decision is that freedom of speech and freedom of assembly are denied as long as gay people are unprotected from housing and employment discrimination (Mohr 1988: 173). That is, I may exercise my freedom of association by going to a gay event, but if my picture appears in the paper the next day and my landlady evicts me after seeing the picture, my First Amendment right is denied me. Similarly, I may exercise my free speech right by publishing an article in a gay newspaper, but if the article causes me to be fired, I do not have the same constitutional protections as a heterosexual person. An extensive study by the National Gay and Lesbian Task Force in 1984 revealed that over 90 percent of gay Americans suffered some form of discrimination (Mohr 1988: 27).

Discrimination based on sexual preference is comparable to discrimination against Jews. Both homosexuals and Jews were targets of the Nazis. One of the earliest attacks on anti-Semitism, "Civil Disabilities of the Jews," was an essay by the English historian Thomas Macaulay in the *Edinburgh Review* in 1830, when Jews were not allowed to become judges or sit in Parliament. Arguments justifying these exclusions were similar to arguments now used to justify discrimination against homosexuals: a belief that the state is fundamentally Christian and a belief that a minority can rightfully be discriminated against in the present because it was persecuted in the past. The US Congress acted on both beliefs in October 1988 when it ordered Washington DC to repeal its gay rights ordinance or lose all its funding. The Orange county congressman who led the repeal fight said that lawmakers must "follow God's plan of one man and one woman who come together for the procreation of children" (*Bay Area Reporter,* 6 October 1988: 2).

The belief that a Christian state can define sex in this narrow way and legitimately punish those who deviate is best expressed in sodomy laws. Still existing in twenty-eight states, sodomy laws make it a crime for two men to engage in sex acts in private. Occasionally these laws are used against lesbians (and theoretically could be used against heterosexuals as well). Usually unenforced, sodomy laws nevertheless have a purpose: they give the heterosexual majority the opportunity to express "raw hatred of gays *systematically and officially* without even having publicly to discuss and so justify that hatred" (Mohr 1988: 60). Sodomy laws are currently being challenged in Michigan and Texas

(Lambda 1990: 8). Until 1988, Irish law allowed sentences up to life imprisonment for gay sex acts, but the European Court of Human Rights ordered Ireland to drop its sodomy law because it violated citizens' right to privacy (*Bay Area Reporter,* 1 December 1988: 26).

Family issues related to lesbians and gay men have predictably stirred up emotions because they undermine the traditional notion of a family as consisting of a heterosexual couple and their children. The high divorce rate and the availability of contraception and abortion have changed the American family far more than gay liberation, but "intentional families" of two women or two men, extended families in which homosexual couples form the core, lesbian or gay male single parents, or friendship circles functioning as families obviously differ from the Ozzie and Harriet model of the heterosexual nuclear family, based on a popular tv show of the 1950's featuring Ozzie and Harriet Nelson and their sons Ricky and David. In ruling that a gay couple together for ten years could be considered a family under New York City rent control regulations, a New York Court of Appeals judge argued that a family can be defined as "two adult lifetime partners whose relationship is characterized by an emotional and financial commitment and interdependence" (*New York Times,* 7 July 1989: A1). This decision is significant because it does not restrict the definition of a family to a child-producing, child-rearing unit or to a relationship only heterosexuals may enter into. Theoretically, if the institution of the family is not inherently heterosexual, neither should the institution of marriage, be, at least marriage as a civil ceremony. But legalized marriage for lesbians and gay men is too revolutionary a change to occur in the United States in this century: it defies the Judeo-Christian idea of marriage which the state reinforces in many ways; it implicitly states that marriage is about personal fulfillment, especially sexual fulfillment, rather than the transmission of private property; and it clearly separates love relationships from procreation. Legalized marriage is not a choice that would be made by gay people who see themselves as rebels and non-conformists, but it ought to be available for those who believe in it.

Domestic partner laws provide a few of the benefits of marriage to lesbians and gay men, for example health care coverage for spouses of city employees. Berkeley passed a domestic partners law in 1984, and Seattle adopted one several years later. The Minneapolis city council approved domestic partners in January 1991. The San Francisco version, which simply provided one day of funeral leave and hospital visitation rights, was rescinded by voters in November 1989, although it had been endorsed by the conservative *San Francisco Chronicle* and the Episcopal Bishop of California. Reinstated in 1990, the law permits unrelated people who live together to register their relationships with the city. They agree to provide food and shelter for the partners and to pay medical expenses not covered by insurance. Some gay activists who oppose domestic partners say that they do not need any official recognition for their lives and fear that the measure will promote assimilation into mainstream culture. Others value the symbolic affirmation of their relationships. Even though few lesbians and gay men today are coerced into heterosexual marriages by their parents, their ministers, or their own ambivalence, domestic partners laws are important for declaring publicly that same-sex unions are common enough to be officially recognized. Heterosexual opponents of domestic partners legislation who see it as an attack upon marriage apparently lack faith in that traditional institution: it can remain strong regardless of the status of homosexuals.

One case involving family relationships pits a lesbian against AT&T. As the surviving partner of an AT&T employee, she claims a death benefit which the company denies, despite personnel policies of no discrimination because of sexual preference (Lambda 1990: 5). In this case the employer had given up the most blatant forms of discrimination—firing or refusing to hire homosexuals—but reserved the right to practice more subtle forms.

For lesbians and gay men, some of the most painful cases are those involving adoption, foster care, and child custody. Five years after barring homosexuals from become foster parents, Massachusetts reversed its policy. An emotional public debate in 1985 followed disclosure that two young boys had been placed with a gay male couple. The reversal results from a lawsuit brought by Gay and Lesbian Legal Advocates and Defenders of Boston and the Civil Liberties Union of Massachusetts.

Custody cases have had mixed results for lesbians and gay men. Usually the courts have denied them custody of their biological children from heterosexual marriages but have occasionally ruled in their favor. Typically, a man whose wife has left him for a woman will seek revenge by attempting to get sole custody, or a woman angry at her homosexual ex-husband will try to deny him access to their children. Less common is the situation in which two women raise children, one dies, and then her parents seek custody on the grounds that the surviving partner's lesbianism makes her an unfit mother. Many lesbians who would prefer to live with their lovers cannot do so, because the courts will take away their children. Some gay fathers may not see their children in the presence of their partners. Jeanne Jullion's book *Long Way Home* describes a lengthy and harrowing battle for her son.[12] In most lesbian mother custody cases, a woman is on trial for her lesbianism. Courts deny custody because lesbianism is perceived as evil (Mohr 1988: 200).[13]

Just as the courts do not protect the parental rights of lesbians and gay men, their constitutional rights are often violated by police. Thirty women arrested during an ACT UP demonstration in New York were unnecessarily strip-searched, a violation of their constitutional protection against unreasonable search and seizure. AIDS demonstrators at the Food and Drug Administration in Portland were strip-searched by federal marshalls. The First Amendment right to free speech is an issue in right-wing attacks on phone sex and gay and lesbian phone services providing, for example, information about events or about safe sex (Lambda 1990: 3–4). For many years gay legal rights advocates have challenged prison rules that deny inmates access to gay and lesbian newspapers.

A less tangible right than the right to read whatever you want, to say whatever you please on the telephone, or to attend a demonstration without being strip-searched, is the right to move about freely without being beaten up for your perceived difference. Gay bashing, violent crimes against gays, is one of the most serious discrimination problems in America and until recently one of the least acknowledged. Many crimes go unreported because the victim is afraid to reveal his or her sexual orientation to authorities. Crimes against lesbians and gay men are reported in the mainstream press only if the victim is prominent. The backlash caused by AIDS led to a 200 percent increase in reported anti-gay violence in the years 1985–88, according to the National Gay and Lesbian Task Force. Physical assaults, threats of violence, vandalism, police abuse, homicide and arson were reported, including many incidents on college campuses. Often gay men are beaten by pairs of attackers or gangs. Groups such as Community United Against Violence (CUAV) in San Francisco try to protect lesbians and gay men from violence and to publicize assault crimes. In Washington DC, Rod Johnson was beaten nearly to death by a group of skinheads armed with baseball bats who yelled, "Die, faggot, die," as they hit him. In June 1990, a group of Marines beat patrons of a gay bar near Capital Hill. While camping with her lover along the Appalachian trail, Rebecca Wright was shot to death by a man who tracked them for a day (Lambda 1990: 5–6). In August 1989, five youths in Lincoln, Nebraska, shot and killed a man they thought was gay. In November 1989, the home of a gay activist in Springfield, Missouri, was destroyed by an arsonist during a controversy over the showing of a play about AIDS. In Greensboro, North Carolina, a high school student was beaten by his parents, who broke his arm and threw him out after finding gay literature in his bedroom. A 500-page compilation of such stories might convey some sense of the brutality and violence directed at gay people in the USA. In addition to the murders, beatings, and attacks on property are the epithets of hatred hurled at them in public places or scrawled on walls.

In the face of this hostility, gay people lobbied for inclusion in the Hate Crimes Statistics Act which became law on April 23, 1990. This was an historic day for the lesbians and gay men of America, as President Bush tacitly admitted by inviting gay leaders to the signing of the bill, because the Hate Crimes Act is the first piece of pro-gay legislation ever passed at the federal level. It requires the Justice Department to collect and publish data for five years on hate-motivated crimes based on religion, race, ethnicity, or sexual orientation. The legislation affirms the worth of homosexuals by equating them with the more established, more powerful minorities, Blacks and Jews. Gay bashing, like the lynching of Blacks, is intended to keep a stigmatized group in line (Mohr 1988: 28). The Hate Crimes Statistics Act will prove what gay people already know: assaults on them are prevalent. An official proclamation that gays do not deserve to be beaten or killed is only a first step, however, towards granting them equal rights.

AIDS has severely tested their claim to equal rights. The full story of discrimination against people with AIDS would require a separate book. Doctors, dentists, hospitals, schools, insurance companies, employers, and landlords have all discriminated. A 1990 study by the American Civil Liberties Union, "Epidemic of Fear," found that AIDS-related discrimination rose 35 percent faster than newly diagnosed AIDS cases in 1988 (*Washington Blade,* 29 June 1990: 19). In Texas, a company changed insurance plans to prevent an employee with AIDS from getting more than $5,000 from a policy that provided $1 million, a violation of the Texas Deceptive Trade Practices Consumer Protection Act (Lambda 1990: 1–2). A man dying of AIDS in a Florida hospital was given a plane ticket for San Francisco and forced to leave; he died forty-eight hours after reaching San Francisco.

A major gay rights case of the 1980s involved two Minnesota women, Karen Thompson and Sharon Kowalski. They were lovers who had lived together for four years when, in November 1983, Sharon was severely injured in a car accident. Karen, a physical education professor, was spending several hours a day on Sharon's rehabilitation when her attempt to become Sharon's guardian, to make medical decisions in her interest, was blocked by Sharon's parents, who denied that she was a lesbian. For several years the Kowalskis and the courts denied Karen the right to see her partner. Even worse, instead of getting the rehabilitation she needed, Sharon was moved to a nursing home in northern Minnesota, far from Karen. She suffered years of sensory deprivation and neglect, even though she was able to type out words indicating that she loved Karen. The case became a *cause célèbre* in the lesbian community: "Free Sharon Kowalski" committees sprang up all over the country, and many fund raisers were held. Karen wrote *Why Can't Sharon Kowalski Come Home,* a book for which movie rights have been sold.[14] Since the case clearly involved issues for the disabled as well as for gay people, Karen was invited to speak to many lawyers, psychologists, and social workers. Often asked why she continued an apparently hopeless struggle, she replied that "Sharon is too beautiful a person to give up on."

Finally, in January 1989, several months after winning the right to get competency tests, Sharon was moved to a rehabilitation hospital in Minneapolis. Karen was allowed to visit her and in February 1990 began to take her on weekends to the home they owned in central Minnesota. But in April 1991, a judge ruled against Karen's petition for guardianship, blaming Karen for revealing Sharon's lesbianism. This was an absurd rationale for the ruling because Karen could not have obtained just treatment for Karen without first revealing the grounds on which it had been wrongly denied her. If the two women had signed durable power of attorney forms giving each other the right to make medical decisions, Sharon's parents would not have been able to force them apart and to deny their daughter rehabilitation. They preferred an irreparably damaged daughter to a lesbian daughter, and the courts of a supposedly progressive state enforced their homophobic decision. Sharon's best interests were disregarded; her disability was conflated with incompetence. She was treated like a single woman even though she had been in a partnership for four years. She was denied the right to control her own medical care, the right to freedom of association, and, worst of all, the right to a full recovery (see Epilogue).

Because lesbians and gay men have been forming more open relationships in the past twenty years, breakups are more public, too, and occasionally when issues are contested the opposing parties go to court. As a consequence, new interpretations of laws which assumed universal heterosexuality are being made to deal with gay "divorces." Palimony cases are an example. Even farther outside the boundaries of legal precedent is the situation that arises when a couple in a long-term relationship who raised children conceived by artificial insemination split up and fight about visitation rights. A New York court ruled that a lesbian co-parent has no legal right to visit the children she once lived with. A vigorous dissent said, however, that the non-biological parent should be allowed to visit the children because she planned her partner's pregnancies and agreed to participate equally in the support and rearing of the children (Lambda 1990: 4).

Cases in which gay people are adversaries obviously differ from cases in which they attempt to redress grievances. These cases are bound to become controversial in the gay community. Some say that people who are outcasts should not voluntarily expose themselves to a judicial system that is homophobic and unjust. From this radical perspective, lesbians and gay men should seek arbiters and mediators within their own community. On the other side, gay people who feel more at home in America than alienated from it will use the courts to get what they want.

A recent court case shows how anti-gay bigotry deforms the American judicial system. A Los Angeles Superior Court judge ruled that the Boy Scouts of America may legally bar an openly gay Eagle Scout from becoming a scoutmaster. The judge reasoned that the opposite ruling would interfere with the right of the Scouts to uphold their belief that homosexuality is immoral (San Francisco *Examiner*, 22 May 1991: A 6). Although this case was a setback for gay rights, widespread media coverage usefully called attention to the arbitrary nature of discrimination, and sophisticated viewers and readers were no doubt aware that homosexuals have been scoutmasters from the earliest days of the movement.

An important political effort by gay people is to monitor mainstream media coverage and respond when it is homophobic or heterosexist. The Gay and Lesbian Alliance Against Defamation (GLAAD), founded in New York in 1985, has chapters in several other cities. Its newsletter notes that stories about gay or lesbian issues often fail to include the viewpoint of anyone who is actually gay and they put homosexuality in the context of social problems such as drug abuse. In addition, "hate-mongers are quoted damning us as if they were responsible spokespersons" (*GLAAD Newsletter,* Summer 1990: 2). To counter this situation, GLAAD meets with media executives, cites examples of fair reporting as well as biased reporting, organizes against the powerful homophobic coalitions attempting to censor lesbian and gay artists and writers, and zaps homophobic comedians. As a result of a two-year letter-writing campaign by GLAAD, the top of the Empire State Building, which is lighted in various colors for national holidays, became lavender during Gay Pride Week in June 1990. In the

1970s, a powerful American symbol would not have been linked to anything gay.

Sometimes gay politics and mainstream politics converge. When Jesse Helms amended the National Endowment for the Arts appropriation bill to read that no funds could be used for "obscene" work, which included homoeroticism, liberals and radicals realized that the threat to the freedom of visual artists, performance artists, and writers was not confined to the gay community. If homoerotic images are suppressed, homosexuality can be made to seem shameful. The NEA drew the wrath of the religious right for failing to regard homosexuality as an abomination, thus defying right-wing ideology. In no sense was the NEA pro-gay when it funded a few gay and lesbian artists in the 1980s. It simply was not anti-gay. The religious right expects government agencies to be anti-gay. Thus the arts funding debate went far beyond questions of taste and censorship to the question of religious interference in essentially secular matters. A survey of national civil rights groups showed that anti-gay amendments proposed in the House and Senate make those groups more willing to advocate gay rights (*Washington Blade,* 11 May 1990: 1).

The impact of gay people on mainstream politics is a many-sided question. Two members of the House of Representatives from Massachusetts, Barney Frank and Gerry Studds, are openly gay, but both were closeted when first elected to office. Two openly gay Minnesota state legislators, Karen Clark and Allan Spear, will probably rise no higher in mainstream politics because of anti-gay prejudice. All of these politicians had to appeal to many voters besides gay voters to be elected. Clark's coalition of the elderly and Native Americans in south Minneapolis gave her a strong base, for example. In cases where gays lack the political power to elect one of their own candidates, they can sometimes at least insure that the winner will not be homophobic, as they did when Dianne Feinstein was elected mayor of San Francisco.

In the 1950s, the movement later called gay rights consisted of a few secretive organizations in several large cities. In the sixties it grew slowly. Inspired by Stonewall and mass comings out, gay rights became a movement. Neither the early German advocates of homosexual rights nor the courageous women and men who joined homophile groups in the years 1950–70 could have foreseen this development. A student looking for articles on homosexuality in *Reader's Guide* in 1949 would have been directed to the headings "sex perversion," "abnormal," and "queer people" (Keen, Part 2: 28). Little had changed by 1966 when *Time* called homosexuality "a pernicious sickness" and a "pitiable flight from life" (21 January 1966: 41). A mass movement was needed to change this way of thinking. Laws ending discrimination against homosexual persons are only a first step, however, because homosexuality as a practice could still retain its inferior status (Epstein 1987: 47). Will gay people ever be regarded as fully equal to heterosexuals? "The acceptance of our erotic choices ultimately depends on the degree to which society is willing to affirm sexual expression as a form of play, positive and life-enhancing."[15] A corollary is that acceptance of lesbians and gay men depends on the degree to which America functions as a secular state and not a religious state.

4

GAY AND LESBIAN LIBERATION AS A MOVEMENT OF IDEAS

When most students hear about gay and lesbian liberation they think of sexual preference or politics. Media images of lesbians and gay men focus on these areas. A lesbian is forced out of the Marines, for example, a school committee disagrees about adding books on gay topics to the library, or a politician "comes out of the closet" (for a discussion of this slang term see the *Encyclopedia of Homosexuality* 1990: 244–5). And of course newspaper stories about AIDS and HIV infection are common. But there is another important side to gay and lesbian liberation that most students are probably not aware of. Gay liberation is a movement of ideas. Even if all political activity of lesbians and gay men stopped, the ideas of gay liberation would still be powerful. But ideas of equality, justice, and self-determination are potent only if there exists at least the possibility that they will alter institutions.

For more than twenty years, many gay people have believed that their struggle for equality is as important as the civil rights movement and the women's movement. The term "gay" has been used for homosexuals since the 1920s in the United States and the 1950s in Britain (*Encyclopedia of Homosexuality* 1990: 456). Its widespread use began in the late 1960s, however, in the same decade when Negroes became Blacks and girls became women. "Gay" had the advantage of being short and snappy, and it lacked the heavy weight of negative connotations attached to the more cumbersome term "homosexual." The slang term carried the connotations of lighthearted and carefree, from the more traditional meaning of "gay," lighthearted in the sense of feeling free to declare one's sexual preference. Above all, "gay" was a name chosen by the group itself, as a sign of its refusal to be named by, judged by, or controlled by the dominant majority. The word "gay" kept its standard English meaning, but ever since the 1970s the newer meaning has been the more important, even though the *New York Times* took nearly twenty years to adopt it. An advantage of "gay" over "homosexual" is that it names an identity rather than a sexual practice and thus is a broader term. By the late 1980s, cosexual groups almost always put the term "lesbian" in their names: the National Gay Task Force, for example, became the National Gay and Lesbian Task Force, a change indicating that lesbians were gaining a higher profile in the movement.

One of the first slogans of gay liberation, adopted in 1968, was "gay is good"—not just acceptable, not just something to tolerate, but a positive identity. "Gay is good" would have been laughed out of existence if lesbians and gay men had been a tiny minority. Because they were a huge minority by the early 1970s, far bigger than they themselves had guessed in the 1960s, their point of view commanded attention, even though many heterosexuals were not ready to agree with them. Like the slogans "Black is Beautiful" and "Women Hold Up Half the Sky" (from China), the "gay is good" slogan expressed pride and defiance at the same time.

Why were gay people able to challenge centuries of prejudice with this assertion? Groundwork for gay liberation had been laid in the late nineteenth and early twentieth centuries, as the last chapter demonstrated. After World War II, more gay people lived in big cities, where relative anonymity gave them a measure of freedom to act on their sexual feelings. The peace movement, the women's movement, and the civil rights movement set examples for a mass protest based on the idea of sexual freedom. As people became more sophisticated about sex they realised that homosexuality was not a vice or a disease. Furthermore, homosexuality seemed universal, or nearly universal, a fact at odds with the belief that it runs contrary to nature. As instances of homosexual behavior among birds and animals began to be documented—among greylag geese, lizards, monkeys, and mountain goats (*Encyclopedia of Homosexuality* 1990: 61)—it became clear that whatever the term "unnatural" meant to preachers and police, it could not mean that the natural world exhibits no homosexuality. After scholars who scrutinized the Bible passages thought to condemn homosexuality found that these passages had been misinterpreted, religious leaders who based their opposition to homosexuality on the Bible lost credibility. Many heterosexuals continued to think of gay people as sick and sinful, but this viewpoint was no longer the only one. The monopoly on ideas about homosexuality was broken.

This chapter will describe some of the ideas of gay and lesbian liberation, the beginning of gay and lesbian studies in American colleges and universities, and gay publishing.

THE IDEAS OF LESBIAN AND GAY LIBERATION

Among the important concepts that gay liberation established are (1) homophobia; (2) heterosexism; (3) heterocentrism; and (4) compulsory heterosexuality.

An early goal of gay liberation was to correct the view that homosexuality is a problem by delineating a real problem, **homophobia**, that is, the irrational fear or hatred of homosexuals or homosexuality.[1] The coinage of this term, which now appears in standard dictionaries, was an effective strategy for shifting from the defensive position of having to justify homosexuality to the offensive, forcing the opposition to justify its stance. Homophobia exists in individuals,—in right-wing extremists, for example—but it is more importantly a widespread social problem. Like racism and sexism, it cannot be eradicated by individual changes of heart but only by institutional change. An individual may decide that his or her hatred of homosexuals is wrong, based on some personal experience, but this change will not be deep or lasting if the individual hears sermons attacking gays, or works with people whose anti-gay bigotry surfaces frequently in conversations, or lives in a town where the idea of a law protecting lesbians and gay men from job and housing discrimination is regarded as a joke.

Researchers who have begun to study homophobia theorize that it originates when (1) men use violence against homosexuals to reassure themselves about their own sexuality; and (2) people motivated by fear and self-righteousness perceive gays as threats to their moral values (*New York Times*, 10 July 1990: B1). A similar theory traces the roots of homophobia to the cultural associations of violence with masculinity. "Aggressive violence seems to be used as a kind of shield to ward off the contaminating, tabooed homosexuality, as if its mere presence constituted a threat to one's male self image . . ." (*Encyclopedia of Homosexuality* 1990: 1375). Other likely origins of homophobia are fear of the unknown or anxiety about sex in any form. Homophobia in the 1950s came from a mistaken notion that homosexuals were more likely than others to be communists (and therefore traitors) or to become spies. Lesbians are hated because their existence proves that not all women are sexually available to men or subject to their control.

One of the most barbarous manifestations of homophobia is the use of electric shock treatment on homosexuals. This technique is practiced today in China, along with the use of herbal medicines to induce vomiting, to stimulate bad reactions that will be associated afterwards with erotic thoughts. This persecution is justified by Gao Caiquin, a sex researcher who heads the Institute of Marriage and Family, on the grounds that homosexuality is abnormal (*New York Times*, 29 January 1990: A2).

Scientists in the United States also exhibit homophobia. Several examples were cited by organizers of a conference titled "Homophobia in the Sciences" held at Caltech in February 1990:

- homosexuals frequently feel uncomfortable confiding in doctors;
- high school students rarely receive accurate information about homosexuality in biology courses;
- historians of science ignore or misinterpret the role of homosexuality in the lives of great scientists such as Leonardo da Vinci and Sir Francis Bacon;
- most professional organizations of scientists have not supported anti-discrimination policies to protect gay and lesbian scientists from being fired or harassed at work (*Los Angeles Times*, 2 February 1990: E9).

Just as homophobia is not confined to uneducated people, it is not confined to whites. "Taking the Home out of Homophobia: Black Lesbians Look in Their Own Backyards," a dialogue between writers Jewelle Gomez and Barbara Smith, examines the ironic situation of an oppressed group oppressing others. Smith challenges a myth held by some Black people that when Black lesbians and gay men go out into the white community they forsake their racial roots. "People say that to be lesbian or gay is to be somehow racially denatured [but] in fact, the cultural and political leadership of the Black community has always had a very high percentage of lesbians and gay men." Usually they are closeted.[2]

In the decades before gay liberation, homosexuals appeared in the news only when they were arrested and thus they seemed to comprise a criminal underclass and were naturally despised for that reason. One of the ironies of homophobia is that middle-class heterosexual parents who worried that their boys might be snatched by some evil stranger lurking in the bushes—the stereotyped fantasy of the homosexual male created in part by the media—had far more to fear from the men to whose care they entrusted their boys—scoutmasters, YMCA leaders, priests, ministers, youth workers. Men who molest boys are now the targets of law suits and newspaper investigations. The growing awareness of the sexual molestation of boys by adult males who know them will fuel homophobia unless a clear distinction is made between gay men in general, who accept their sexual orientation and seek sex with consenting adults, and homosexual or heterosexual men who sexually coerce children because they are sick. The term "gay" does not accurately describe men who molest boys because "gay" connotes proud self-acceptance and openness about one's emotional/sexual identity. Some gay men approve of consensual sex with children, however; their views are circulated by the North American Man Boy Love Association, or NAMBLA.

Another source of homophobia is the need for scapegoats. Just as Jews were blamed for Germany's economic collapse in the 1930s, homosexuals are accused of destroying the American family by promoting a hedonistic, selfish, childless way of life. The family, of course, has been weakened by many twentieth-century developments, beginning with the automobile, which gave young people a way to escape from parental control and a place for sexual exploration. Compared to the impact of the automobile on the family, or of television, economic dislocations, wars, declining religious influence, and women's liberation, the impact of newly visible homosexuals has been minimal. Homosexuals are convenient scapegoats because of the widespread uneasiness about sex that still characterizes puritan America. Homosexuality represents all hidden and forbidden sexual feelings. When it is not kept taboo, people are more likely to realize that sex is powerful, irrepressible, and sometimes hard to keep within fixed boundaries. Moreover, because gay sex is non-procreative, pleasure and emotional bonding are its only purposes and thus gay people symbolize sexual pleasure, whether or not they are sexually active as individuals. Gay people often say that heterosexuals who fully accept their own sexual natures do not condemn them. Widespread alcoholism, drug abuse, and other addictive behavior suggests a high level of sexual dysfunction in this culture, and people who feel sexually inadequate or unloved may turn their anger on homosexuals, projecting upon them their own feelings of shame and confusion. Merely by existing, gay people prove that sex cannot be policed.

Homophobia also results from rigid ideas about gender. A man who appears womanly by conventional norms or a woman who appears manly threatens the sharp gender separation which most people take for granted. Even though many male homosexuals are masculine in appearance and many lesbians are feminine appearing, those most visible to heterosexuals are the ones who seem to cross gender lines. Gender is one of the first things we perceive about a person and when we cannot immediately make the right designation we may feel frustrated. Many homosexuals enjoy "gender bending," that is, blurring the distinction between male and female or suggesting that these divisions are fluid, not fixed by biology. If they appear to be making fun of a basic human line of demarcation, fear or dislike of them is one response. Perhaps in a time of extremely rapid social change, when people cannot rely on the truths they learned at home or at church, they have a particular need to believe that the categories of male and female are absolutely unchanging. The idea that a person could be male one day and female the next, which seems playful and exhilarating to many gay people, may seem threatening to heterosexuals. Calling sex roles into question fundamentally challenges power inequalities based on them. Those who want to preserve a male/female power imbalance naturally cannot tolerate gender bending. Even androgyny, the idea that male and female characteristics can co-exist within a person, is threatening. The androgynous ideal is very attractive for many homosexuals, but if their dress or behavior suggest androgyny, they may be scorned by heterosexuals.

Homophobia leads to violent attacks on gay people and even murder. When four Latino teenagers beat a gay man to death recently in San Francisco, they were tried as individuals, but the anti-gay attitudes they learned at the Catholic school they attend must certainly have fueled their hatred. The official Vatican document on homosexuality issued in October 1986 comes close to condoning violence against gay people by saying that if they persist in demonstrating for their rights they should not be surprised to be beaten up, a message Catholic leaders would not dare to send to Blacks, Jews, women, or other minority groups who demonstrated for their rights.

The AIDS epidemic has made homophobia a more serious problem than it would otherwise have been in the 1980s and 1990s. The perceived link between homosexuality and disease has allowed people who might earlier have been ashamed to express anti-gay bigotry to condemn gays openly. At the same time, the hatred of people with

AIDS by some Americans has prompted others to pay attention to homophobia for the first time because they see how vicious and irrational it is.

An aspect of the problem that is not yet well understood is "internalized homophobia." This phrase means negative attitudes or stereotyped view of homosexuals held by homosexuals themselves. The anti-gay rhetoric of conservative Republican politicians who frequent gay bars and are known to be gay is an example. Closeted gays in power positions sometimes prevent other gays from being promoted or fairly evaluated. Gays who can "pass" for straight may avoid more obvious gays because they are uncomfortable with their gay identity. Sometimes a lesbian or a gay man cannot clearly distinguish between a personal problem such as drinking, compulsive eating, or severe depression and the condition of being gay, and they experience some degree of self-loathing. Sometimes gay teenagers and college students accept themselves until their families reject them, and then they begin to feel unsure of their worth. A lesbian or a gay man whose long-term relationship ends may respond to loss by feeling ashamed to be gay. Given the homophobia of the culture it is remarkable that so few people appear to be emotionally crippled by internalized homophobia, but probably all of them experience it at one time or another, especially if they lack positive gay role models or gay friends. Like the low life expectancy of American Indians, internalized homophobia is not the focus of social science research because gay people, like Native Americans, are not a respected group. But it would be useful to know a great deal more about the mechanism of internalized homophobia, to consider it in psychology classes, and to make high school and college counselors more aware of the damage it causes.

Many examples of homophobia were given in Chapter 1 to demonstrate that gay men and lesbians are an oppressed minority. Another example may make homophobia seem real to college students. During a recent "cross-cultural week" at Michigan State, Jerry Mattioli led a candlelight vigil for lesbian and gay rights. The next day, after his name appeared in the campus paper, he noticed people whispering and staring at him. A bridge in the middle of the campus was covered by violent slogans such as "death to gays" and "abolish faggots." Since other slogans specifically attacked Mattioli, university officials asked him to leave school for the weekend for his own safety. A few hours after he left, he received a call from a friend telling him that his dorm room had been torched. Everything in the room was destroyed.

Some enemies of gay people do not kill them or destroy their property but they do advocate discrimination. **Heterosexism** is prejudice or discrimination against gay people, analogous to racism and sexism. Students who have some grasp of racism and sexism will more readily understand heterosexism than students for whom the first two terms are unfamiliar. But any student can understand that prejudice directed against a class of people is unjust.

Like the concepts of racism and sexism, the concept of heterosexism challenges the dominant group's claim to superiority. Heterosexuality is more common than homosexuality, but it is not inherently better for that reason, any more than right-handedness is preferable to left-handedness. Gay people reach that conclusion from their own experience. If homosexuality were a lesser form of being, millions of people would not choose it for a lifetime. No one would leave a socially sanctioned heterosexual marriage for a devalued same-sex relationship unless she or he found deeply fulfilling benefits from this change. Homosexuality has survived all attempts to stamp it out, including imprisonment and death. As soon as social prohibitions were slightly eased, it formed the basis for a mass movement.

But the idea that a homosexual state of being is equal to heterosexuality is not yet a majority opinion in America and may not be for another hundred years. Feminism began in mid-Victorian England but did not have a major impact until the years preceding World War I, and it did not change the way many American women viewed themselves until the 1970s and 1980s. The idea of Black–white equality circulated for many decades before even the most virulently racist policies were challenged in the 1950s and 1960s. The terms "racism" and "sexism" are signs of social progress because they mean that the superiority of the dominant group will no longer be conceded by the less powerful group. Similarly, the coining of a term not yet in the dictionary, "heterosexist," challenges the assumption of heterosexual superiority, an assumption so pervasive that until recently it passed for a fact. The shaky assumption of the superiority of heterosexuality would have been exposed before the 1970s if specialists in history, politics, sexuality, philosophy, and other disciplines had not been as blinded by prejudice as the students they were instructing. Many university professors used to believe that Blacks were genetically inferior to whites and that men were superior to women in every way. Having been wrong in these basic matters, having mixed up assumptions with conclusions drawn from evidence, it is not surprising that they are also wrong about homosexuality when they teach that it is a disorder.

One of the ways Blacks responded to racism in the 1960s and women responded to sexism in the 1970s was to say: we are not only your equals, we are actually better than you are. This may have been a rhetorical ploy more often than a deeply held belief, but the psychological benefit for the oppressed person is obvious. When gay people claim superiority they point out that their relationships are often characterized by equality whereas heterosexual relationships are often not. Even though many heterosexuals in the 1990s are consciously trying to create a spirit of equality in their partnerships, the pattern of dominance/submission is built into heterosexuality and the whole weight of the dominant culture reinforces this pattern. Differences of money, power, and age can work against equality in gay relationships, however. Although some lesbians and gay men believe in their superiority to heterosexuals, a more common view is expressed in the slogan often chanted in Gay Pride parades: "Two Four Six Eight. Gay is Just as Good as Straight."

This is not the view of the Defense Department, which subjects homosexual applicants for "secret" and "top secret" security clearances to more intense scrutiny than other applicants and describes undesirable sexual conduct as including "homosexuality and bestiality" (*Los Angeles Times*, 6 February 1990: 1). Linking homosexuality to sex between humans and animals is heterosexist; it illustrates both contempt for gay people and gross ignorance of them. Similarly, it is heterosexist to list homosexuality with social problems or diseases such as drug abuse and alcoholism.

Some of the most blatant examples of heterosexism come from

colleges and universities and in some cases indicate a backlash against vocal campus gay and lesbian groups. Denying these groups space on campus is heterosexist, as is the toleration of anti-gay jokes in campus newspapers or on campus radio stations. If a college library does not include many recent books on homosexuality, including books on gay liberation and books published by gay presses, it is heterosexist. If the counseling center staff includes no one sensitive to the needs of gay students, its policy is heterosexist. Married students' housing on nearly every campus is restricted to heterosexual students, a guarantee of second-class citizenship for lesbians and gay men. The Army and the Navy use campuses for recruiting even though they flagrantly discriminate against homosexuals. This is a bad policy at private schools but is intolerable at state-supported schools, whose funds come from all the taxpayers, gay as well as heterosexual.

A sociology course on the family that covers only the traditional family is heterosexist. A psychology department in which homosexuality is discussed only in the abnormal psych class is heterosexist. The hiring policies of nearly all academic departments are covertly heterosexist, and lesbians and gay men are often denied tenure, although the stated reason is rarely sexual preference. If a lesbian is denied tenure because she "doesn't fit in" or a gay man denied tenure because his publications are on homosexual topics, they are victims of heterosexist bias. More subtly, they are discriminated against by being prevented from having significant numbers of colleagues who are like themselves, either in their own departments or in others.

In a call for papers for the book *Censorship and Self-Censorship: Anti-Feminist Harassment in the Academy*,[3] examples of intellectual harassment include ridicule of scholars for lesbian feminist ideas; heckling at conferences and in classes; homophobic slurs; physical threats; and refusal of support for graduate students based on their choice of lesbian research topics.

Anti-gay harassment takes petty forms as well. Flyers or posters advertising campus events are defaced or destroyed; descriptions of the campus gay and lesbian alliance are kept out of the school catalogue; graffiti insult lesbians and gay men. A freshman English teacher at a Catholic college in the East found that her students were afraid to write an assigned essay on social attitudes towards homosexuality because they thought students in their dorms would brand them as homosexuals simply because they wrote on the topic. In such a climate of fear and intimidation, the free discussion of ideas is difficult and the very purpose of higher education thwarted.

What would a gay positive campus look like? On this campus, many professors would be comfortable enough with their sexuality and secure enough in their jobs to be openly gay. Fifteen percent of the counseling staff would either be gay themselves or specially trained to be sensitive to the needs of lesbian and gay students. Visiting lecturers would speak on gay topics. Campus film festivals would include gay and lesbian films. Gay and lesbian books would be prominently displayed in the bookstore and the library would occasionally have an exhibit on gay history or gay writers. Dormitory residents could be openly gay without fear of harassment. They could ask questions about homosexuality in any class without fear of ridicule either from the professor or from other students. Anti-gay graffiti would not appear in campus bathrooms. The gay student group would have an office in the union and a budget. Students and teachers who had AIDS would be treated with respect. The military would not be allowed to recruit on campus until it ended its discriminatory policies, and the Newman Center would close until the Catholic Church gave up its campaign against gay people. An openly gay man or a lesbian would have a chance of being named academic dean or president of the college. Assuredly this is a utopian vision of American colleges and universities in a conservative age; on the other hand, many of these changes will take place in the lifetime of students reading this text, and some may even take place in this decade.

Academic research is often heterosexist, in its assumptions, its choice of subjects for study, or its conclusions. The author of a sociological study of lesbians concludes that her view of lesbian identity is better than the views of the women she interviewed because they think of their lesbianism as an essence, a true self, whereas she sees lesbian identity as fluid and changing.[4] Similarly, when biographers who have little insight into homosexuality or who confuse serial monogamy (having a succession of partners) with promiscuity attempt to interpret the lives of major writers who were gay, the results often trivialize or distort the writer's life. This is the case with works intended to be definitive, such as Phyllis Robinson's *Willa: the Life of Willa Cather*, now superseded by Sharon O'Brien's *Willa Cather: the Emerging Voice*; Victoria Glendinning's *Vita: a Biography of Vita Sackville-West*; and Michael Holroyd's *Lytton Strachey*.[5] The women biographers are at least sympathetic to their subjects, but Holroyd's acceptance of the arrested development theory of homosexuality prevents him not only from fairly interpreting Strachey's emotional and sexual life but also from understanding other important aspects of his experience such as his intimate relationship with the painter Carrington.

Besides outright prejudice against gay people, a more subtle form of bias can be identified, **heterocentrism**. This is the (often unconscious) attitude that heterosexuality is the norm by which all human experience is measured. Homosexuality is ignored. When two teenagers at a girls' boarding school fell in love, their favorite teacher told them that their love had no future. Since the teacher could only imagine heterosexual love, her viewpoint was heterocentric. While homosexuality was hidden or repressed, heterocentrism could not be identified as a flaw in thinking.

To maintain the supremacy of heterosexuality, English scholars of the nineteenth century altered translations of Greek poetry celebrating love between men so that the real import was obliterated. In nineteenth-century America, the obviously sexual nature of the love between male comrades extolled by Walt Whitman caused some alarm, but it was possible for many decades to overlook the erotic meaning of this poetry because heterosexual experience was assumed to be universal. Emily Dickinson's passionate love letters to women and her poems were altered by her family after her death. This deception survived a hundred years because of the power of heterocentrism. People are presumed to be heterosexual even when, like Whitman and Dickinson, they leave behind explicit evidence that they were not.

Most research in the humanities and the social sciences is heterocentric. It purports to be about humankind when in fact it is about heterosexuals. A good example can be found in the article "Demographic Perspectives on the Long-Lived Society" by Siegel and

Taeuber. Noting that women outlive men, the authors refer to the "massive excess of females at ages sixty-five and over, now numbering five and one half million . . ."[6] This statement assumes that old women could only be partnered with men *their own age*. If we assume that some women over 65 will have female partners, some will be happily single, and others will pair off with younger men, the statistic might not be as massive as the authors assume. Informed that many women over 65 lack partners, a student free of heterocentric thinking might conclude that an enlightened social policy reflecting women's greater longevity would be to encourage lesbian relationships.

In addition, gay men and lesbians are often completely missing from college textbooks. Literature by and about them will not be found, for example, in the anthologies compiled for freshman and sophomore English courses by the major textbook publishers. Social science texts sometimes mention homosexuality in discussions of sex but say nothing about the lives of homosexual *persons*.

Now that heterocentric thinking can be identified as a point of view needing correction one can ask who is harmed by it. Obviously, gay people are harmed by being excluded from consideration. But heterocentrism harms all students and teachers in the university because it reflects a distorted, incomplete view of reality. Heterocentric teaching and research is conceptually flawed. Even worse, the blinders of heterosexism prevent researchers from asking many interesting questions. Gerontologists believe that the family is the chief support of older persons. But what happens when their life choices have alienated families or greatly minimized reliance on them? Even when families of gay men and lesbians are relatively tolerant, the gay person often moves to a large city to live more freely and his or her nearest biological relative may live hundreds of miles away. Researchers need to ask what these facts mean for the aging patterns of homosexuals.

Gay and lesbian liberation has also introduced the idea of **compulsory heterosexuality**, meaning that at present people must be pressured and coerced into heterosexual behavior (see Adrienne Rich, p. 206). The fact that many resist this pressure does not make heterosexuality any less compulsory. If homosexuality and heterosexuality were presented to young people as equally desirable, then many more of them would act on their homosexual desires and feelings. The anti-gay fury of fundamentalists tacitly acknowledges this. If homosexuals by nature truly were a tiny minority, there would be no need to prop up heterosexuality by condemning homosexuality. Every image of love, romance, and partnership held up for admiration to children and adolescents is a heterosexual image. Television and advertising reinforce these images. Books, magazines, and films promote hetero-sexual sex as the norm. Churches and schools prepare young people for traditional heterosexual partnerships, and these partnerships are honored throughout the college curriculum. At nearly every work-place in America, people are assumed to be married or dating people of the opposite sex. The combined weight of all of these expectations is very heavy. Females are coerced into heterosexuality by the lie that women choose women out of hatred for men.[7] Men are told that they can prove their manhood only by the sexual conquest of women. When gay boys and adolescents are denounced as sissies, their offense often is an unwillingness to assert dominance over others.

Some other terms besides compulsory heterosexuality which stu-dents may find in reading about gay liberation are "homoeroticism," "erotophobia," and "erasure." Erotic means tending to arouse sexual love or strongly affected by sexual desire. The adjective "homoerotic" describes painting, photography, writing (or even advertising) in which same-sex love is suggested. There is a distinction between suggestions of overt homosexuality, however, and suggestions of strong feelings of attraction between two men or two women. The latter may or may not be linked to genital sex. Scenes of nude men and boys bathing, both in painting and in poetry, for example, are often homoerotic; the same-sex passion in them is usually more obvious to the gay viewer/reader than to others. "Erotophobia" means an irratio-nal fear or hatred of the erotic. It is used to explain attempts to censor sexually explicit literature, art, or AIDS information pamphlets. "Era-sure" simply means that lesbians and gay men were missing from the historical record until very recently. It also means, for example, that AIDS deaths are sometimes covered up as cancer deaths, that the 1990 census assumed all citizens are heterosexual, and that the alumni magazines of many American colleges do not print news of graduates' gay and lesbian activities. Lesbians are erased when the national press treats homosexuality as a male phenomenon. *Newsweek*'s cover "The Future of Gay America" (12 March 1990) showing two men holding hands pictured only half of gay America. Gay people of color are erased when white lesbians and gay men are taken to represent the whole gay liberation movement.

Advocates of gay and lesbian liberation not only want to popularize concepts such as homophobia, heterosexism, heterocentrism and compulsory heterosexuality and to make terms such as homoerotic and erotophobic more common, they also seek to correct misconceptions about gay people. Four common ones are: (1) homosexuality is an illness that can be cured; (2) people are gay because they were seduced when young; (3) children raised by lesbians and gay men will turn out to be gay themselves; and (4) if homosexuality is not discouraged, the human race will die out.

Ever since 1974, when the American Psychiatric Association removed homosexuality from its category of disorders, most progressive people have accepted the fact that homosexuality is a normal expression of feeling and a normal behavior. Early research supported the illness hypothesis because it was conducted on patients in prisons and mental hospitals. Homosexuality itself can only be studied through more representative samples and, as soon as research used comparisons between heterosexuals and homosexuals, the myth of illness was exposed. Consequently, the claims of right-wing ministers and a few psychologists to "cure" homosexuals are false. People may be coerced into repressing feelings and desires; they may force themselves to seek opposite-sex partners. If they are genuinely homosexual, however, they cannot stop being homosexual; they can only conform outwardly to religious or psychological pressure. From the 1940s through the 1960s when only negative images of homosexuality existed, it was understandable that people trying to repress or control their homosexuality would try marriage as a "cure." Many thousands did. Today when most people have at least some access to unbiased information about homosexuality, the choice of marriage to eradicate one's same-sex drives is a serious mistake.

No one becomes gay simply because of an early sexual experience.

The condition of being gay presupposes a pattern of feelings and attachments based on a strong drive. An early sexual experience may reveal one's gay identity but does not cause it. This misconception attributes great power and predatory instincts to homosexuals, making them mythic creatures of evil who threaten the young. In fact, some gay people do not discover their true sexual identity until their twenties or later. Their early sexual experience is heterosexual.

Most children raised by gay men or lesbians, either biological or adopted, will grow up to be heterosexual. The relative unimportance of family influence in determining sexual preference is clearly demonstrated by the fact that the overwhelming majority of gay people grow up in traditional heterosexual families. If their families didn't make them heterosexual, despite all the social pressure to be heterosexual, neither will gay families make their children gay. So far, children raised by gay parents appear to be more tolerant of difference of all kinds than traditionally raised children, but conclusions about these families can only be tentative since they are a new form of alternative family. The long-range effects of growing up in a lesbian or gay male household may not interest heterocentric researchers, but it will be worth knowing, in the twenty-first century, how these families evolved. Many families made up of lesbians, of gay men, or of lesbians and gay men together, will remain hidden, to protect the privacy of family members.

If homosexuality is tolerated, the human race will not die out. Lesbians and gay men have the same reproductive capacity as heterosexuals and some choose to become parents. Same-sex desire and emotional histories can co-exist with the bearing and rearing of children. Some advocates of gay liberation have touted the movement as much-needed population control, and it is probably true that a huge increase in the gay population would be reflected in a lower birth rate. On the other hand, in the early 1980s, no one could have predicted the popularity of gay and lesbian-created families.

The concept of racism was not much discussed in colleges until the civil rights movement prompted the development of Black studies, and, until women's studies grew out of the women's liberation movement, sexism was not acknowledged as a major influence on campus life. Even though the ideas presented in this chapter are relevant to all courses in the humanities and the social sciences, they will be considered in only a few courses until a third reform movement within universities grows stronger—gay and lesbian studies. With its roots going back to the 1950s, it began in the 1970s; its "breakthrough decade" was the 1980s.[8]

GAY AND LESBIAN STUDIES

Like Black studies and women's studies, gay and lesbian studies seeks to gain greater visibility for the minority it represents, to challenge stereotypes, and to eliminate bias from college courses. Just as Black studies looks at knowledge from a Black perspective and women's studies takes a feminist perspective, gay and lesbian studies re-examines the curriculum from a gay perspective. Although it originates in a political movement outside of the university, gay and lesbian studies is an intellectual discipline. It considers not only acts and behavior, but "the specific beliefs and social forms that lend meaning to these acts."[9] That is, same-sex love and affection between college students may be very different from same-sex acts in a tribal initiation rite or from the erotic passion of sixteenth-century nuns, as shown for example in the 1985 Spanish film *Extramuros*. Gay and lesbian studies also functions as a support group for gay students, faculty, administrators, and staff.

Two types of courses are offered: (1) those which use a standard college course format to explore gay dimensions of a subject, for example, gay history; and (2) those specifically focused on issues or topics of special concern to the gay community, such as AIDS prevention, workplace issues for lesbian and gay men, or relationships between women and between men.

Gay and lesbian studies is now offered at many schools including Stanford, UC Berkeley, Yale, Amherst, MIT, and Brooklyn College. Mildred Dickemann asks students in her "Anthropology of Homosexualities" course at Sonoma State to look at the classification of homosexuality throughout the topical subheadings in the card catalogue of the college library, to deduce what is being implied or assumed about the subject from this classification. S. Diane Bogus assigns essays and stories by Black lesbians and Black gay men in her course "The Homosexual in American Literature" at Cal State Stanislaus.

In 1989, City College of San Francisco became the first college in the country to have a department of gay and lesbian studies and in 1991 to create the first full-time, tenure-track position in the field. The aims of the department, headed by Jack Collins, are to explore the social and cultural dimensions of homosexuality, to further an objective understanding of it, and to increase social awareness of the gay and lesbian subculture. Courses include literature, history, anthropology, creative writing, psychology, and film.

Gay literature has been taught at City College of San Francisco since 1972. One course is a survey from Sappho to Christopher Isherwood. Many assigned works would be familiar to students in mainstream literature classes, for example, Walt Whitman's *Leaves of Grass*, the short stories of E. M. Forster, and the poetry of W. H. Auden and Adrienne Rich, but the questions raised might be unfamiliar: How does the writer's homosexuality influence his or her work? Can we trace a homosexual tradition in literature? How do gay students feel in literature classes when the only instances of romantic love they read about and discuss in class are heterosexual? Which gay or lesbian writers are Native American, Asian American, Hispanic, or Black? How does having to conceal one's identity shape a literary text? What major works have gay subtexts? Students in this course read works they would not find in other literature courses, for example, "Lanval," from the *Lais* of Marie de France, in which Guinevere reproaches her lover for being more interested in his squire than he is in her.

But special courses on gay topics are not enough. Gay studies teachers aim to influence their colleagues in all academic disciplines so that information on gay people and issues is included in many classes besides gay and lesbian studies classes. In "Marriage and the Family," for example, students should learn about alternative families and analyze social pressures to be heterosexual. In other sociology classes they should read books like *The Mirror Dance*, Susan Krieger's study of a Midwestern lesbian community presented entirely through the voices of the community members.[10] In psychology, students should be assigned positive or at least neutral readings on homosexuality. In anthropology classes, homosexual behavior in other cultures should be acknowledged.

The phrase "lesbian studies" became familiar to some college students in the 1980s as books and articles were published by lesbian scholars,[11] but few courses are devoted entirely to lesbian studies, and many women's studies programs do not yet cover lesbian topics at all, in some cases for fear of provoking opposition on campuses where the programs are already controversial. The field of women's studies is slowly shedding some of its heterosexist bias, however, as textbooks begin to acknowledge the existence of lesbians. Both the essays and the bibliography of *Modern American Women, A Documentary History* include material on lesbians for example, and lesbian scholars are well represented in the essay collection *Women, Knowledge, and Reality: Explorations in Feminist Philosophy.*[12]

A few gay and lesbian studies conferences were held in the 1980s and will be held more frequently in the 1990s. A highlight of "Queer Theory," a two-day conference at the UC Santa Cruz in February 1990, was a film titled *Tongues Untied* (1989). Produced and directed by Marlon Riggs, the film deals with Black gay male identity, racism in the gay community, and homophobia in the Black community. The fourth annual lesbian, bisexual, and gay studies conference at Harvard in October 1990, "Pleasure/Politics," featured a wide variety of topics including rural gay life, censorship, anti-homophobia education, gay and lesbian marriage, sexual orientation and the law, sexuality among indigenous peoples, and "What We Do: (Homo) Sexual Practices." Topics from these two conferences illustrate the interweaving of politics and sexuality in gay and lesbian studies. In addition to conferences devoted entirely to homosexuality, others include a significant number of panels and papers on the topic, for example "Gender at the Crossroads," a conference at Stanford in March 1990; and the annual meetings of the National Women's Studies Association, many of whose founding members are lesbian feminists.

Because gay and lesbian studies, like women's studies and ethnic studies, has grassroots origins, it shares with those fields the dilemma of sometimes being too radical for the university but not radical enough for the movement. Dennis Altman cautions that gay and lesbian studies so far has been too timid in attempting to fit itself into existing academic disciplines at the expense of grappling with "the larger questions of constructing a meaningful language and theory of liberation."[13] Altman's point is supported by the fact that some of the most creative and boundary-challenging research does not fit into conventional academic categories but nevertheless greatly increases our knowledge of gay people, for example, slideshows developed by several scholars: Will Roscoe's on the Zuni man-woman; Tee Corinne's on lesbian erotic art; Karla Jay's on Paris lesbians Natalie Barney and her lover Renée Vivien; and Judith Niemi's on women adventurers and explorers. A journal of art history or a journal of sexuality probably would not welcome research on lesbian erotic art, nor would a traditional historical journal be likely to print an article on nineteenth-century women explorers, some of whom were lesbians.

The launching of gay and lesbian studies has been somewhat more problematic than the launching of ethnic studies or women's studies because a smaller number of teachers, students, and researchers has been involved in this work. In addition, gay and lesbian studies faces a problem not characteristic of the other academic reform movements: it is made up of two very different constituencies whose agendas sometimes clash. The difficulty of smoothly aligning lesbians with gay men was alluded to in the title of a discussion topic formulated by the gay and lesbian studies academic study seminar at MIT in the fall of 1989: "Lesbian-gay studies: a shotgun marriage?" Unquestionably, some gay male academics have been and still are misogynist, and some lesbian academics are staunch separatists. Between them lies no common ground. But the phrase "gay and lesbian studies" (or "lesbian and gay") presupposes that cosexual programs are desirable. Because of the historic inequality of women and men, however, gay men hold many more power positions in academia than lesbians do, and thus coalitions between them are nearly always coalitions of the more and the less powerful. Lesbians must guard against any tendency to become marginalized.

One of the most important facts about gay and lesbian studies today is that its development has been tragically impeded by the AIDS deaths of many scholars, teachers, administrators, and students. In addition, many men currently living with AIDS are too weak to do the research and teaching that would normally be furthering gay and lesbian studies. Both grassroots and university-based scholars whose partners have AIDS may be full-time caregivers unable to pursue their research. Many writers whose work helped create gay and lesbian studies have died of AIDS. Gay professional caucuses would be larger and stronger if many members and potential members had not died. At the same time, the many books about AIDS, those documenting the disease itself, those discussing the social and political meanings of the epidemic, and personal narratives have strengthened gay studies. Among the best are *Personal Dispatches: Writers Confront AIDS*, edited by John Preston, and Dennis Altman's *AIDS in the Mind of America*.[14]

Gay and lesbian studies will have greater impact in the 1990s than in the 1980s because of the widening scope of research by gay male and lesbian academics and because the number of publications about gay people, both popular and scholarly, will greatly increase. These two trends will make access to ideas about homosexuality easier for most college students and will enable them to reconsider any myths and stereotypes about homosexuals they may have acquired from families, schools, churches, and the mass media.

People who do research on gay topics should not be presumed to be gay, but often their research interests reflect their own homosexuality. Some would have begun their research much earlier if intellectuals in general had been open-minded about homosexuality and if good work on this topic had a chance of being published before the 1970s. But, in many cases, scholarly interests grew out of participation in the gay liberation and women's liberation movements. For some gay academics, research on homosexuality can be only a sideline because of prejudice in their departments; the work of others is grudgingly accepted; and a few gay scholars are strongly encouraged in their work by colleagues and superiors. Thus far few grants have underwritten research on gay topics, and little prestige accompanies the work. Consequently, the existence of professional support groups for gay scholars is crucial. Two of the first gay professional caucuses were formed in the early 1970s in the American Library Association by Barbara Gittings and in the Modern Language Association by Dolores Noll and Louis Crompton. Similar groups are the National Organization of Gay and Lesbian Scientists; the gay caucus of the American Historical Society; the Committee on Lesbian and Gay History; the Society of Lesbian and Gay Anthropologists; the Society for Lesbian and Gay Philosophy; the National Association of Lesbian and Gay Gerontologists; and the Gay Studies Special Interest Group of the American Educational Research Association. Most of these groups publish newsletters containing information about new work and research in progress. The Gay Academic Union is a nationwide network of scholars and students. Several cities including Boston and San Francisco have lesbian and gay history projects. Libraries and archives have been founded by gay researchers in several European countries and Canada. Two of the largest in the US are the National Gay Archives in Hollywood and the Lesbian Herstory Archives in New York.

The impetus for research on homosexuality is very strong because until recently homosexuality was a forbidden topic. Erased from history, lesbians and gay men were invisible to themselves as well as to heterosexuals. People who belong to a racial or ethnic minority grow up knowing that their group exists, and girls grow up knowing that women exist. But many homosexuals alive today, perhaps most, grew up not knowing that people with feelings similar to their own existed at all, much less existed in large numbers. Liberation from ignorance has motivated them to learn all they can about homosexuals in the past and about the great diversity of gay and lesbian life today. This knowledge is not only intrinsically interesting but necessary for their survival.

As they try to overcome obstacles to their research created by censorship, reticence, and the dearth of evidence, gay and lesbian scholars resemble scholars working in any controversial area, but they face specific problems such as subjects' fear of exposure (leading for example to child custody suits or job termination) or the destruction of documents by friends or lovers. When Edith Lewis destroyed Willa Cather's letters, for example, at Cather's request, she facilitated heterosexist research on her partner.

Nevertheless, because research focusing on gay people or gay issues is relatively new, scholars and graduate students are finding opportunities to make original contributions to knowledge, the old ideal of scholarship which has all but disappeared from American universities. Undergraduates can also participate in gay and lesbian studies, for example by preserving the experiences of old lesbians and gay men through oral histories or by following leads in such sources as Clare Potter's *Index to Lesbian Periodicals*, Barbara Grier's *The Lesbian in Literature*, and J.R. Roberts' *Black Lesbian Bibliography*,[15] and the two-volume *Encyclopedia of Homosexuality*, edited by Wayne Dynes (1990).

The following examples show the diversity of gay studies. Mike Hippler's *Matlovich* is a biography of the Air Force sergeant and gay rights leader Leonard Matlovich who fought his discharge for being gay. Paula Gunn Allen's essay "Lesbians in American Indian Cultures" appears in *Hidden from History*. Sociologist James G. Wolf edited the collection *Gay Priests*. The anthology *Lesbian Nuns: Breaking Silence* includes a scholarly discussion of convent lesbianism in the past by Nancy Manahan.[16] Important historical works listed in the bibliography are Boswell's *Christianity, Social Tolerance, and Homosexuality* (1980); Faderman's *Surpassing the Love of Men* (1981); D'Emilio's *Sexual Politics, Sexual Communities* (1983b); and *Gay American History* by Katz (1976).[17] Research in progress includes lesbians over 60 who were in the military (Monika Kehoe); gender (Mildred Dickemann); a bibliography of lesbian studies articles from 1970 to 1989 (Linda Garber); homosexuality in China and Japan (Louis Crompton); gay politics and theatricality (David Thomas); and images of lesbians on book covers (Michele Barale).

From a radical perspective, the new academic respectability of gay and lesbian studies brings problems as well as opportunities. The field was created by risk-taking academics and grass-roots scholars, teachers and students. Now, people who have come to it recently are beginning to use it for career advancement. Because of homophobia in the universities, the founders had nothing to gain and much to lose by involvement in gay and lesbian studies. While this may still be true for some scholars, others have many new publishing opportunities as a result of the growth of gay studies, and sometimes their research is directed not at lesbian and gay students and teachers (or a broad academic audience) but rather at their colleagues in narrow disciplines. Thus there is a natural tension between generalists in gay studies and those with an interdisciplinary focus on the one hand and highly specialized academicians who seek to fit lesbian and gay topics into pre-determined categories on the other.

The Journal of Homosexuality has played an important role in stimulating research. Two of its special issues are on lesbian and gay aging, edited by John Allen Lee (1990) and homosexuality and education, edited by Karen Harbeck (in progress). The journal editor, John De-Cecco, directs CERES, the Center for Research and Education in Sexuality at San Francisco State University. *Matrices* is a newsletter for lesbian feminist scholars published at the University of Minnesota.

The lives of lesbians offer many topics for investigation in literature, history, psychology, health, sociology, education, political science and other fields.[18] How do lesbians of color deal with the double jeopardy of membership in a racial minority and a sexual minority, for example? How do lesbians adapt to the corporate world? Can homophobic attitudes towards women in physical education be measured? How have lesbians been visually represented? Why are lesbians more frequently expelled from the military than gay men? What patterns can be seen in case histories of lesbians fired from academic jobs? Do the experiences of lesbians in long-term partnerships have any relevance for gay male relationships or heterosexual marriages? Do the lives of old lesbians provide evidence to support the theory that the resilience and toughness needed by minority group members to survive in a hostile culture help them adapt well to aging? Among old lesbians who hold advanced degrees is identification with a profession stronger than identification as women or as lesbians? Because the stigma attached to lesbianism was universal and harsh before the 1970s, women who chose that life in the five decades before women's liberation had a very strong need to prove their worth by education and professional achievement. Women's historians do not yet know how lesbians coped over lifetimes with the stigma of an identity judged sick and sinful.

College classes will become more interesting when ideas and

knowledge about homosexuality are incorporated into them. But the impact of gay and lesbian scholarship must extend beyond the campus. A sign of the importance of this work is that academic presses are beginning to publish it. Karla Jay is editing *The Cutting Edge: Twentieth Century Lesbian Studies* for New York University Press, for example, and Richard Mohr edits a gay and lesbian series published by Columbia. When the department of continuing education of Harvard Medical School and the department of psychiatry at Cambridge Hospital sponsored a conference on women in May 1990, two of the fifteen sessions dealt with lesbian issues, an indication that gay and lesbian research has begun to be acknowledged in a way that it was not ten or even five years ago.

Although extremely important for creating a climate in which homosexuality can be discussed rationally and more fully understood than in the past, scholarly research, even when intended for readers beyond the academic world, is read by only a relatively small audience and thus would not by itself be enough to challenge widely held stereotypes and discriminatory practices. The dissemination of popular books is necessary to do that.

GAY AND LESBIAN PUBLISHING

Books and articles about lesbians and gay men have been published by the gay press since the early 1970s and by mainstream presses since the late 1970s, but the explosion of this work since 1985 has been so great that a *Publisher's Weekly* report of several pages (8 December 1989) could give only some highlights of one of the most remarkable changes in American publishing. The entry of lesbians and gay men into mainstream publishing is as momentous for them as the dismantling of the Berlin wall was for Germans. More clearly than any other cultural or intellectual development, the rise of gay and lesbian publishing demonstrates that gay liberation is a movement of ideas.

When 1,200 people gathered for the first national convention of lesbian and gay writers in San Francisco in March 1990, they were astonished by their numbers and by the distance they had come in twenty years. Like two of their folk heroes, Allen Ginsberg and Judy Grahn, many remembered when gay writing was an underground movement in the 1950s. Others became writers in the 1970s, when describing their experience still took courage but was a choice made within the context of a liberation movement, and still others, in their twenties, are only beginning to write. Within the lifetimes of many at the conference, gay literature had changed from "a literature of guilt and apology to one of political defiance and celebration of sexual difference."[19]

The original audience for gay writing was created by a few small lesbian presses such as Daughters, Diana Press, Persephone and Naiad and by a few gay male presses such as Sunshine Press and Grey Fox. Like the power to name themselves gay, the power to write the truth about lives which had so often been condemned or misunderstood was extraordinarily liberating. The works of these presses inspired readers not only to seek out more books on gay life but to become writers themselves, because for the first time they had a subject to write about. Joined by Alyson, Seal Press, Cleis, Spinsters Ink, and a few other independents, these presses demonstrated a great potential audience for gay books, so that when mainstream houses finally began acquiring lesbian and gay authors it was commercially safe to do so. Without the pioneering work of the small lesbian and gay presses, however, most mainstream houses would never have discovered either gay writers or gay readers. Today a few major publishers are encouraging the growth of lesbian and gay literature, most notably St Martin's and New American Library, but lesbian writers have far less access than gay men to mainstream publishing. Women and men have joined forces, however, to create Publishers' Triangle, a support group for gay publicists, agents, editors, writers, and publishers.

The emergence of independent lesbian and gay publishing is part of a major small press expansion in America. At a time when mainstream houses are owned by huge conglomerates, the literary life of American publishing is in the small presses. Kitchen Table: Women of Color Press exemplifies this vitality as do Firebrand, a lesbian press, and Beacon Press, publisher of many gay and lesbian authors. In addition, self-publishing has played a role in the growth of gay publishing, especially poetry; for example, *Earth Life* by Essex Hemphill and *Eat Thunder, Drink Rain* by Doris Davenport.

Besides books, periodical articles are an important part of gay and lesbian publishing. Pioneering lesbian periodicals of the 1970s, *Conditions* and *Sinister Wisdom*, remain in print today. *Gay Community News* and *The Advocate* publish reviews and interviews with gay and lesbian writers. In the 1990s, *The European Gay Review, Outlook*, and *Lambda Book Report* are devoted to the writings of both lesbians and gay men, while other publications focus on one sex, for example, *The James White Review* and *Common Lives/Lesbian Lives*.

The frequency with which the term "heterosexual" is used now, compared to ten or fifteen years ago, signals a victory for gay liberation. This is a basic change in American English, reflecting a change in consciousness. The prefix "hetero," meaning many, does not as accurately designate opposite-sex attraction as the prefix "homo" (same) designates same-sex attraction. When only one form of sexual behavior seemed to exist, there was no need to define it. Now, every time a young person entering puberty hears the word "homosexual," it reminds him or her that more than one sexual orientation is possible. And every time Jesse Helms defends the "heterosexual American family," he scores a point for gay liberation because he is forced, by a political movement, to make a distinction he would not have had to make twenty years ago. The openness of homosexuals has made them, paradoxically, "at once dangerous and in danger, powerful and oppressed"[20]—In danger, in the sense that bigoted politicians like Helm can lead crusades to censor creative work and intimidate people who believe in the free discussion of homosexuality, but dangerous in the sense that, having experienced the power of their ideas, lesbians and gay men will never go back into hiding.

5

GAY CULTURE AND COMMUNITY

Gay liberation is one of several sexual freedom movements in twentieth-century America, including the birth control campaign led by
Margaret Sanger, the hippie subculture of the 1960s, and the women's
liberation movement, with its emphasis on reproductive freedom. As
a political protest movement, gay liberation also has analogues, noted
in Chapter 3: civil rights, the anti-war movement, and women's liberation. But gay and lesbian culture is unique. Because homosexuals have
no common country or language to bind them, gay culture is especially
important in creating a sense of community (Altman 1983: 155). "Gay
community" refers to the lesbians and gay men who consider them-

selves part of a political movement. Membership in the community is thus chosen rather than automatic. The phrase "gay culture" designates their attitudes, values, tastes, artistic and literary works, groups and organizations, common experiences, festivals, special events, rituals, and their sense of a shared history. This chapter describes some aspects of gay culture and discusses its significance.

Gay culture existed before Stonewall but its remarkable growth in the 1970s changed it qualitatively. What had been a few sparks became a great blaze. In the decades before 1970, the need of homosexuals to be protected from the dominant groups made a subculture necessary. When fired from jobs, evicted from apartments, jeered in the streets, or caught in bar raids, homosexuals experienced this treatment as individuals who were defying every recognized authority. Some felt inferior and ashamed; others who were proud of their homosexuality felt common bonds with those like themselves; but all had to make private accommodation to discrimination. The group they belonged to was their circle of friends, and the dangers of being found out insured that the circle was small. Only a few outspoken and courageous individuals, such as the founders of Mattachine and the Daughters of Bilitis, saw themselves as part of a potentially much larger group. Originally, gay culture was an adaptation to a bad situation, a defense. Later it became a catalyst for social change. Without a pre-existing gay culture, gay liberation could not have become a huge protest movement in the 1970s, but without that movement, gay culture could not have grown so dramatically. The new visibility of the 1970s, resulting from the birth of group consciousness, transformed gay cultures from isolation and fragmentation into relative cohesiveness.

The basis for a gay subculture is the perception of being different. Eighteenth-century Englishmen who gathered at "mollyhouses" (public houses where homosexuals met), New Yorkers in the 1880s who had special meeting places, German students who patronized gay and lesbian clubs in the 1920s in Berlin and other university towns, Black and white homosexuals who socialized in Harlem clubs in the same era, soldiers and sailors in World War II who turned hotel bars into their own gathering places, all expressed their sense of difference. They were sexual outlaws who wanted to be with their own kind.[1] The urban homosexual subculture was created by people looking for sexual partners at a time when their desires were unmentionable in the dominant culture. Friendship was an equally important need for some. Both before and after Stonewall, the subculture allowed gays to have a sense of belonging that was especially important because many had been rejected by families and friends.

To some degree, gay culture depends on opposition to homosexuality, which sharpens both the sense of difference and the need to band together. But even if all opposition to homosexuality were to disappear, it is likely that gay men and lesbians would continue to form their own groups. In the future, as these groups grow stronger, they may constitute a satellite culture rather than a subculture.

Coming out has a central place in gay culture. No matter how much gay people differ from each other in class, race, economic status, or age, no matter how much women differ from men, all share this experience. It involves changing one's self-concept, reinterpreting past emotional history, and changing relations with others. When people come out, they naturally feel that only those who have experienced a similar transformation will fully understand them. In the 1930s, the expression "come out" meant having one's first sexual experience, but during World War II its meaning expanded to finding gay and lesbian friends and discovering the gay life (Berube 1990: 6). Today it also means acceptance of one's gay identity and a self-conscious association with a mass movement. The process of coming out links gay politics, the politics of pride in being gay, to gay culture, which reinforces that pride. Sexuality is central to both gay politics and gay culture. Similarly, feminism is rooted in a belief that women must control their own bodies and be treated equally. But women do not have to argue first that they deserve to exist. Gay culture is a many-faceted expression of the right to be.

Examples in the following pages show the diversity of gay and lesbian culture. It may be a lesbian softball game, a gay Native American powwow, a novel with gay characters, a women's music festival, a drag ball, a cruising spot, a campus gay group, a meditation group for lesbians and gay men, the lambda symbol (a Greek letter appropriated by early gay activists), safe-sex posters, the AIDS quilt, a picnic for gay fathers and their children, or a same-sex wedding. It may be private—photo albums, clothing, jokes, favorite sayings of a small friendship circle—or public, for example the Vancouver Gay Games of August 1990, one of the largest sports event in the world that year.

BARS

The bar has a central place in gay culture. Until the 1970s, bars were the only public meeting places for homosexuals (except for the meeting places of a few political groups, which were not public in the same way). It was in bars that homosexuals learned they were not the only ones. Some bars catered to both men and women; others were primarily for women. Their chief functions were socializing and cruising, and they were often located in unfrequented warehouse districts (*Encyclopedia of Homosexuality* 1990: 111). In the bar, homosexuals won "the first of their civil rights, the right to assemble, in public, as homosexuals."[2] But an atmosphere of danger surrounded bar life because of frequent police raids. When Monika Kehoe, a writer who came out in her seventies, went to lesbian bars in Greenwich Village in the 1950s, she knew that she would lose her job as Dean of Women at a local college if a bar raid led to lists of names appearing in the newspapers. At Mona's, a lesbian bar in San Francisco, the marquee read, "Where Girls Will Be Boys." At the Black Cat, well-known San Francisco drag queen José Sarria sang songs from operas and led men in singing "God Save Us Nelly Queens" to the tune of "God Save the Queen." ("Nelly" is a slang term for a male homosexual). In the years before gay liberation, the bars took the place of family and church for many homosexuals (Altman 1983: 21).

Lesbian bar life in the 1940s and 1950s foreshadowed gay liberation because (1) lesbians formed a distinctive culture there; and (2) the bar was the central place from which they confronted a hostile world (Davis and Kennedy in Duberman *et al.* 1989: 427). Lesbians identified themselves as butches or femmes, roles that allows some latitude for women who felt they were neither. Joan Nestle recalls that in the 1950s at the Sea Colony, a working-class lesbian bar in New York, it was a crime for women to dance together. Even though the bar world was restricted by "Mafia nets, clean up New York nets and vice squad nets," lesbians needed such gathering places because the dominant culture told them, "hate yourself because you are a freak . . . hate yourself because you are sexual" (Nestle 1987: 37–8). The bars represented sexual and economic independence (Nestle, 105).

A harmful result of bar life for both women and men has been a high rate of alcoholism, a problem addressed by gay community centers in the 1970s and vigorously attacked throughout the 1980s by gay AA and Al-Anon groups, other recovery groups, counseling programs, and "Living Sober" conferences. Lesbians and gay men today meet very openly in a wide variety of settings, but for some the bar remains the only institution that links them to other gay people.

DRAG

The bar concealed homosexuals literally, while drag is a symbolic concealment. Men who dress in women's clothes are a diverse group, whose work-day manner of clothing may give no clue to their love of drag. Although the total identity of drag queen seems to be disappearing, drag is an enduring part of gay male culture, partly because the gap between the (heterosexual) lives homosexuals were raised to lead and their actual lives is a constant source of ironic humor. In the documentary "Word is Out," Tede Matthews gives drag a political interpretation as a conscious statement of rebellion against traditional gender roles. An explicit criticism of anti-gay bigotry in the Catholic Church is conveyed by the San Francisco charitable organization called The Sisters of Perpetual Indulgence, whose members include Sadie, Sadie, the Rabbi Lady and Sister Missionary Position. The Imperial Court is a large social service organization of drag queens who have extravagant balls and coronations. One of its officials, Empress Toby of San Jose, told a reporter, "I like the attention I get in drag. I don't fantasize that I'm a women" (*Gay in America* 1989: 53). Some ardent assimilationists in the gay community dislike the image drag queens project, but a more common attitude is that the outrageousness of drag accurately mirrors the nonconformity of homosexuality itself. For lesbians, drag is more tangential. They may joke about wearing drag when they dress for professional jobs or a family wedding. Black singer Gladys Bentley performed in a tuxedo at Mona's and in Harlem clubs in the 1930s and 1940s. The link between clothing and homosexual identity is complex: cross-dressing can signal homosexuality, but a complete association of the two goes back to the erroneous Victorian idea, which persisted in the twentieth century, that homosexuals are people trapped in the wrong body.

CAMP

Like drag, camp pokes fun at middle-class respectability (*Encyclopedia of Homosexuality* 1990: 189). Camp is a style of humor based on love of the exaggerated, of artifice, and of androgyny.[3] At a gay bar in Sydney, for example, after patrons watched the wedding of Prince Charles on television, they performed a drag version of the royal ceremony (Altman 1983: 153). According to Jack Collins, chair of the gay and lesbian studies department at City College of San Francisco, mimicry is the essence of camp (as the drag version of Prince Charles' wedding illustrates), and camp expresses a range of emotional tones.[4] It "stresses form over content, deflates pomposity, mocks pretention, and subverts values." It may be but is not necessarily effeminate (*Encyclopedia of Homosexuality* 1990: 413). In the past, gay men used camp humor to deflect the hostility directed at them; it was a form of self-defense (Altman 1983: 152). Camp defies the moral authority of those who condemn homosexuality. Out of context, however, camp humor may not seem funny. It exists in same-sex groups in which homosexuality is latent rather than openly expressed—among boy scouts, for example, in barracks, or in monasteries. When a southern bishop gave a retreat at a large Benedictine monastery in the Midwest, he jokingly referred to himself as "Magnolia Dei," a play on the familiar Latin tag, "Mater Dei," Mother of God, and an allusion to his region. The use of a female-sounding name is campy because it crosses gender boundaries in a humorous way. The bishop's nickname would have no meaning if a flourishing drag queen culture did not exist. Gay men use the phrase "camping it up" to mean behavior that is silly, outrageous, or irreverent.

FIGURES

Another way gay people cope with stigma is to identify famous figures from the past who were homosexual, such as Leonardo da Vinci, Michelangelo, André Gide, Emily Dickinson, the British composer Benjamin Britten and his lover, tenor Peter Pears. Gay people have great curiosity about those who may have been "one of them." Freud's daughter Anna, for example, herself an analyst and theoretician, lived with her colleague Dorothy Burlingham for fifty years. For decades scholars denied or ignored Walt Whitman's homosexuality, a central theme in his poetry. When the biographer of journalist Lorena Hickok published love letters written to her by Eleanor Roosevelt, Arthur Schlesinger, writing in the *New York Times*, had a hard time explaining that the language of sexual love was really some other kind of language. Even in the 1980s, hints of homosexuality of a distinguished person were considered scandalous. Well-known figures in sports, in Hollywood, and in business often marry to conceal their homosexuality from the public. Tennis champion Martina Navratilova has disregarded this custom, however.

Equally important to gay culture is recovering the lives of those homosexuals who were not famous. Collections such as the National Gay Archives in Hollywood and the Lesbian Herstory Archives in New York City preserve valuable records from the lives of ordinary people. Slideshows created by grassroots social historians have taught gay men and lesbians about aspects of their past.[5] Edythe Eyde took the name Lisa Ben, an anagram of lesbian, when she began to publish the first US lesbian magazine, *vice versa*, in 1947. Today she writes parodies of popular songs to give them a gay twist, for example, "Fairy from Tulare," a take-off on Merle Haggard's "Okie from Muskogee."

PLACES

Many large cities have sizeable gay and lesbian populations including Seattle, Minneapolis, Chicago, Los Angeles, Miami, and Boston. Northern California, western Massachusetts, and the Santa Fe area have large lesbian populations. Where lesbians live when they can choose the place is a research topic of University of Colorado geographer Jacqueline Beyer. Today visitors to major US cities who come from other states or other countries can easily find gay places to visit such as bars, restaurants, hotels, and bookstores. Just as traveling Methodist ministers or union officials can find their own people when they are on the road, gay men and lesbians have their special networks. Some resorts cater to them. The Russian River area of northern California is a predominantly gay vacation spot. After gay investors revitalized Key West in the 1970s, its economy was bolstered by gay tourists. Provincetown at the tip of Cape Cod, long known as a haven for artists, writers, and theater people, has more recently become a popular resort town for both lesbians and gay men. Other places are created within the gay and lesbian community—several lesbian land collectives in Oregon, for example; a base for the men's group Radical Faeries in Wolf Creek, Oregon; and Crone Haven, a lesbian land group in British Columbia, begun as an alternative to nursing homes for lesbians. In the 1970s, many lesbian and gay colonies were founded in rural areas; some still exist.

SPIRITUALITY

The desire to live apart from the dominant culture is a manifestation of lesbian and gay spirituality, which has many facets. Radical Faeries, for example, and many feminists create goddess-worshipping rituals and study Native American and Zen Buddhist religious practices.

More traditional gay people have formed groups to express their religious affiliation: Integrity for gay Episcopalians, Dignity for Catholics, Kinship for Seventh Day Adventists, Quaker groups, and gay synagogues. Others worship at Metropolitan Community Church, a church founded by Protestant lesbians and gay men. Although some homosexuals are atheists and materialists, a recurring emphasis on spirituality has sometimes served the political and psychological function of buttressing the gay community's rationale for acceptance. The "love that dare not speak its name" has been portrayed as originating in a spiritual bond or existing solely on a spiritual plane. Walt Whitman envisioned American democracy becoming purified by manly love, the emotional and sexual union of comrades which he called "adhesiveness." More recently, Judy Grahn's *Another Mother Tongue* and Arthur Evans' *Witchcraft and the Gay Counterculture* suggest that lesbians and gay men have special spiritual powers and thus are linked to shamans, healers, and poets. Similarly, Mark Thompson's anthology *Gay Spirit: Meaning and Myth* ascribes a special spiritual sensitivity to gay men.[6]

The spirit of solidarity among gay people, rising out of a shared oppression (from a radical view) or lesser status (from a reformist view), has created loving bonds among people who may have little in common besides their sexual preference. The love gay people feel for each other is not as easily described as more tangible aspects of their culture such as the music, clothing, films, or books they favor. People who have been despised and rejected because of their emotional/sexual identity naturally feel great empathy for others in the same situation. But the loving bonds among lesbians and gay men do not come only from negative experiences. They come too from a sense of being pioneers together. The mixed feelings of danger and opportunity experienced by those who enter a new land together unite gay people. At their public events and celebrations, especially on their Gay Pride days, they express affectionate caring for each other. This spirit in the gay community is especially evident in the response to AIDS, which has meant death and dying, funerals and bereavement, but has also meant extraordinary caring and devotion.

THEATER AND FILMS

Theater and films have always been important to lesbians and gay men as emotional outlets and as workplaces. Traditionally, gay men have identified with females stars. For many gay men, the movies are a place "to experience strong feelings and sexuality with others in a socially acceptable environment" (Bronski 1984: 93). Lesbians have been drawn to androgynous stars such as Greta Garbo, Marlene Dietrich and Katharine Hepburn, who occasionally wore male clothes in their films. Two of the first films about gay life to reach a broad audience were *Desert Hearts*, based on a Jane Rule novel, and *Longtime Companion*, a film about AIDS. Inspired by Vito Russo's film lectures and his book *The Celluloid Closet: Homosexuality in the Movies*,[7] gay and lesbian film festivals were created to show experimental and avant garde work by both gay and non-gay film makers, documentaries, and occasionally cartoons. Popular films by gay artists include the documentaries *Before Stonewall* and *The Silent Pioneers*. Each February a subsection of the Berlin film festival is devoted to new lesbian and gay films. A favorite of lesbians since the 1930s is *Madchen in Uniform*, a film about lesbian feelings in a boarding school (with a veiled anti-fascist theme), based on a novel by Christa Winsloe. In the German version, the main character is persuaded not to kill herself by her devoted classmates, but American censors required an altered ending, a suicide jump, before permitting the film to be shown (*Washington Blade*, 22 June 1990: 27).

The contrived image of the homosexual as troubled to the point of suicide or as deserving death for his or her "perversion" has been fairly common in novels and plays, but often gay images were entirely suppressed. The furor over Mae West's play *The Drag* in 1927 led to a law banning portrayals of homosexuals on the New York stage which lasted until 1967 (Bronski 1984: 111). In that social climate, the homosexuality of famous playwrights such as Noel Coward, Tennessee Williams, and Somerset Maugham was known only in theater circles. As with film, lesbians and gay men had to create their own images in plays. To encourage this work, a gay theater company was formed in New York, the Glines, joined by Theater Rhinoceros in San Francisco. In July 1990, the Alice B. Theater of Seattle, taking its name from the lover of Gertrude Stein, sponsored a ten-day national gay and lesbian theater festival. Gay playwrights include Harvey Fierstein, Robert Patrick, William Hoffman, Jane Chambers, and Kate Bornstein.

VISUAL ARTS

Emmanuel Cooper's book *The Sexual Perspective:* Homosexuality and Art in the Last 100 Years in the West focuses on the lives and works of individual artists.[8] In the late 1980s, photographer Robert Mapplethorpe became one of the first openly gay artists to be recognized in the mainstream art world.[9] British painter David Hockney is a well-known homosexual artist. Lesbian visual artists are more likely to be recognized only within their own circles, partly because of sexism and partly because they have created their own outlets for their works. Tee Corinne and JEB (Joan E. Biren) have researched lesbian images in the work of important photographers of the past such as Alice Austin and Berenice Abbott. JEB's slideshow "Lesbian Images in Photography, 1850–1980" presents the work of thirty women. One of Tee Corinne's slideshows (with Frances Doughty) is called "Styles of Being a Lesbian in Paris, 1890–1945." Other notable lesbian photographers working today are Lynda Koolish, Cathy Cade, and Morgan Gwenwald.

WRITING

For many lesbians and gay men, books are the introduction to homosexuality and the key to understanding the self. The crucial importance of writing in gay culture is summed up by activist Barbara Gittings, remembering what she thought in the 1950s when searching for books that would illuminate her feelings: "I'm looking for my people."[10] Pre-liberation books helped many figure out they were gay, but positive images of gay men and lesbians did not become common until the

1970s when literature by openly gay people began to be published, often by small gay-owned presses. The coming out story, which lesbians and gay men had always told to their friends, became more public as writers published autobiographical poems, short stories, novels, and plays. The task of gay writers, according to Michael Denneny of St Martin's Press, who has encouraged many of them, has been to create "a cultural space, a clearing of the mind where we could imagine our own lives."[11] Writers could not do that without the influence of a liberation movement to clear their minds of negative notions of homosexuality. Literature was an important vehicle for building solidarity among gay people of color. Latinas collaborated on the anthology *Companeras,* edited by Juanita Ramos, for example; Black women on *Home Girls,* edited by Barbara Smith; and Black men on *In the Life: A Black Gay Anthology,* edited by Joseph Beam.[12] A few gay writers, more men than women, were published by mainstream presses in the 1980s, making the existence of a gay literary subculture more visible than before. By the early 1990s, the catalogues of two major booksellers, Lambda Rising in Washington DC and A Different Light in New York, Los Angeles, and San Francisco, had grown into book reviews.

In addition to the literature that grew out of gay and lesbian liberation were newspapers and magazines that chronicled gay life and reported on political issues. The newspapers include *Philadelphia Gay News, Gay Community News* (Boston), *The Washington Blade, The New York Native, The Bay Area Times,* and *Equal Times* in Minneapolis. Among the magazines are *Outlook, The Advocate,* and *Christopher Street.* Reading the gay press is essential to understanding gay politics and culture. Because of the explosion of gay books and periodicals in the last ten years, college libraries require extensive collections of this material to be up to date.

Like other subcultures, the gay subculture has its own slang and particular interpretation of words. In Chinese, for example, homosexuality is called "the love of the cut sleeve" from the story of the Han emperor Ai who cut off his sleeve rather than disturb his sleeping lover. A B-D woman is Black slang for a bulldagger, a tough, swaggering butch. Code words and phrases helped homosexuals make contact cautiously. In the 1940s, the phrase "dropping hair pins" meant hinting you were homosexual, and "letting down your hair" meant you were completely open (Berube 1990: 6), a phrase that has passed into mainstream English. A lesbian attracted to another woman would ask, "Don't we go to the same church?" to signal her identity in a way that would be meaningless to a heterosexual woman. "Coming out" is a powerful expression which heterosexuals have appropriated for non-sexual uses. Someone will say, for example, that she comes out as a chocolate addict or compulsive shopper. This usage is probably intended to characterize the speaker as hip but it trivializes the experiences of lesbians and gay men.

Controlling the interpretation of labels given them is a function of gay power, most obvious in the word "gay" itself. The intensely derogatory "queer" has been reclaimed as a term of affection, comparable to "nigger" used only among Blacks. Common newspaper usage of the term "gay lifestyle" may not offend most gay people, but their identities are not accurately described by this phrase. We assume or change a lifestyle, but gay identity, even though it may be more fluid rather than fixed in particular individuals, is nonetheless an essential part of their emotional/sexual being; it is hardly a "style." The media guidelines of the Gay and Lesbian Alliance Against Defamation recommend that the phrase "avowed homosexual" be avoided, since the adjective "avowed" rarely precedes any other noun, and that those who have AIDS be called "people with AIDS" (PWAs) rather than AIDS victims. The former phrase denotes individuals who happen to have a disease, while the latter suggests that the only important fact about a person is his or her illness. This distinction was insisted on by gay activists at an early AIDS conference in Denver in 1983. They were influenced by the women's health movement, which popularized the notion that women are *survivors* of rape rather than victims. Thus people who have AIDS often emphasize that they are "*living* with AIDS."[13]

In the following excerpt from *Movement in Black* by Pat Parker, one of the best-known lesbian poets and activists, the word "perversion" is given a particular slant:

> Everytime we watched
> a queer hassled in the

streets and said nothing—
It was an act of perversion.

Everytime we lied about
The boyfriend or girlfriend
at coffee break—
It was an act of perversion.

Everytime we heard,
"I don't mind gays
but why must they
be blatant?" and said nothing—
It was an act of perversion.

Everytime we let a lesbian mother
lose her child and did not fill
the courtrooms—
It was an act of perversion.

Everytime we let straights
make out in bars while
we couldn't touch because
of laws—
It was an act of perversion.

Everytime we put on the proper
clothing to go to a family
wedding and left our lovers
at home—
It was an act of perversion.[14]

The act of reinterpreting their lives, exemplified in Pat Parker's poem, encouraged gay men and lesbians in the 1980s to define "family" on their own terms. In the heady days of sexual freedom in the 1970s, when gay liberation seemed a movement of the young, "family" meant only the oppressive structure that they had left behind. To some, its chief function was to reproduce capitalism. Later it meant an intentionally created unit based on love and mutual support. For those without children it often meant the special friends with whom holidays were celebrated. Increasingly, the word "family" meant that lesbians and gay men were fully capable of raising children, either from heterosexual marriage or those born through artificial insemination. The decision of gay people to be parents *as gay people* "marked a major change in gay and lesbian life" (Miller 1989: 109). It showed that gay culture was more deeply rooted than in the 1970s and that many gays wanted to create a better world for others besides themselves. To some extent, it also demonstrated the maturing and the increasing self-confidence of the gay community, but there were disagreements about the meaning of the new family—did it signify a waning radical spirit and a mere imitation of heterosexual life, or did it hold the promise of a radical revision of marriage and family? The complexity of the new families is suggested by a classification of lesbian families into three kinds: (1) nuclear—children born to or adopted by the couple; (2) blended—children from the mother's previous heterosexual relationship; and (3) extra blended—children from both sources.[15] Although child rearing was less common for gay men, the possibility of gay families encouraged them to seek joint custody of their children after divorce or to share parenting with lesbian friends. Surveys by *Partners*, a newsletter for gay and lesbian couples, will shed light on the families lesbians and gay men are creating in the 1990s.

A concomitant development is an emphasis on committed relationships in the gay community. Partly this results from AIDS and the manifest dangers of casual sex and partly from the aging of gay men and lesbians. Whether or not they choose formal ceremonies of commitment, in increasing numbers they are settling down as couples. This pattern, always strong in small towns and rural areas and among lesbians, is now more characteristic of the urban gay male community.

GROUPS AND ORGANIZATIONS

Today in America there are literally thousands of lesbian and gay organizations, an astonishing proliferation given the fairly recent development of group consciousness among gay people. No little girl ever grew up hearing that one day she might belong to Dykes of the American Revolution. *The Lavender Network* is an Oregon newspaper that lists gay groups throughout the state—for example, Blue Collar Gays, a lesbian art group, the Sacred Band (pagan spirituality for gay men), business and professional lesbians, a group creating a television program, a lesbian chorus, campus groups, youth groups, athletic groups, gardening groups, Jewish lesbians, a blood donor's club, an imperial court (drag queens), and a club for lesbians over 35 called Funny Ladies Afternoon Tea and Posey Society. A recent issue of the *Washington Blade* listed 266 gay groups. They include a social group for men interested in southern culture, a Zen meditation group, a lesbian cancer project, groups for Asians, Blacks, and Hispanics, a support group for federal employees, deaf gays, a teachers' caucus, a band, a country western dance group, a literary discussion club, and a group for married gay men. The Latino Lesbian and Gay Organization of Austin has 1,000 members, and a smaller group, Ellas, serves Latina lesbians. Les Ballets Trockadero is a ballet company made up of gay men. Black and White Men Together, a group committed to fighting racism, celebrated its tenth anniversary in 1990. It has chapters in many cities. The Gay Asian Pacific Alliance (GAPA) was founded in 1987 in San Francisco. The Black lesbian collective Nia takes its name from the Swahili word for purpose. Bay Area Career Women, a lesbian organization, has 1,500 members. In 1979, gay students at Howard formed the first gay organization at a Black college. San Francisco State University has had a gay group since 1970. Originally called the Gay Liberation Front, it is now known as the Lesbian and Gay Alliance. Lesbian and gay elders have their own groups in New York and San Francisco. In Seattle they call themselves Lavender Panthers.

Gay elders did not become visible until the 1980s. Those interviewed for Keith Vacha's book *Quiet Fire: Memoirs of Older Gay Men*, lived in a world of danger because of their emotional/sexual identities: both psychological danger, of being fired, receiving dishonorable discharges from the military, or being rejected by families; and physical danger, not only from random beatings and police brutality but also from assault by men they brought home as casual sexual partners. Marcy Adelman's book on older lesbians, *Long Time Passing*, is made up of articles and interviews with a professional athlete, a doctor, army veterans, life-long lesbians, those who came out in mid-life or later, women closely identified with the lesbian community, and women not part of that politicized world.[16]

SAN FRANCISCO

San Francisco holds a special place in the affections of gay people across America because more than any other city it stands for gay and lesbian liberation. But San Francisco was a mecca for homosexuals long before the seventies: purges of homosexuals from the armed forces in the Pacific in World War II sent many of them to San Francisco, where they stayed rather than return home in disgrace. Thus San Francisco symbolized a freer, less restricted life than was possible elsewhere. This impression was heightened by the Beat poets whose headquarters was North Beach. Their subculture helped to create gay consciousness. Allen Ginsberg's poem "Howl" celebrated homosexuality, linking his generation of gay men with Walt Whitman and his comrades. But in 1957 the publisher of "Howl," Lawrence Ferlinghetti of City Lights Books, was tried for selling an obscene book. It sells well to this day. From 1950 to 1960, single-person households in San Francisco doubled, a clue to the attractiveness of the city to homosexuals. By 1968, the Society for Individual Rights, with 1,000 members, was the largest homophile organization in the country.[17]

The exodus of gay men and lesbians from cities and rural areas all over America and their relocation to San Francisco in the 1970s showed that gay identity could be the center of one's life. This was a significant change from the 1950s and 1960s. Moving to be near other lesbians and gay men had the same draw for them that nearness to other Asians had for Asian immigrants to San Francisco in the 1980s. The city could not expand much because of its geography and thus the newly enlarged gay population had a big impact on the city. Newcomers to San Francisco had the immigrants' faith in a better future. But to make the transition from homosexual to gay, that is, to assume a political identity, they needed to feel safe. How did they know they would not be arrested or harassed? In San Francisco their numbers protected them.

Lesbians and gay men were safe, too, because they began creating their own places to congregate, such as bars, clubs, and restaurants, where they could openly show affection for someone of the same sex. Exposure to that freedom made a deep impression on gay visitors, some of whom wanted it for themselves and moved to San Francisco. The rise of gay neighborhoods also influenced the belief that it was safe to be gay in San Francisco. The experience of being around large numbers of other gay people was extraordinarily liberating. At the founding convention of the National Women's Studies Association in San Francisco in 1977, for example, when lesbians were asked to stand, hundreds of women rose to their feet and looked in astonishment at their numbers. Many gay people who moved to San Francisco gave up professions and prosperity in order to feel free. Those who did not move thought of San Francisco as a magical place; trips there strengthened them for life in more hostile environments.

Visitors love the Castro district, heavily populated by gay men, a national and even international symbol of open gay life. Castro Street itself is the commercial center of the gay male community in San Francisco. A guide to gay San Francisco published in a recent issue of *The Sentinel*, a local gay paper, listed forty-seven bars and thirty-four restaurants. A directory published by the Lesbian Rights Task Force listed eight pages of organizations for lesbians.

WOMEN AND MEN

$$\left[\text{men} \quad \left[\text{men} \quad \text{[cosexual]} \quad \text{women} \right] \quad \text{women} \right]$$

The diagram shows one way of understanding where women and men stand in relation to one another. The men on the far left and the women on the far right inhabit a single-sex world; they want a separate existence. The men on the left tend to be older than men in the other groups, but lesbian separatists come in all ages. Next to these two groups are men and women whose social lives are largely but not exclusively shared with others of the same sex. Finally, at the center are women and men whose only experience of the movement is a cosexual experience. They tend to be young, the members of the militant group ACT UP, for example. The men in the middle and center groups have been strongly influenced by feminism, and the women in the center group tend to be more accepting of all aspects of gay male sexuality than either of the other groups of women. Gay male culture has not had the impact on lesbian life that feminism and lesbian feminism have had on men's lives. Gay men discarding macho roles and exploring their feelings gained much from feminist thinking, whereas lesbians creating a separate women's culture distanced themselves from both heterosexual and gay men. Women separated because they wanted to strengthen themselves by healing from the damage of childhood sexual abuse, rape, psychological abuse in families, or from the less tangible harmful effects of growing up in a sexist culture. Women also separated because of gay misogyny.

Lesbian life is the subject of the next chapter, but a few characteristics of lesbian culture will be noted here. The community from which it springs has four characteristics: (1) interacting social networks; (2) group identity based on sexual preference; (3) subcultural values, basically feminist; and (4) an institutional base of organizations and settings.[18] Lesbian culture is first of all more of a *counter*-culture than gay culture as a whole, less dependent on commercial success, more antagonistic to the dominant culture. Singers Holly Near, Meg Christian, and Chris Williamson eventually reached a very broad audience, but in the early days of women's music they were underground classics whose songs helped women come out. Similarly, early lesbian feminist literature had a powerful impact on women making the transition from straight to gay. Women's poetry readings have held a special place in lesbian culture. Among the most respected figures are Audre Lorde, Adrienne Rich, and Judy Grahn. The largest lesbian press, Naiad, founded by Barbara Grier, has published mysteries, romances, bibliographies, and the best-selling anthology *Lesbian Nuns: Breaking Silence*, edited by Rosemary Curb and Nancy Manahan (1985). Naiad's best-known author is Jane Rule, whose *Lesbian Images* (1975) is a pioneering work of literary criticism. Lesbian culture encompasses "culture" in the traditional sense of literature, art, and music, but also means diverse activities, productions, and places such as craft work, coffeehouses, women's studies conferences, country retreats, mothers' groups, therapy groups, and Mothertongue Readers' Theater. Lesbian culture is less visible to the heterosexual world than gay male culture. An exception is Valencia Street in San Francisco: within a few blocks are a lesbian bar, a women's bookstore, a Japanese-style women's bathhouse, and an arts and crafts store, and on a nearby street is the four-story Women's Building. All of this activity must seem remarkable to lesbians in their fifties and older who read *The Ladder* in the 1950s and 1960s when lesbianism was a secret society.

Gay culture of course does not exist wholly separate from mainstream culture. When lesbians and gay men choose traditional marriage ceremonies, for example, or become parents, they invest old roles with a meaning unimaginable two decades ago. Occasionally, gay culture and the dominant culture intersect more publicly. A special ceremony was held on Flag Day, June 14, 1989, at the Harvey Milk library in San Francisco, named for the city supervisor slain in 1978. The Alexander Hamilton post of the American Legion, a gay post, presented an American flag and a rainbow flag (symbol of the gay community) to branch librarian Florence Mitchell as the City Librarian and other officials looked on. After the flags were raised, the Gay and Lesbian Freedom Day Marching Band played the national anthem. The Harvey Milk library thus became the first public institution in America to fly the gay flag. This branch was a logical choice both because it is near the Castro and because it houses a large collection of gay and lesbian books and the beginning of an archive. Important elements of gay culture came together on Flag Day: pageantry and fun (the band); civic spirit (American Legion post); the written word; and, above all, a spirit of community (the multicolored flag).

When gay culture manifests itself in clothing styles, chic decor, trendy bars, and expensive resorts, it is just as consumption-oriented as mainstream culture and barely distinguishable from it. But a gay and lesbian avant garde, made up of film makers, experimental writers, performance artists, visual artists, musicians, comics, and others, clearly stands apart from mainstream culture.

A flourishing gay culture says to the heterosexual majority: our behavior cannot be stamped out, so tolerate it. A strong gay culture may be more threatening than a political movement because it emphasizes the existence of a separate people. It is as if a large colony of dissenters turned up inside a religious kingdom. Before, the king's subjects had access to only one world view; now they know alternatives exist. Gay people threaten the established order by saying it is a construct, an arrangement, not a fixed law like the rotation of the planets. Just as Renaissance Christians had to admit that the earth was not the center of the universe, modern people must acknowledge that heterosexuality is no longer the whole emotional/sexual universe. Seeing the sexual world only through the pairing of man/woman is as rigidly dualistic as seeing the international world as sharply divided between communists and capitalists. The pairing man/woman is so basic to Western thought, however, that the alternatives of woman/woman and man/man, the substitution of sameness for antithesis, will not take its place, but the belief in heterosexuality as the only natural form of sexual expression is no longer tenable. Although many people still hold it, the inescapable refutation of gay culture surrounds them.

Gay people have been dismissed as narcissists because of the principle of sameness in their intimate relations, but this misconception is based on the false assumption that one is exactly mirrored by a same sex partner. The narcissism jibe does get at an essential feature of gay culture, however—its emphasis on self-development. This is inevitable, given the difficulty of merely establishing a positive gay identity in a homophobic culture. Self-awareness is heightened by the experience of being different. Gay culture necessarily involves a great deal of self-affirmation. Gay people often have the advantage of an outsider's perspective, the clear-sightedness that comes from seeing the essential artifice of social arrangements. Just as Blacks must be able to traverse both white territory and their own, gay people must figure out two worlds, the heterosexual one and their own. Consequently, they develop a feeling for nuances, contradictions, ironic juxtapositions. Anyone who defies one of the central expectations placed upon young people, the expectation of a heterosexual adult life, must, in the process of evolving differently, emphasize his or her self-development. The question "Who am I?" has such special urgency for gay people, at some point in their lives, that the presumptions of a state that would impose uniformity are easily exposed by them. By temperament, of course, not all gay people are dissenters and nonconformists, but gay culture tends to encourage these attitudes.

If gay culture simply meant a new way of loving it would not provoke intense opposition, but it undermines traditional notions of sex, gender, and family. Visual images of women with women and men with men suggest an end to the non–consensual dominant/submissive pattern of traditional relationships and blur gender distinctions. Gay culture says a manly man may put on a dress and a woman is womanly no matter what she wears or how much power she wields. For a long time, the family has not adhered to the religious norm of two adults married for life and their offspring. Gay and lesbian families further erode this image. Their families exist only to enhance their well-being.

The essence of gay culture has been defined as "the broadening and extension of sexuality," for gay liberation, like feminism, has brought about a more tolerant and more complex view of sexuality in the dominant culture (Bronski 1984: 184). In broader terms, the essence of gay culture is self-determination. Like everyone else, lesbians and gay men are bombarded daily with messages about the primacy of heterosexuality. To follow a different path openly and wholeheartedly rather than furtively, they have created a culture in which homosexuality is the norm. That psychic space allows them more control over their emotional and sexual lives than they would have by measuring themselves against heterosexual norms.

The Society for Individual Rights was founded at a time when homophile groups disguised their purpose by innocuous sounding names. A culture of concealment preceded a culture of exuberant self-celebration. But the sixties group was aptly named because individual rights was then and remains today the unifying thread running through the diversity of gay culture.

6

LESBIAN FEMINISM

This chapter describes one of the most significant changes in the lives of American women since the 1950s, the development of a new lesbian identity. The appearance of lesbian feminists in the late 1960s but especially in the late 1970s dramatically changed the way lesbians perceive themselves and are perceived by others. This shift resulted partly from forces and influences discussed in previous chapters, but the main cause was feminism (women's liberation). Feminists who came out of the closet gave a political meaning to lesbianism. They challenged and to some extent removed a centuries-old stigma by proudly proclaiming their identities. Although lesbian feminism grew out of feminism (as its name indicates), many lesbian feminists today identify with both the women's movement and gay liberation, and to some extent the two overlap. Lesbian feminism is treated separately here because accounts of both gay liberation and women's liberation often gloss over it.

This chapter considers lesbianism in general before narrowing its focus to lesbian feminism.

LESBIANISM

The essence of lesbianism is preference for women, not rejection of men. If a woman chooses other women for her sexual partners because her deepest feelings and needs can only be satisfied with women and if she has a history of strong emotional attachments to women, she is a lesbian. In the 1950s and earlier this identity was despised and trivialized. Today many thousands of American women affirm it because their own experience tells them it is natural. They approvingly quote the poet Elsa Gidlow, who expressed her sense of difference by saying, "In a land of apples I am faithful to oranges."

Lesbian groups exist in many countries, including China, Poland, Germany, Yugoslavia, Switzerland, France, Holland, the UK, Canada, Nicaragua, Peru, Australia, New Zealand, South Africa, and Japan, where they are called "regumi," meaning circle of lesbians. In all of these countries, as in the United States, lesbians challenge traditional notions of womanhood by exemplifying another way for women to be; by leaving marriages; by reproducing on their own terms, thereby separating motherhood from male control; by assuming positions of power in various mainstream jobs; and by demolishing the stereotype of the aging woman as frail and sexless.

American lesbians can be found in all social classes and income brackets. They are old, middle-aged and young; range from very radical to conservative politically; live in big cities, on farms, and in small towns; are secretive or open about their identity; are childless or mothers; come from happy families and unhappy families; cultivate friendships with men or avoid men; include Ph.Ds and high school drop outs. Some are life-long lesbians, while others come out after age 50, 60, or 70. Some women fairly quickly become totally comfortable with the emotional/sexual identity of lesbian, while others name themselves lesbians only after long, painful struggles. Some lesbians look obvious to the straight world because of their manner or dress, while others can easily pass for heterosexual.

The lesbian world includes women who are highly unconventional in most aspects of their lives as well as women who are conventional in every way except for their sexual preference. Some emphasize the sexual aspect of their identities, believing that sex between women is the essence of lesbianism, while for others emotional bonding and intimate companionship are more important. Some lesbians choose long-term relationships; others are single or coupled for short periods. Some believe lesbianism is an essence they were born with, not an identity they have taken on. For others, lesbianism is a self-conscious political statement which any woman can make. Many lesbians never marry; some come out after a marriage ends; and others choose relationships with women while remaining married. Lesbians often describe their former marriages as relatively happy until they discovered that all of their emotional and sexual needs were not being satisfied. A woman whose clothes do not quite fit her may be only vaguely dissatisfied until the day she finds clothing that fits perfectly. Once she has the right fit, she understands what was missing before. She doesn't hate her old clothes but she cannot express her true self in them.

To use another metaphor, lesbians are like immigrants:

> Even if we have not moved geographically, we have travelled enormous distances socially, spiritually, sexually. Coming out is a kind of migration, leaving behind an old, unsatisfactory way of life to search for a new source of sustenance. . . . Just as our immigrant grandparents believed that in New York City the streets were paved with gold, so lesbians have made San Francisco one of our chosen places. Here and in other lesbian communities urban and rural, scattered across the country, we have searched for a home, a place to find work, happiness, freedom, a chance to make a better life. We have searched for what was previously denied us: the wholeness of loving women.[1]

Lesbians are like immigrants in other sense because they, too, face prejudice, hostility, and discrimination. They no longer have these experiences as isolated individuals, however, but as members of a minority. While the quest for wholeness is an important goal for individual lesbians, as a group they seek to make this quest conceivable and attainable for large numbers of women. To the extent that a male-controlled society cannot tolerate such a change, lesbians threaten the existing social order, not only by their political organizing but merely by living openly as lesbians.

American lesbians are a diverse group:

- Carrie and Consuella are Latina lesbians who met while stationed in the Persian Gulf. Carrie discovered her lesbianism through her participation in women's softball. After Consuella confided to her lesbian aunt that she had strong feelings for women, her aunt encouraged her to read anthologies in which Latina lesbians published their stories.
- Ingrid and Toni are radical activists at the Midwestern university both attend. They helped found the lesbian group on their campus. Lesbian feminism is central to their lives and nearly all of their friends are lesbians. They read lesbian publications and have relatively little contact with gay liberation.
- Sandy is a public health nurse who works on the reservation of the Ojibway tribe she belongs to. Several times a year she goes to Minneapolis to meet with other gay and lesbian Native Americans.
- Gail, a lawyer for a gay and lesbian rights organization, has a women's studies background. For a time she lived in a lesbian land collective. Although her work for a gay organization makes her radical in the eyes of her biological family, in her own eyes she has become part of the establishment because she works with men and has a law degree.
- Sabrina is a Black journalist. In college she considered herself bisexual but later gradually began to identify as lesbian. She is in the closet at her newspaper job but intends to come out after she has repeatedly demonstrated her reporting skills and established a rapport with her co-workers.
- Mary and Marge are a lesbian couple in their mid-forties. Ten years ago when they first got together they were very active politically, helping to found the gay rights center in their city. Now their energies are focused on raising an adopted child and a child Mary had by artificial insemination. If a particular issue arose that touched their lives, they would quickly become politically active again.
- Muggs, a waitress who has also worked on an assembly line, knows

a few other lesbians through her union but usually socializes with gay men rather than with women.

- Reena and Dot met in a lesbian bar. Sometimes they march in the Gay Pride parade in the largest city of their state, but they have no contact with women's culture, the music, the books, the art, the newspapers, or the coffeehouses. They know a few gay men but no other lesbians.
- Gretchen is an 80-year-old male-identified lesbian who moved to Los Angeles when she was 68. At that time she had no connection with either gay rights or the women's movement. Closeted all her life, she prided herself on her rugged individualism and her skill in sports. Gradually she found a niche for herself in the lesbian community and in her late seventies published a book about older lesbians.
- Rachael and Rebecca are the only Jewish women in their Adult Children of Alcoholics group. Judaism is central to Rachael's life but she is very new to lesbianism; Rebecca, a long-time lesbian, is just beginning to explore the meaning of her Jewish identity.
- Kate is a Protestant missionary in Central America who fell in love with Maureen, a Catholic missionary in the same country. Neither woman previously had considered herself a lesbian, but the intense passion of their relationship challenged them to reconsider their self-definitions. They know that the women's movement has increased their self-esteem but they find it largely irrelevant to the lives of the poor women they work with. They are secretive about their relationship. Committed to radical social change for the people of Central America, they do not consider gay liberation to be part of their "liberation theology."
- Doris and Barbara are friends. Both are Black. Their friendship circles include Black gay men and Black feminists. They have experienced racism in both the women's movement and the gay movement. Their primary political identification is with other Blacks, but they support both women's liberation and gay liberation.
- Wing Yee and Le Hao met in the Gay Asian Pacific Alliance. Wing Yee's Chinese American parents accept her lesbianism, but Le Hao is afraid to tell her Vietnamese American family about herself because she expects a very negative reaction. Through the Alliance, Wing Yee and Le Hao discovered the work of Asian American lesbian writers such as Canyon Sam, Willyce Kim, and Merle Woo.
- Edna aspires to be a "diesal dyke," a tough butch, but her friends tease her that she has not yet learned to swagger. She knows that the people at the insurance company where she works would be amazed if they knew how she dressed on weekends.

- Joan considers herself a lesbian separatist. She spends time only with other separatists and works as a gardener to be independent. Depictions of women in the mass media disgust her. She occasionally writes sketches for a separatist magazine.
- Nan and Rosemary are a couple who fell in love while each was married. They decided to stay married because of affectionate feelings for their husbands and for the economic advantages of marriage. Their health insurance, for example, was far better than coverage they could have gotten as 60-year-old single women. When Nan's husband died, Rosemary began to feel impatient for the time when she could live with Nan. These women do not label themselves lesbians and know no women who do. They believe they just happened to choose a lover who is female. Since they do not feel discriminated against, they have no interest in the gay rights movement.
- Ruth and Mary Beth teach math at a community college in a conservative town. Most of the other teachers know they have lived together for years and think of them as a couple. But Ruth and Mary Beth act as if they are just roommates. They go to department meetings in separate cars. If a student mentions the gay rights movement, they express disdain for it.

The last example, of women apparently lesbians who do not adopt that label, indicates that some women may not be free to choose a stigmatized identity. Often such women lead harmonious lives because they have found a suitable partner. Their denial may seem to be a personal choice, but it is made in a milieu where heterosexuality is compulsory. That is, if they grew up in traditional families where they had no access to dissenting points of view, met no open lesbians in their formative years, and later chose the relatively conventional life of academics, they may not be *free* to adopt an unconventional sexual identity.

Friends of Ruth and Mary Beth assume they have a sexual relationship. But what if they do not—are they lesbians? Some lesbians would argue that they are not because sexual intimacy with another woman is to them the distinguishing sign of lesbianism. Others believe that a deep emotional bond with another woman, such as one growing out of years of close companionship, is a truer mark of lesbianism than sexual behavior. Lillian Faderman, author of *Surpassing the Love of Men* (1981), thinks that many of the intense friendships between women in the nineteenth century and earlier were not sexual but should be included in lesbian history. On the other hand, Susan Johnson's book *Staying Power* (1990), on long-term lesbian couples, includes in her study only women whose relationships are now, or once were, sexual.

Defining lesbianism as a specific sexual behavior rather than as an identity reduces a complex state of being to acts. A woman may feel profoundly connected to other women for a lifetime and have no desire for heterosexual relationships without wanting to have sex with women, or a woman may have sex with another woman without being a lesbian. The meaning she attaches to the experience determines whether or not she is a lesbian. Lesbians often must struggle to overcome obstacles to free sexual expression, however, and thus to de-emphasize the sexual nature of lesbianism is to misrepresent it. Sexual attraction to women is usually essential to lesbianism.

Other generalizations are difficult to make because of the diversity obvious in the examples given above. Clearly, women like Ingrid and Toni may have nothing in common with women like Ruth and Mary Beth except for their choice of women as partners. The experiences of lesbians of color differ from those of white lesbians. Nevertheless, the lives of the women named here suggest four broad categories of lesbians:

(1) Women whose lives are female centered who do not choose the label "lesbian" or "homosexual" but probably would if the identity were not stigmatized.

(2) Women who consider themselves female homosexuals or lesbians but derive no political meaning from that description. Some who became lesbians at a time when secrecy was necessary for survival view the openness of lesbian/gay life today as flamboyant and even dangerous. They say they prefer the days when homosexuals formed a secret society.

(3) Women who see their lesbianism in a political context, as part of gay liberation, and identify more with gay men than with other women.

(4) Women who define themselves as lesbian feminists. Their self-concept has been profoundly influenced by the women's liberation movement.

LESBIAN FEMINISM

To understand present-day lesbian feminism it is necessary to consider lesbianism in the two decades before the women's movement began, the impact of the movement on lesbian life, patterns of lesbian feminism from the 1970s to the 1990s, and a few of the issues that concern lesbians today.

LESBIANISM BEFORE THE CONTEMPORARY WOMEN'S LIBERATION MOVEMENT

During World War I, women who volunteered to drive ambulances and to nurse wounded soldiers had many more opportunities to discover their lesbianism than they had at home. Similarly in World War II, some women were able to explore lesbian feelings more safely in anonymous settings than they could have in their home towns. For a time, they held desirable jobs and could live independently. In her autobiography *Zami*, Audre Lorde describes working in a factory in Bridgeport during the war and coming out with another Black woman, whom she met at work.[2] Women who were unaware of lesbian feelings at the time they enlisted were thrown into a milieu where homosexual relationships, if not common, were at least more visible than they had been in the small towns of America before the war. During the war, military officials did not expel many homosexuals because winning the war was more important than purging the ranks of them. In the 1950s there was less tolerance; the attempt of Senator Joseph McCarthy to link homosexuals to communists is well known. Many gay men and lesbians lost government jobs at that time, more than were fired for allegedly being communists.

Persecution sometimes emboldens people to stand up for their rights, and thus the roots of modern-day gay liberation and lesbianism can be traced to the 1950s. Paradoxically, this was an inauspicious time for the first lesbian groups to appear because of the great emphasis on nuclear families and child rearing; but lesbians who had experienced the loosening of social restraints during the war could not be driven into marriage and motherhood because they saw alternatives, especially if they stayed in the large cities they had first come to during the war.

For many lesbians in the 1950s the center of social life and the one place where it was safe to be openly gay and to seek prospective sexual partners was the lesbian bar (or any bar which lesbians were known to frequent). The solidarity experienced by lesbians who knew each other through bars foreshadowed the later solidarity created by lesbian feminism, but lesbian feminists often did not know who their fore-mothers were. They learned in the 1980s and 1990s by reading works such as *Zami* and Joan Nestle's essay collection *A Restricted Country* (1987) and by hearing accounts of 1950s' bar life from those who experienced it or later recreated it through oral histories and interviews.

Lesbians who wanted an alternative to the bar found it in small friendship circles and in a social club, the Daughters of Bilitis (DOB), founded in 1955 by eight San Francisco women, including two who later became well-known activists, Del Martin and Phyllis Lyon. The name, taken from *Songs of Bilitis* by Pierre Louys, was deliberately obscure: open lesbians would not have been allowed to rent meeting space or use the mails. During the 1950s, DOB chapters were formed in most major cities. Their publication, *The Ladder*, lasted until 1974. In San Francisco, DOB sponsored monthly discussions intended to dispel myths about lesbians and to tell women their legal rights. In the 1950s the few novels featuring lesbian characters usually ended tragically, and newspapers and magazines did not mention homosexuality except in stories about bar raids or murders. DOB laid the groundwork for lesbian feminism of the next decade by its social events, referrals, and confrontations with public officials, and by its work with accepting professionals in fields such as religion, law, and the social sciences.[3]

DOB members called themselves "homophiles," from the Greek work for love of same. Rejecting the label "deviant" because of its negative connotations, they chose instead "variant woman," a more neutral term. One difference between these women and those who came out later through participation in the women's movement is that many DOB members found support from gay men important to them.

Today, lesbians who live in rural areas or small towns often befriend gay men because the number of gay people "out" enough to socialize with other gays is rather small.

In the 1960s, many of the lesbians who would later become feminists gained political experience in the civil rights movement and the anti-war movement. They kept quiet about their lesbianism, if they were aware of it, in order to be accepted in these groups. Some lesbians became hippies. Even in the radical sixties, heterosexuality was the only conceivable sexual orientation for most people. When feminism was reborn in the late 1960s, lesbians took the slogan "the personal is the political" to mean that for the first time they could disclose their emotional/sexual identities. They proclaimed their right to be "dykes" and "queers." Without the examples of the civil rights and anti-war movements, however, lesbians would not have been able to imagine radical social change. The earlier movements helped them believe in the justice of their cause and gave them techniques for organizing and demonstrating.

LESBIANS IN THE WOMEN'S MOVEMENT

Why was feminism so attractive to lesbians? It made the lives of women central instead of marginal; it relieved the pressure to date and marry and said that single was no longer second class; it provided the concepts of oppression and internalized self-hatred; it presented women with a greatly expanded range of choices about work and private life; and it promoted group consciousness and solidarity among women. All of these were necessary foundations to the development of a deeper level of self-acceptance among lesbians than was possible in the 1950s, except for a few very strong individuals. Women's liberation told women that they could be heterosexual, homosexual, bisexual, or asexual and that these choices were equally valid.

Although some heterosexual feminists spurned their sisters who came out of the closet, the women's movement encouraged lesbians to declare themselves. Coming out was the ultimate rejection of ladylike behavior. It was a defiant cry of self-determination. Not every lesbian feminist made this choice, but most believed that it was an essential political statement because the ignorance and prejudice which had surrounded lesbianism for centuries could only end if the true numbers of lesbians were known.

It would have been impossible to mobilize large numbers of lesbians before 1970: the taboos were too strong and the fears too great. Most educated women had not even read a book portraying a lesbian character much less met one. But as large numbers of women came together to discuss their lives, myths about lesbians began to be challenged. They were no longer the secretive and troubled creatures of the underworld, or the misfits of the abnormal psychology texts, but the women across the room, in the coffeehouse, at the movies, at marches, at work, and at school. They were even the wife and mother. Women discovered that feelings they had judged sick or neurotic were in fact completely natural and life enhancing. They saw that their desire to place women at the center of their lives did not make them man haters or imitation men. It did not make them narcissistic, arrested in their development, or inclined to molest children. Lesbianism was ordinary—that was the great discovery of those who joined women's liberation.

The subordinate social position of women worked against the formation of lesbian identity before the late 1960s when women were rarely independent enough to escape the net of compulsory heterosexuality. Feminism was radical because it taught women that their subjugation and the dominance of men, far from being inevitable or rooted in nature, were the product of complex social, historical, political, and economic forces that could change. Once they understood that, they saw that the dominance of heterosexuality itself could be challenged. Simply naming heterosexuality and considering it as an institution was liberating, for it had previously seemed, like air and water, a fact of nature needing no elucidation. The next step was to conceive of lesbianism as an alternative to heterosexuality, a possible choice for large numbers of women rather than the aberrant choice of a few. Lesbianism could then be viewed as more than a personal preference; it was a stand against male domination. The early lesbian feminists saw that they could not entirely escape the confining rules for women laid down by family, church, and state and could be persecuted for their rebellion, but acting on their attraction to other women freed them from many restraints. Sometimes the fear of negative consequences was far more damaging than the punishments themselves.

Lesbianism existed but could not flourish before women's liberation (except in the coteries of the privileged) because women saw themselves only as individuals. The movement created group consciousness. As individuals, women who loved women, or tried to, or wanted to, could be silenced, punished, made fearful, or kept in isolation. As part of the mass movement of women's liberation, lesbians could exist in relative safety. To label one's self "lesbian" before women's liberation was to take on the heavy weight of a despised identity; the assumptions about the sickness and sinfulness of lesbians were powerful. Only a dramatic and far-reaching struggle could dispel prejudice of that magnitude. Although the stigma attached to lesbianism was not entirely dispelled by the new movement, lesbians freed themselves from much of the homophobia they had internalized. Individual women in earlier times believed themselves to be normal and happy—Gertrude Stein and Alice B. Toklas, for example—but no public voices echoed their private voices.

Because feminism encouraged women to honor the women who came before them by learning their history, information about notable women who had passionate attachments to other women began to be widely shared among lesbian feminists. These discoveries showed that lesbianism was more common than lesbians of the 1950s would have guessed. Eleanor Roosevelt's love letters to the journalist Lorena Hickok were revealed, for example, and similar romantic friendships which were probably sexual were found to have existed among presidents, deans, and professors at Eastern women's colleges. The lesbianism of writers associated with the modernist movement such as Amy Lowell, H.D., Angelina Grimke, Margaret Anderson, and Sylvia Beach became obvious. In some cases, it was difficult to decide if a well-known athlete, writer, artist, or movie star had been a lesbian. Virginia Woolf, for example, had a passionate affair with Vita Sackville-West and loved other women intensely but in her journals referred to "sapphists" as if they were different from herself. On the other hand, she wrote to her sister, Vanessa Bell, "You will never succumb to the charms of any of your own sex—What an arid garden the world must be for you" (May 22, 1927).[4] Whether or not the lesbianism of any one public figure could be established, the stereotype of the lesbian as a sordid, menacing creature was shattered by the discovery that many women in the past had chosen other women for their lovers and partners. Thus the early lesbian feminists saw themselves not only as radically departing from the norms of the 1950s but also as continuing a *tradition* of love between women that had been "hidden from history."

Since lesbianism seemed very radical in the early 1970s, heterosexual feminist leaders tried to discount its impact on the fledgling feminist movement so that the movement would have broad appeal. Betty Friedan called lesbians "the lavender menace," for example, a tag many of them exuberantly adopted. But it was hard for feminists' spokeswomen to distance themselves from a group whose energy fueled the movement: many of the first women's centers, bookstores, abortion clinics, festivals, marches, and protests were organized by lesbians, who did not want to become invisible every time a reporter asked if women's liberation was a lesbian plot. At first they kept a low profile, joking among themselves that the press was right. But by the mid 1970s lesbians were more visible in leadership roles and more aware of their significant numbers within the movement. "Closets are for clothes," their buttons said. In some communities, lesbians *were* the women's movement, and in many others they made up more than half of its membership. Grassroots feminist leaders who were lesbians—Charlotte Bunch, for example—never got the media attention heterosexual leaders such as Gloria Steinem and Betty Friedan enjoyed, although Kate Millett's bisexuality was announced by a *Time* cover in the early 1970s. Slogans such as "Feminism is the theory, lesbianism is the practice," were not mentioned in the media. By suggesting that lesbianism was the highest form of woman bonding, the slogan naturally caused tension between heterosexual feminists and lesbians, but it allowed lesbians to make two important points: their lives could not be reduced to sex and they were not trying to be men.

Feminism tended to be a more urgent cause for lesbians than for other women because it was all they had. Heterosexual women quite rightly resented being criticized for "sleeping with the enemy" but they undeniably benefited from living in a socially approved role they could fall back on if the movement died out. Lesbians needed the new security and sense of power only the movement could provide. Thus they threw themselves into feminism with great zeal and often their whole lives were taken up by the cause. They championed its most radical position, an end to male control of women's lives. Lesbians read only women's books and women's periodicals and listened only to women's music—Meg Christian, Holly Near, and Chris Williamson were early favorites. Lesbians patronized women's businesses. They voted women into leadership roles in unions. On sexist ads they slapped stickers saying "This degrades women." They protested sexism in children's books and on television. They organized boycotts. They demonstrated against beauty contests. They began to publish their own work, which was unacceptable to mainstream presses. They fought for women's studies programs at hundreds of colleges and universities. Although some lesbians continued to work for civil rights and against the Viet Nam war, they felt that their home was in the women's movement.

Of the many institutions which encouraged the growth of lesbian feminism in the 1970s and 1980s—bookstores, festivals, marches, consciousness-raising groups, friendship circles, resource centers—none was more important than the National Women's Studies Association. Founded in 1977 by college teachers, administrators, counselors, librarians, writers, publishers, and grassroots activists, NWSA brought together hundreds of lesbian feminists who would not otherwise have found each other, advocated inclusion of lesbian material in women's studies classes, sponsored a wide variety of panel discussions and presentations on lesbian topics at its annual conferences, and provided a forum for women who were discriminated against for being lesbians. In addition, women's studies programs targeted by homophobic right wingers could rally support through NWSA. Many lesbians found lovers and partners at NWSA events. Others found publishers, contributors to their anthologies, or buyers for their products or services.

Lesbian feminists working in isolation gained strength through NWSA, among them teachers treated as outcasts on their campuses but honored as pioneers by their national organization.

LESBIAN FEMINISM FROM THE 1970s TO THE 1990s

Euphoria and a playful spirit characterized the social and political gatherings of lesbian feminists in the late 1960s and 1970s. Women who had been hiding their true identities, in some cases for decades, or punished for revealing them, joined the liberation movement feeling that the conditions of their lives would improve dramatically. For those who had never been in groups of gay women (a term some preferred to the more direct name "lesbian" in the early 1970s), the first experience of that solidarity were extraordinarily intense. At my first lesbian brunch in Minneapolis in 1974, I was fascinated by the stories women told, of discovering their lesbianism, of falling in love, and of their amazement upon learning that former teachers, or students, or neighbors, or even ex-boyfriends were gay too. An article of faith was that the lesbian population was huge. Thus Jill Johnston titled a book *Lesbian Nation*[5] and a popular tee shirt advertised "Lesbian National Forest." The slogan "We Are Everywhere" was a defiant cry. Bertha Harris (1973) titled her essay about expatriate lesbians in Paris in the 1920s "The More Profound Nationality of their Lesbianism," meaning that women like Natalie Barney, Renee Vivien, and Romaine Brooks were not really Americans because they had left their native country, and not really French, but had an identity deeper than nationalism, their lesbian identity.

Lesbians of the 1970s who were inspired by the vision of great numbers of their own kind held a monolithic view of lesbianism. They believed that any two women having it in common shared a bond so transcendent that no other traits or experiences could be as important. Knowing themselves to be marked by their choice of a despised identity, lesbians felt an instantaneous and deep rapport with any other woman who announced her lesbianism. The strength of this bond came from the newness of making one's lesbian identity known. In addition, women whose families and friends had rejected them felt that they could be understood only by their lesbian sisters. Lesbians of the 1990s sometimes joke about the strict dress codes adopted by 1970s lesbians: jeans, boots, flannel shirts, and short hair. Nail polish, lipstick, and makeup were forbidden and bras abandoned. Clothing statements reflected hippie nonconformity but were more importantly a sign of rebellion against the traditional female role. Women tended to look and dress like their lovers; androgyny was valued. What later came to be called the "clone look" or the "twins look" was more than a clothing choice. Lesbians wanted to express their sameness and they wanted to spot other lesbians. Psychologically it was important for them to see mirror images of themselves in order to compensate for their earlier invisibility and to celebrate their existence. Not all lesbians adopted a severe dress style, of course; but there was definitely a certain look to lesbians during the first several years of the women's movement.

One of the first and most powerful challenges to the monolithic view of lesbianism was the anthology *This Bridge Called My Back: Writings by Radical Women of Color*, edited by Cherrie Moraga and Gloria Anzaldúa.[6] Many lesbian contributors to this volume identified as much with their cultural or racial group as they did with lesbianism, and they eloquently described experiences of racism within the feminist and lesbian feminist communities. In the same year, the National Women's Studies Association convention was devoted to consciousness raising about racism. Lesbian feminists experienced their differences from each other in very painful, angry, and soul-searching confrontations. Women of color denounced tokenism. Adrienne Rich and Audre Lorde spoke of racism and anti-lesbian prejudice. Many white lesbians at this conference learned that lesbianism, which had seemed such a unifying force, was more complex than they realized and that an exclusive focus on it was to some degree a function of class privilege.

If race made a fundamental difference in the way one experienced lesbianism, so, too, did class. Working-class women were as likely to be lesbians as middle-class and upper-middle class women, but to some extent the writing, speaking, song writing, and political organizing that built lesbian feminism required leisure and freedom from economic pressure, privileges more available to middle-class than to working-class women. Working-class women often found middle-class women oblivious to the stresses and obstacles to self-development which they experienced daily and unwilling to examine differences obscured by slogans such as "Sisterhood is Powerful." For some working-class lesbians, for example, coming out at work was an unattainable luxury, and the costs of women's concerts, books, retreats, and celebrations often made them feel excluded.

At the same time, working-class lesbians have been in the forefront of lesbian feminism from its earliest days—poets Judy Grahn and Pat Parker, for example, and novelist Rita Mae Brown. Many of the women's studies teachers who created lesbian feminist enclaves within universities have working-class backgrounds, as do many of the lesbians who nurtured the growth of women's publishing from a very small enterprise in the early 1970s to a national network of writers, publishers, editors, distributors, agents, and book reviewers in the 1990s. The energy of many working-class lesbians helped women's music evolve from occasional coffeehouse performances for small audiences to a major industry whose strength is most apparent at the annual Michigan Women's Music Festival.

Other differences besides race and class emerged in the 1980s. Jewish lesbians published their stories in the anthology *Nice Jewish Girls*;[7] lesbian mothers began organizing; lesbians with disabilities began to speak and write. Catholic lesbians formed their own organization. Lesbians were looking for their roots; lesbian identity alone was no longer enough. Many West Coast lesbians turned to Buddhism. Old lesbians sponsored conferences that excluded women under 60. Therapy groups became popular. Lesbian feminism seemed fragmented by all of these developments; the high-spirited unity and militancy of the 1970s passed away. Some lesbians deplored the inward-gazing tendencies of many lesbians in the 1980s. To others it seemed inevitable that lesbian feminists changed with the times and that women who had been encouraged by feminism to develop themselves wanted to continue that process in the 1980s, even to the detriment of political organizing.

From the vantage point of the 1990s, the high-energy public lesbianism of the 1970s has been followed by a less political and more private movement, sometimes called "lifestyle lesbianism" to distinguish it from the radical activist lesbianism inspired by women's liberation. As lesbianism became less shocking and was articulately defended and even celebrated in a few major cities and on a few college campuses, newcomers did not need to feel radical fervor in order to join its ranks. Women new to lesbianism in the 1980s who had not participated in women's liberation often did not regard themselves as belonging to an oppressed minority and thus did not join political organizations. They were likely to identify with a broad lesbian community, however, by membership in social groups. Other lesbians were politically aware without being politically active. The decline of radical lesbianism in the 1980s has been explained by "the historical convergence of Reaganism, the aging of lesbian feminist activities, the emergence of internal splits within lesbian communities, and the desire for something new."[8]

The desire for something new took many forms in the 1980s. Some lesbians left big cities to live on the land. Some who had decided against motherhood reconsidered their options when artificial insemination became feasible. Some chose self-employment for the first time, because open lesbianism was not compatible with their jobs in factories, corporations, or schools. Some who had thought non-monogamy synonymous with healthy lesbianism in the 1970s formed monogamous relationships in the 1980s. Many who had long since left the mainstream religions of their families explored alternative forms of spirituality such as woman-church, a radical movement in Roman Catholicism; goddess spirituality (a broad term for customs, beliefs, and rituals created by women to honor their lives); gay synagogues; gay groups within liberal Protestant denominations; and Metropolitan Community Church, a gay church. Some lesbians remained staunchly materialist. Underlying these disparate choices was a realization that lesbianism per se could not fulfill all one's emotional, psychological, and spiritual needs, as it seemed to do in the early days of lesbian feminism.

Although radical lesbian feminism declined in the 1980s, the broad lesbian feminist movement gained momentum, not only because it survived right-wing backlash but also because many women who came out in the 1980s formed new organizations. Lesbianism became demystified. To the degree that it seemed normal and ordinary to the women choosing it, lesbianism had become a fixture of American life, an institution rather than a handful of women who met only in each others' living rooms or socialized in bars. Once largely an urban movement, lesbian feminism in the 1980s spread to the small towns and rural areas of the country, although lesbians outside of major cities tended to keep a low profile. Women over 50 were much more conspicuous at lesbian events than they had been before, and in the 1980s it was easier for teenaged lesbians to come out because information on lesbianism was far more accessible than it had been before.

One of the most important developments strengthening lesbian feminism in the 1980s was the increased visibility of lesbians of color as speakers, writers, musicians, business women, teachers, and organizers. Kitchen Table, the only US press run by women of color, published or distributed many books in which lesbian voices were heard, those for example of Beth Brant, Pat Parker, Cheryl Clarke, Chrystos, Jewelle Gomez, Audre Lorde, Michelle Cliff, Kitty Tsui, and Paula Gunn Allen. The Black a cappella group Sweet Honey in the Rock drew large audiences. In addition, articles by lesbians of color appeared in many anthologies, for example, in *We Are Everywhere: Writings by and about Lesbian Parents*.[9] A related development was anti-racism work shared by lesbians of color and white lesbians; for example, Elly Bulkin, Barbara Smith, and Minnie Bruce Pratt, who published *Yours in Struggle: Three Feminist Perspectives on Anti-Semitism and Racism*.[10]

In the 1980s lesbian feminism not only grew stronger within itself, it also made a greater impact on the outside world. More lesbian magazines and newspapers were published than in the previous decade, giving lesbian writers more opportunities to publish. Women's bookstores, often run by lesbians, flourished. Lesbian publishing grew from a few very small ephemeral grassroots projects to several well-established presses such as Seal, Cleis, Spinsters Ink, and Firebrand. Naiad, a lesbian press, expanded rapidly. Kitchen Table Women of Color Press introduced new lesbian writers. Mainstream publishers belatedly discovered a market for books about lesbians. Occasionally the mass media portrayed lesbians in an unbiased way or described unjust treatment of them, and a few lesbians appeared on talk shows. Lesbian and gay caucuses were formed in many professional groups. Lesbians were hired for high-profile leadership jobs in national gay rights organizations. Lesbians who had been denied tenure successfully sued their universities, and a few cases received national attention. As women's studies expanded, the academic base for lesbian issues became more solid, even though some women's studies programs were targets of homophobic attacks.

In the 1990s, two kinds of lesbian feminists can be identified, those who have found a place for themselves somewhat apart from but somewhat connected to mainstream America and the more radical women known as separatists. Another way of expressing this difference is to say that the former take feminism as their ideology while the latter make lesbianism itself an ideology.

Many lesbian feminists who came out in the late 1960s or early 1970s are less active politically than they were then. Although they remain committed to feminism, they are no longer as singlemindedly focused on it as they once were. One reason is that they hold better jobs than would have been available to them in the 1950s and work takes up much of their energy. Another is simply that they are twenty years older than they were when the women's movement began. In addition, many have settled into relationships in which politics is not the central shared activity, although it may be an important link. Often the political energy of these women has been directed to fairly new issues like environmental illness (multiple chemical sensitivities) or the epidemic of breast cancer among American women. Or they work on issues such as aging, preservation of the forests, or censorship. After the United States began bombing Iraq, thousands of lesbian feminists took part in anti-war demonstrations. The social changes of the past two decades have allowed them to integrate their lesbianism into other aspects of their lives so that it is not the distinguishing mark that it once was. Many of these lesbian feminists identify to some degree with the gay liberation movement.

For other women, the single most important thing about their lives is that they are lesbians. Women of all ages and backgrounds hold this view, and many define themselves as separatists.[11] The word "separatist" means that these lesbians dissociate themselves from men, including gay men, in every way possible and also from heterosexual women. Sometimes they also dissociate themselves from other lesbian feminists whose politics they disagree with. Similarly, separatists do not believe in coalition building, for example with leftists or pacifists. They believe only lesbian groups will give priority to lesbian issues and that the survival of lesbianism depends on seeing it as a single issue. For separatists, lesbianism has the force of an ideology. Consequently, their theorists believe that the emphasis many lesbian feminists place on personal relationships is misguided. In her book *The Social Construction of Lesbianism* (1987), for example, Celia Kitzinger argues that the core meaning of lesbianism is not personal sexuality but a political stance. The aim of lesbianism is to overthrow patriarchy; presenting it as a matter of personal choice de-politicizes it. Thus, for Kitzinger, the liberal social scientists who accept lesbianism but emphasize personal happiness and fulfillment are as suspect as their homophobic predecessors who regarded it as pathological.

In the 1970s the popularity of separatism led to the creation of a radical women's culture through organizations such as land collectives, print collectives, alternative businesses, and lesbian resource centers. For the first time, lesbians could live almost entirely in a lesbian world which reinforced their sense of pride in themselves and their identification with other lesbians. Some women who adopted separatism in the 1970s moved away from it later, while others remain firmly committed. In the 1990s, separatists are among the most articulate spokeswomen for lesbian feminism. Differences between separatists and other lesbian feminists mentioned here and those discussed in the next chapter are significant, but at times the difference seems to be a matter of tone—muted anger at male domination as opposed to vociferously expressed anger, for example. Despite differences among them, all lesbian feminists belong to a radical culture in which women's experience is taken as the norm and institutions such as family, church, and state are seen as enforcers of heterosexuality.

CURRENT ISSUES

Issues lesbians face have been noted throughout this book; only three will be discussed here: relationships; jobs; and invisibility.

Relationships

The popularity of Susan Johnson's book on long-term lesbian relationships, *Staying Power* (1990) and *Lesbian Couples* by D. Merilee Clunis and G. Dorsey Green,[12] both of which sold thousands of copies in the first few months after publication, suggests that lesbians today value committed relationships more than they did in the 1970s. Because of the great value they place on autonomy, lesbians in couples are more likely than heterosexuals to maintain separate friends, separate interests, and sometimes separate residences, although this is probably more true for urban couples than for those in small towns or rural areas. A lesbian is likely to have as a lover or partner someone able to give and receive nurturing. Her chances of being physically assaulted or psychologically abused in a relationship are far less than for her heterosexual counterpart. Not all lesbian relationships show equal power distribution, but they are more likely to be egalitarian than heterosexual relationships. On the other hand, since a great number of American women are survivors of incest, rape, and alcoholic families, a female–female couple is likely to include one partner who was abused in some way; and the problems resulting from these traumas can undermine even strong relationships. In addition, lesbians suffer an economic disadvantage because the earning power of two women is very likely to be less than the earning power of a heterosexual couple or a gay male couple.

On February 14, 1991, 150 lesbian couples took part in an historic event. They joined gay male couples in celebrating their unions publicly, on the first day domestic partners could register in San Francisco. First they stood on the steps of City Hall while gay and lesbian ministers blessed their relationships; then, as their names were read, each couple walked down a large marble staircase inside City Hall where their friends had gathered.

Work

In the 1970s, some of the first women to become construction workers, truck drivers, carpenters, electricians, plumbers, heavy equipment operators, and printers were lesbians. They were also among the first women to integrate police and fire departments. Many were harassed by male workers. In the 1980s many lesbians became lawyers, doctors, engineers, financial planners, park rangers, and school principals—all jobs formerly held only by men. The harassment they experienced was more subtle than that directed at lesbians in blue-collar jobs. A problem common to nearly all lesbians who work is that most businesses, schools, factories, and other workplaces have male bosses. Despite efforts to rid the workplace of sexist attitudes and behavior, deference to men is still an unstated job requirement for most American women. Heterosexual women are somewhat more likely to tolerate and adjust to this fact of work life. If a lesbian is perceived as different, she may not be promoted as quickly as women who are comfortable in a heterosexual milieu. Even where workers accept lesbian colleagues, homophobia may color perceptions of them. For example, college English teachers who are lesbians report that if they mention two or three times in a semester that a writer was gay or lesbian, student evaluations of the class will usually include the comment "All she talks about is homosexuality." Because the student is uncomfortable hearing *any* mention of the subject, he or she greatly exaggerates the actual number of references made during the semester.

In addition, if a woman worker wants to be open about her lesbianism, many jobs will be closed to her and she will be limited in the number of places she can comfortably live. Thus her career choices may be influenced in part by self-protective decisions she would not have to make if she were heterosexual.

Early in 1991, when the US attacked Iraq and thousands of reserv-

ists were activated, lesbians who came out to their commanding officers were told that they would be sent to the Gulf but dishonorably
discharged as soon as they returned home. Nearly all lesbians in the
service conceal their identities. "It's outrageous that they have to lie
for the right to serve their country," according to Miriam Ben Shalom,
a former reservist who heads a national lesbian and gay veterans' group
(*San Francisco Chronicle*, 18 February 1991: A12).

Invisibility

Although lesbians are more visible to each other than ever before, their
existence is not often acknowledged in mainstream America. When
the war between the US and Iraq began, for example, newspapers and
television stations interviewed many mothers of soldiers in the war,
but lesbian mothers were not among them. Anti-war protestors from
various groups were quoted, but not representatives of huge contingents of lesbian and gay marchers. When lesbians are mentioned by
the media, the effect is often to reinforce negative stereotypes. For
years reporters ignored the presence of lesbians in professional tennis,
but when a former tennis star claimed that Martina Navratilova set a
bad example because of her lesbianism, the slur was treated as news
by sports reporters. Lesbians, like Blacks, make news if they commit
crimes, do something outrageous, or cause anxiety to the dominant
group. *Newsweek* has reported, for example, that many Bay Area lesbians have become pregnant through artificial insemination. This is true,
but it is hardly the only significant aspect of lesbian life in the 1990s.
Lesbianism would be better understood if the mass media portrayed
civic leaders like the two lesbians elected to the San Francisco Board of
Supervisors, if women of color were acknowledged to be lesbians, if the
diversity of lesbians were even alluded to. Because lesbians remain a
hidden population, their exact numbers cannot be known. They probably make up at least 15 percent of the female population.

Today, although not all college students will meet women who
are out of the closet, many more students than in the past will be
able to learn about lesbian lives from novels, short stories, poems,

autobiographical essays, textbooks, and classroom presentations. One of the best ways to begin to know lesbians is to look at pictures of them taken by lesbian photographers. In *Eye to Eye*, JEB (Joan E. Biren) presents women in couples, by themselves, and with friends.[13] Self-acceptance and energy are the dominant impressions in this collection. Since hardly anyone grows up with positive images of lesbians, either verbal or visual, books like *Eye to Eye* challenge traditional ideas about women's experience.

Given the stigma still associated with lesbianism, it seems logical to suppose that only unusually bold, unconventional, radical, independent, free-thinking, defiant, or eccentric women would be able to act on lesbian feelings. In fact, lesbianism is common and ordinary, so much so that lesbians are the woman next door, the gym teacher, the camp counselor, the postal clerk, the prom queen, the PTA president, the minister's wife, the union organizer, the UPS driver, or the seven Oakland women featured in *A Lesbian Photo Album* by Cathy Cade.[14] By temperament, lesbians are probably no more adventurous than other women; by circumstance they are sometimes forced to be.

Women who grew up believing they were sick or sinful for feeling attraction to other women need healing experiences before they can fully accept themselves. The psychological harm caused by stigma does not disappear when social attitudes are slightly modified. In the 1990s lesbian feminism is strong because many women are able to claim their lesbian identities fully as a result of twenty-five years of self-love and struggle, or ten years, or five. The lesbians just now coming out—as young, middle-aged, or old women—do not have to be pioneers in the same way that lesbians of the early 1970s were pioneers. Because of lesbian feminism, they can find support for their feelings in books, classes, women's music, and in social and political groups. In other words, today a few institutions *encourage* the intellectual, moral, emotional, and sexual development of women who name themselves lesbians. Furthermore, when lesbians attend a meeting of the National Organization of Women today, they are not told to stay in the closet, as they were told in the 1970s. When they come out to their college counselors, they are not sent to ministers and psychiatrists. Most of the people with whom they come in contact do not believe they molest children and have probably heard of the gay and lesbian liberation movement. Today women can come out to their friends and be readily accepted.

But these women coming out in the 1990s are coming out in a homophobic culture in which women have not yet achieved full equality with men, and they are very likely to experience some form of anti-gay discrimination. Even though lesbian feminism offers them a group identity, coming out will require courage and a strong sense of independence until lesbianism is completely accepted as a way of feeling and being.

7

CONFLICTS AND DEBATES IN THE GAY AND LESBIAN LIBERATION MOVEMENT

Another way to approach gay liberation is to consider some of the debates, dilemmas, and conflicts in the movement. Although the gay world may seem uniform to outsiders, especially to those who do not know lesbians and gay men, it is made up of many subgroups, and people who identify as lesbian or gay often disagree among themselves on many topics. Most of the debates involve gay people in their relation to the dominant culture, while a few occur within the movement. The AIDS epidemic has intensified both.

EXTERNAL DEBATES

A debate alluded to in Chapter 1 is whether gay and lesbian liberation is one movement or two. Lesbian feminism originated in the women's movement rather than in the homophile movement. Even though lesbians were not accepted by all heterosexual feminists, many felt more at home organizing with women than with gay men. In the 1970s, however, gay liberation was cosexual: some lesbians affiliated with both feminism and gay liberation; some who considered feminism their main political cause were peripherally involved in gay liberation; and others, who had never been feminists, maintained their longstanding ties to gay organizations which were mostly male. Without the women's movement to encourage thousands of lesbians to become activists, gay liberation would have drawn small numbers of women in the pattern of the earlier homophile movement.

Women and men who have homosexuality in common form a single movement. The most obvious proof is the annual turn-out for Gay Pride events on the last Sunday of June. In most of the cities where this day is celebrated, at least half of the marchers and half of the observers are women. Less numerous and less affluent than men, women are not yet equals in the struggle for gay liberation, but in the 1990s they have many more positions of power in the movement than they previously had, in national, state, and local organizations. Despite these gains for women, many lesbian feminists see themselves as an autonomous group, and some wish to stay entirely separate from men and from gay liberation. Not all of the women who espouse lesbian feminism see it as incompatible with gay male liberation, but many believe that, without some separate focus on lesbian issues, lesbian voices will be drowned out in gay liberation.

ORIGINS

Another debate, over the origins of homosexuality, has political implications. If homosexuality is biologically determined, then obviously it is not chosen and gay people can claim that they should not be discriminated against for their sexual orientation. But if people are found to be biologically predisposed to homosexuality, bigots may then advocate research to discover ways of preventing it. If, on the other hand, homosexuality is not biologically determined, bigots will say it is chosen and ought not to be the basis for any rights. In some cases, homosexuality probably does result from choice. More often it seems to be such a fundamental part of one's identity, so fixed and permanent, that the only choice is whether to acknowledge or suppress it. However homosexuals come to be, they deserve to exist because human variability is intrinsically good and because, as Ruth Benedict wrote in 1934, "Wherever homosexuality has been given an honorable place in any society, those to whom it is congenial have filled adequately the honorable roles society assigns to them."[1] More recently, John Boswell noted that reclaiming the homosexuality of a renowned person such as Michelangelo "lends welcome support to the work of political activists seeking to counteract negative stereotypes of gay people." But taking the view that no one in Michelangelo's time can be called a homosexual because that social category came much later may appear to undermine the argument that homosexuals are a minority (Boswell in Duberman *et al.* 1989: 12)

STEREOTYPES

A dilemma for gay men and lesbians mentioned in Chapter 2 is that they must vigorously defend sexual freedom in order to carve out a place for their sexuality but they do not want to be stereotyped as obsessed by sex or as promiscuous. For many heterosexuals, the only salient feature of a gay person is his or her sexual preference. To gay people themselves, this view is limiting and demeaning because it overlooks their individualizing traits. To be seen only as sexual actors is not to be seen at all. Similarly, the directive to gay Catholics that they remain celibate is ludicrous, because sex is a fundamental part of life, and oppressive, for it creates a special inferior status for gay people. Whether typecast as insatiable sexual predators, as they are by the right wing, or told they have no right to sex at all, or blamed for AIDS, gay people must counter negative and distorted images of their sexuality. If they have several relationships over a period of time (serial monogamy), or if free sexual expression is their most important value, they do not want to be branded as promiscuous. If they are writers, artists, or photographers, they do not want uproars over sexual images to prevent fair-minded appraisals of their creative work.

OUTING

A controversy arose in 1990 over the practice of "outing," which means forcing public figures out of the closet, that is, revealing their homosexuality. Politicians and movie stars were targets. Three positions on outing are:

(1) it is a good tactic;
(2) it is questionable but may be used against closeted officials whose votes or stands seriously harm the gay rights movement;
(3) it is completely unjustifiable.

According to a code almost universally followed in the past, homosexuals did not reveal the homosexuality of a closeted person. Those who disregard the code today tend to be young activists angry at the continuing deaths from AIDS who want to expose people whom they view as hypocrites and liars. Unlike middle-aged gays who often took a long time to reach total self-acceptance, the young have no empathy for the closeted. Prominent closeted gays, in their view, reinforce the myth that being gay is so terrible that it must be covered up. In addition, the closeted deprive gay people of role models by their invisibility and prevent heterosexuals from knowing the true extent of homosexuality. Proponents of outing note that AIDS was not taken seriously until Rock Hudson's homosexuality was revealed shortly before his death from AIDS.

Some opponents of outing think an exception can be made for powerful closeted gays who repeatedly use their influence to block gay rights legislation or harm community interests in some other way.

Others, who oppose outing under any circumstances, believe the right to privacy is absolute and should not be assailed by the very people who benefit from it. Coming out is a decision individuals must make for themselves. Dragging a person out of the closet is an act of psychic violence. Furthermore, people cannot be forced to be role models. Judith Stevenson, the director of a large gay and lesbian counseling center in San Francisco, sees outing as the misguided action of white men. A working-class lesbian whose daughter was taken away by the courts, she believes that minority people risk far more than others when they disclose their sexual preference (*Bay Area Reporter,* 10 May 1990). Urvashi Vaid, head of the National Gay and Lesbian Task Force, rejects outing because "our movement stands not for coercion but empowerment" (*Washington Blade,* 1 June 1990: 1).

Even those most vehemently opposed to outing acknowledge the legitimacy of the frustration and rage of its advocates, and they mistrust the motives of the newspapers that played up the issue, knowing sensationalism mattered more to reporters than the welfare of the gay community. Also, the issue gave the media a chance to pit gay leaders against each other, a familiar ploy used on minority groups.

MEDIA DISTORTIONS

The outing debate points up a more general dilemma: gay liberation needs the mainstream media to show that it is a mass movement with an ambitious agenda, to bring out a fundamental change in American society, but the media often distorts, trivializes, or ignores gay issues. The October 1987 gay rights march on Washington, for example, which drew 600,000 people, was not mentioned in either *Time* or *Newsweek,* even though it was the largest political demonstration since the Viet Nam era. In the 1980s, the *San Francisco Chronicle*'s coverage of the annual Gay Pride parade was predictable: one shot of a flamboyant drag queen and one of a fundamentalist with a sign saying "Gays Repent." The accompanying story always quoted anti-gay hecklers at the parade. No newspaper would cover a Black march by pictures of KKK counter-demonstrators or quote a woman-hating observer in a story about a women's event. Anti-Semites do not get a forum in the press when Jewish issues are discussed. Stories about AIDS implicitly or explicitly contrast the "innocent" victims of the disease—children, hemophiliacs, or those who got it through a blood transfusion—with the "guilty" victims—gay men, who got it through sex.

Mass media coverage of gay men and lesbians is not as biased as it was ten years ago, partly because a few openly gay reporters work for a few major papers, but the movement must guard against interpretations of it by opinion makers who see lesbians and gay men as outsiders, good copy when scandals or sex stories surface but not full participants in community life. *Chronicle* columnist Herb Caen mocked the slogan chosen by the 1990 San Francisco Gay Freedom Day committee, "The Future is Ours," a sign that gays are tolerated as long as they do not appear powerful. Those who see the media more positively cite increased coverage of gay and lesbian issues in the *New York Times* and a special sixteen-part series, "Gay in America," published by the *San Francisco Examiner* in June 1989. Despite these small gains, however, American television viewers can "watch men killing men every hour in the name of entertainment [while] men expressing open affection toward one another remains taboo" (Adam 1987: 164).

A specific problem with the media is that it tends to portray gay life as a male phenomenon, a misperception strengthened by the AIDS epidemic. Women play a much greater role in the radical group ACT UP, for example, than readers of the mainstream press know. The image of gays as affluent is largely an image of urban professional gay men. Gay men outnumber lesbians, and lesbians keep a low profile by choice, but the cosexual character of gay liberation has not been discovered by the media.

MEDIA IMAGES

A related concern is the image gay and lesbian leaders choose to convey to the media: should they be respectable or unconventional? To some gay people, pictures of men in drag or "dykes on bikes" in their leather clothes harm the cause by calling attention to people whom the media can portray as bizarre, freakish, or at least, very different. Those uncomfortable with such images want gay life to look unthreatening and ordinary, so that heterosexuals will be able to accept it. It is true that "flaming queens" and macha lesbians are not representative of all gay people, but a desire to keep them invisible shows a limited understanding of the history and politics of the movement. The Stonewall rioters were not white-collar workers; they were Black and Puerto Rican drag queens and working-class lesbians. The rowdy, raucous, outrageous, or cross-dressing members of the gay population are as central to the movement as those who are outwardly more conventional and thus more palatable to heterosexuals. Lesbians and gay men who can "pass" (be taken for heterosexual), who dislike the "obvious" gays, may not fully accept their own gay identity. Diversity is a major strength of gay liberation. Attempts to deny it or down-play it for the sake of presenting a respectable image falsify the movement.

VISIBILITY

The question of visibility is a perplexing one. For the homophile movement of the 1950s, visibility was a "two-edged sword," according to historian John D'Emilio: it was a basic goal for homosexuals but it could also result in unwelcome publicity from the homophobic mainstream press (1983b:122). For the last twenty years the movement has stressed coming out, and the willingness of thousands of people to begin that process has been the key element in the growing strength of gay and lesbian liberation. But visibility also creates a backlash: gay bashing has increased as gay liberation has grown. The slogan "Silence-Death" is undeniably true; but speaking out sometimes equals retaliation, for example when homophobic individuals lash out at their perceived enemies, or when the state uses police violence at gay demonstrations to suppress speech. A large-scale return to the closet is inconceivable. But for the foreseeable future, lesbians and gay men who choose to be "out" will risk verbal and physical assaults. Even those who live in gay neighborhoods are endangered because the visibility of these neighborhoods encourages violent homophobes to hunt victims there.

Visibility became an issue at the time of the 1990 census. Should gay people answer the question about unmarried partners living together to show they not only exist but constitute a large minority, or should they pass over the question to prevent the government from finding out who and where they are? Since the census did not count single lesbians and gay men or those in committed relationships who do not live with their partners, it could not have provided even a rough estimate of the gay population. Nonetheless, the mistrust of the government on the part of some gay citizens, who would never reveal their identity, insures that their community remains, to some degree, a hidden one.

PEOPLE OF COLOR LESS VISIBLE THAN WHITES

Another side to the invisibility dilemma is the challenge of portraying the gay movement adequately. Its adherents know that it is not a whites-only movement, as it nearly always appears to be in the mainstream media, but many gays themselves probably do not realize how multicultural their minority is. A special feature on Black lesbians and gay men in Washington showed that great diversity exists even within a single community (*Washington Blade,* 22 January 1990). In the Mission district of San Francisco, a flourishing gay Latino culture exists, but people in that neighborhood are not asked for their opinions on gay issues by the national press. Many lesbians and gay men who are white have probably never met a gay Native American. Observers of the Gay Freedom Day parade in San Francisco in June 1990 who saw the sign "Arab Lesbians" had perhaps never thought of those two words together.

Class differences also make difficult the task of portraying homosexual life adequately. Gay students at Ivy League schools are easier to identify for interviews than working-class, often closeted lesbians and gay men. When most Americans hear the word "gay" they probably do not think of waitresses, truck drivers, clerks, factory workers, mechanics, or bus drivers. Half of the young people chosen for a special San Francisco program to train future gay leaders were people of color and many were women. This commitment to cultural pluralism is unfortunately rare in the gay community.

SINGLE-ISSUE OR COALITION STRATEGY

In addition to the problem of invisibility—of gay people in general and of gay people of color in particular—the lesbian and gay rights movement faces a fundamental question: should it pursue a single-issue strategy or a coalition strategy? Should lesbians and gay men take a stand against the Persian Gulf war, for example? (Gay newspapers estimated that 70 percent of the gay population opposed the war). The argument for a single-issue strategy is that gay liberation will have a better chance of success if it concentrates on a few specific issues such as repeal of sodomy laws and passage of a federal gay rights bill. Some gay activists say they have worked hard for other movements and now must focus on their own. Others believe that gay liberation must seek allies in other social change movements so that the combined power of all will bring about change.

To frame the debate a little differently, should lesbian and gay leaders be radical reformers bent on restructuring the society they live in or should they be moderate reformers trying to get a bigger piece of the existing pie. The differences between radical and moderate are not only ideological but temperamental, i.e. some people are impatient, anti-authoritarian and comfortable with rapid change, while others emphasize what is good in their present situation. The homophile movement was made up primarily of people who wanted to fit into American society. In the 1940s and 1950s, of course, that was a much more universal attitude than it became in the 1960s. Today radicals note that if all the demands of AIDS activists were met, that would be a major change—many more resources would be devoted to the sick and the dying. But the grossly inadequate health care system of the United States would be left intact. An end to military harassment, imprisonment, and expulsion of gay people would be a great victory, comparable to the end of racial discrimination in the service, but would not in itself make the country less militaristic. From this perspective, radical reform is the correct stance for gay and lesbian liberationists.

On the other hand, since anti-gay forces are very powerful in the US, one might argue that simple reforms will be so difficult to achieve that, if they are achieved, a radical change will have occurred. If custody cases involving lesbian mothers or gay fathers are decided in the best interests of the children and not on the judge's homophobia, that change will be radical. If all psychiatrists and therapists give up attempts to "cure" gay people, if all gay and lesbian workers know they will be judged on their job performance and not on their sexual preference, if all gay and lesbian tenants feel secure in their right to privacy, if anti-gay hate crimes subside, if all mainstream religions begin to ordain homosexuals, America will surely be transformed.

TACTICS

Disagreements about the nature of gay liberation—radical or moderate—are closely related to disagreements about tactics, for example, the tactics of the most militant gay group, ACT UP. The AIDS Coalition to Unleash Power began in March 1987 after gay playwright Larry Kramer told an audience of gay men that two-thirds of them might be dead within five years. By their marches and demonstrations, ACT UP called attention to bureaucratic delays undercutting efforts to save men's lives. Pressure, confrontations, and sit-ins forced the Food and Drug Administration to speed up drug trials for AIDS and to consider "parallel track," an ACT UP proposal that men with AIDS be given drugs before they are approved by the usual lengthy FDA process. The drug AZT which prolongs the lives of AIDS patients was outrageously overpriced until ACT UP protests led to a 200 percent reduction in its cost.

When ACT UP closed Golden Gate Bridge to protest inadequate AIDS funding, some gay San Franciscans objected, thinking the demonstrations would alienate a majority of the citizens, and the same criticism was voiced when opening night of the San Francisco Opera in September 1989 was disrupted by chanting and shouting gay men angry about AIDS. For some lesbians and gay men, however, disruptive tactics are more appropriate for times of crisis than polite speeches, arguments, and meetings. Newspapers cover dramatic protests. At the International AIDS conference in San Francisco in June 1990, ACT UP got nearly as much publicity as AIDS researchers. If they had protested the closing speech by Health and Human Services director Louis Sullivan by leafletting outside of the conventional hall, they would have been ignored. By shouting and disrupting the speech, by waving banners and blowing whistles, they obtained front-page coverage. Some gay leaders were troubled by the silencing of a Black man, however, and by tactics which have been used in the past to drown out gay voices. In April 1991, protesters in San Francisco tried to block filming of the homophobic movie "Basic Instincts." This action was applauded by some gay men and lesbians as an appropriate response to an attack on their community but repudiated by others on the grounds that the filmmaker's freedom of expression was violated. The constitutional argument was weakened by the near certainty that the movie would cause gay bashing.

Civil disobedience and direct action will probably become increasingly important in the gay and lesbian liberation movement. The older generation remembers the civil rights movement, and young activists repudiate the assimilationist stance that gay liberation sometimes took in the 1970s and 1980s. The concentrated fury of ACT UP reflects the understandable desperation of many of its members who have AIDS or are HIV positive. The continuing inadequacy of the government response to AIDS, at all levels, is a provocation comparable to continued racial segregation in the 1960s. "This government is letting us die" sums up the activists' position.

Queer Nation was founded in New York in the spring of 1990 to protest a TV commentator's homophobic diatribes. Its rapid spread to many other cities showed the vitality of the grassroots gay liberation movement. Queer Nation has no formal structure and a fluid membership. It has invaded San Francisco bars in affluent neighborhoods to stage kiss-ins, visited malls in huge numbers, and ridden on commuter trains to announce the presence of gay people. Slogans chalked on sidewalks say "We're Here. Get Used to It." Queer Nation demonstrations have been satirical and playful compared to those of ACT UP, but it has a serious purpose. It proposed, for example, that the San Francisco Board of Supervisors declare the city a sanctuary for lesbians and gay men persecuted anywhere in the world.

The tactics of Queer Nation illustrate the frustration many gay people feel at the slow pace of reform, at the tenacity of homophobic attitudes, and at media resistance to balanced coverage of gay and lesbian issues. The tag "queer," however, is deeply offensive to many active in gay politics because they want to root out a word they consider degrading. "Queer" has long been used among gay people themselves but only in the 1990s has it been used in public as a synonym for gay or lesbian. Members of Queer Nation say to the rest of society, We are as different from you as we can possibly be.

INTERNAL DEBATES

In addition to debates about topics such as media representation of gay people, tactics, outing, and others discussed above, involving gays in relation to the larger society, there are internal debates.

LESBIANS VS. GAY MEN

To gay men, feminism has sometimes seemed an anti-sex movement, while lesbians have viewed gay men as hedonists. The issue of police harassment of gay men in cruising areas lacks importance for most lesbians. A recurring controversy aired in the letters to the editor section of gay newspapers is man/boy love. Citing the example of ancient Greece, the North American Man Boy Love Association (NAMBLA) argues that children have a right to be sexual. The power imbalance in such relationships leads lesbians to condemn them. They are less opposed to relationships between late adolescents and adult men than to relationships involving children, and they oppose erotic photographing of children. In the eyes of lesbian feminists, NAMBLA exploits children. But because sex is central to gay male life, any attempt to restrict it or any support for censorship seems antithetical to the spirit of gay liberation. For most gay men, sexual freedom is an absolute value. On the other hand, Sam Steward's novels about hustlers have been kept out of some bookstores owned by gay men.

Lesbian feminists tend to see gay men as less aware of racism and classism in the movement than they are. Sometimes the men bear the brunt of lesbians' anger because they are a nearer and more convenient target than right-wing anti-gay extremists. Lesbian feminists and gay men also do not agree on the place of women's issues in gay liberation. Several years ago a few male readers of *Gay Community News,* a national paper based in Boston, complained that they were tired of reading about abortion in a gay paper; it did not concern them. Lesbians replied that government control of women's bodies is a gay issue. Whatever their differences, however, lesbians and gay men have banded together in the face of external threats to their welfare, such as Anita Bryant's campaign, the attempt in California to fire gay teachers, and, more recently, right-wing attacks on homoerotic art.

MARRIAGE AND FAMILY ISSUES

Other debates within the gay community concern marriage and family issues. Legalized marriage for homosexuals is an important goal for many, while others scorn the idea—legitimacy of gay relationships comes from the participants in them; seeking approval from church or state is demeaning. Other lesbians and gay men who have formally united their lives in church ceremonies or private rites believe that their relationships are fully equal to heterosexual marriages and thus they deserve benefits such as health insurance coverage and hospital visiting rights. Even if gay people were not allowed to marry they could still get some of the benefits of marriage through domestic partnership laws.

A controversial family-related issue for lesbians is whether they should become mothers and raise children in units resembling the traditional nuclear family. Some radical lesbians see motherhood as an oppressive institution, draining the energies of women who might otherwise be working to undermine patriarchy. Lesbians should not contribute to overpopulation, according to this view. Furthermore, lesbians do not freely choose motherhood; they are so conditioned by a heterosexual society that they seek approval for bearing children. The more common view is that both motherhood and co-parenting are appropriate choices for lesbians. The "lesbian baby boom," one of the major changes in lesbian life in the 1980s, is likely to continue through the 1990s. Some lesbians become pregnant through artificial insemination at a clinic, while others obtain sperm from a gay male friend or brother. Some lesbian mothers want their children raised in an all-female atmosphere; others want gay male friends to help raise the children. The 'intentional family' of a lesbian couple, their gay male friends and their children is likely to become more common, as is single parenting by lesbians and adoption by both gay male and lesbian couples.

Another trend from the 1980s that lesbians disagree about is the increasing popularity of the recovery movement and therapy. These look like personal solutions to lesbian separatists, who locate the chief source of lesbians' problems in institutionalized sexism, racism, and homophobia. They find women who are dealing with past family traumas or using couples counseling to be excessively self-absorbed, and they deplore the widespread use of therapy by lesbians. Political activism and reliance on therapy are not mutually exclusive, but separatists tend to view therapy as a tool for de-politicizing women. Therapists and their clients, on the other hand, say that so many women grow up in alcoholic or abusive families that they must deal with the consequences of the past in order to lead healthy lives.

Gay men, like lesbians, have become heavily involved in AA, Adult Children of Alcoholics, and other recovery groups, but the struggle against AIDS often takes precedence. In recent years, the social meanings of HIV infection and AIDS have been vigorously debated in the gay male community. To some, these dangers mean that gay men must now prefer monogamy and long-term commitments to their earlier uninhibited sexual patterns. Others say that this view comes from internalized homophobia, that sexual adventure and exploration are good, and that, if the HIV virus or AIDS leads men to de-emphasize sex, the gay movement will be weakened.

UNITY IN DISAGREEMENT

In a movement as diverse as gay rights, disagreement is inevitable. Men with AIDS are more critical of the health care establishment, for example, than upwardly mobile lesbians and gay men. At the National Gay Writers Conference in San Francisco in March 1991, John Rechy and Edward Albee challenged the label "gay writer," saying they think of themselves as writers who are gay. For many in the audience who disagreed, "gay writer" or "lesbian writer" has a political as well as an artistic meaning. Not everyone who watches a Gay Pride parade in San Francisco likes the costumes or the antics of the Sisters of Perpetual Indulgence, gay men in nuns' habits. Those who are in recovery may not feel comfortable seeing lavish floats sponsored by gay bars. The marchers in the huge contingents of Latino, Asian American, Native American and Black gays are no doubt more keenly aware than most other marchers of racism in the gay community. But writers' conferences and parades are unifying experiences for people in a movement made up of many parts. Common enemies also unite lesbians and gay men. With one voice, lesbian and gay writers and artists denounce censorship. The loudest cheers in the 1990 parade greeted marchers from North Carolina who carried a huge picture of anti-gay Senator Jesse Helms with a line drawn diagonally across it. They had come to raise money to defeat him in a Senate race, and they nearly succeeded. No matter what debates spring up among lesbians and gay men, they agree on their right to exist and the need to fight back when they are attacked.

AIDS

The debates and dilemmas discussed thus far are overshadowed by the most serious problem facing the gay community: how to sustain the gay rights movement in the face of AIDS. AIDS has killed so many men, weakened so many others, and taken over so many gay community resources that it sometimes seems that the movement and the fight against AIDS are the same. First identified in 1981, AIDS had decimated the gay male communities of the major cities of the US, especially New York and San Francisco, by the late 1980s. As the new decade began, the post World War I condition of England seemed a fitting comparison: a generation of men had been wiped out. In the introduction to his book *Personal Dispatches: Writers Confront AIDS* (1989), John Preston writes that "AIDS is like war in the way it insults nature. It reverses the order of life and death." Like survivors of war, those who love and nurse the dying feel that their experience is incommunicable to those not directly affected, for AIDS not only kills, it kills in particularly horrifying ways, through dementia, blindness, and excruciatingly painful diseases that strike one after another. Frail men walking with canes, men who look as gaunt as prisoners of war, can be seen in gay neighborhoods. By the late 1980s the death toll from AIDS was higher than the number of soldiers killed in Viet Nam. By mid 1991, nearly 100,000 had died. The war analogy fits because "AIDS has robbed us of a sense of the future as we have mourned our terrible losses and buried our dead."[2] A difference between war and AIDS is that war often kills the very young, aged 18–25, whereas AIDS tends to kill men in their thirties and forties. Because HIV has a long incubation period, many men were probably infected in their twenties.

AIDS is shocking in that it seems a throwback to an earlier era, before antibiotics, when people were more vulnerable to disease. It seems unthinkable that an infectious disease could kill large numbers of Americans in the late twentieth century. A sexually transmitted disease creates a special fear, different from the fear surrounding polio or influenza. This is especially true of AIDS because the totally uninhibited sexual freedom once thought to be the keystone of gay male liberation suddenly became life-threatening. While a flu epidemic may be seen as a simple public health problem, an epidemic among a despised group was inevitably politicized. The Reagan administration's response to AIDS was: gay men are expendable; drug users are expendable; Black men are expendable. Not until heterosexuals were threatened by AIDS did the government begin to pay attention to the disease. After the San Francisco earthquake, which killed fewer than 100 people, President Bush came to look at the damage, but the epidemic that killed thousands "brought no more than token recognition from the White House" (*Bay Area Reporter,* 4 January 1990: 6).

In addition to traumatizing the gay community by killing large numbers of men in a relatively short time, including some of the most dedicated and talented gay organizers of the 1970s, AIDS has had an enormous impact on the survivors of these men, especially lovers and friends. Many made great sacrifices of time, money, and careers to care for the dying and often they had no energy left for the gay or lesbian political work that would have engaged them in normal times. Thus gay organizations lost workers and supporters at the same time that their resources were drained by the AIDS crisis. When death seemed to be everywhere, traditional goals of gay liberation naturally seemed far less important than caring for the dying. The Human Rights Campaign Fund, the largest gay lobby, described the proposed federal gay rights law as a long term project, and the National Gay and Lesbian Task Force in New York took a similar view of repealing sodomy laws (Miller 1989: 296).

At the same time, however, the AIDS crisis mobilized the gay and lesbian community by concentrating its focus on a single threat and by involving many people who had not been politically active before. The government's initial response of callous indifference forced gay men and their lesbian allies to fight for their own survival. Even after city, state, and federal agencies began to sponsor research and to grant funds for caregiving, the main response to AIDS came from the gay community itself. Hundreds of organizations sprang up to help men with AIDS. Thousands of lesbians and gay men sustained community-based groups such as Shanti, which provides services and support to people with AIDS; Coming Home Hospice; and Project Open Hand, a food provider (all in San Francisco) and Food and Friends in Washington DC. The Gay Men's Health Crisis in New York raised nearly four million dollars in its 1990 walkathon. Ironically, those who had been labeled misfits and unAmerican perverts launched a typically American self-help movement which was probably one of the largest volunteer efforts in the nation's history. In addition, some gay men and lesbians got paid jobs related to AIDS. For them and for many others, the political emphasis of gay liberation shifted from an effort to get government off their backs to an attempt to work with the various government agencies on AIDS.[3]

One of the most dramatic political consequences of AIDS is that a large number of men were catapulted out of the closet when their illness became obvious. Movie stars, fashion designers, government officials, professors, priests, and many others who would normally never have come out were reluctant witnesses to the frequency of homosexual acts in America. The AIDS virus "doesn't care whether you wear drag or leather or a three-piece suit. It doesn't care whether you live in a gay ghetto or with your wife and family in the suburbs. In short, gay men cannot hide anymore than could the Jews of Europe."[4] In a sense, the closeted gay men were more at risk than those who were open about their sexual preference because they were more likely to seek anonymous sexual contacts. The tragic opening of many closet doors has forced heterosexuals to become aware of homosexuality in a way they were not before, when it was more hidden.

AIDS had other political ramifications as well. Drugs not approved by the FDA were smuggled into the country by an AIDS underground, which also encouraged experimental treatments outside of the health care system. People interested in non-drug treatment of immune diseases raised questions about the bias of the medical establishment. Men who had kept themselves alive by a variety of alternative medical treatments communicated their experiences to others with AIDS.

An unexpected development was the new spirit of cooperation and solidarity between lesbians and gay men. AIDS work brought together people who ordinarily would not have struck up alliances or even known much about each others' lives. The very important caregiving role of lesbians is one of many aspects of AIDS overlooked by the mainstream media. AIDS also unexpectedly brought many new supporters to the gay cause: parents whose sons died of the disease; heterosexuals in the medical profession (which remained largely homophobic); and heterosexuals not directly touched by AIDS who understood for the first time the problems and discrimination gay people often encounter.

These became obvious because of a predictable outcome of AIDS: an increase in prejudice, bigotry, and gay-bashing. Jerry Falwell, a fundamentalist minister whose Moral Majority was founded to condemn gay men and lesbians, told his followers that AIDS was God's punishment for homosexuality, but also claimed that gay people were gaining control of American cities, a rather difficult feat for a people dying from divine wrath. Right-wingers spoke of an "international homosexual conspiracy," a new twist to their grandparents' line about an "international Jewish conspiracy." The enemy group changed but the paranoid fears remained the same.

Leaders of Community United Against Violence (CUAV) in San Francisco and other gay groups reported dramatic increases in violent attacks on gay men in which gangs usually singled out one or two individuals. And just as rape victims used to be blamed for somehow provoking the attacks upon them, gay men were blamed for supposedly upsetting the skinheads, punks, and thugs who beat and sometimes maimed them. A murder charge could usually be evaded if the attacker claimed that the gay man made a pass at him. Lawyers beat attempted murder charges even when their clients carried lethal weapons and severely injured their victims. Comedians made sick jokes connecting homosexuality and death, and Americans who would never have joked about the high death rate of young Black men or made fun of the disabled laughed at gay men.

The realization that their lives were not as valued as the lives of heterosexuals prompted many gay men to identify with each other more strongly than before. The AIDS epidemic created a "new basis of community among gay men," based on caring and different from the past in that it did not depend on either the search for a sexual partner or the desire for social change (Miller 1989: 135). But many gay men expressed their caring by militant action, sometimes using humor and satire. While the Archbishop of Los Angeles was preaching a sermon at midnight Mass in 1989, demonstrators walked out to protest a statement he had made earlier, that the use of condoms to prevent AIDS is "both a lie and a fraud." Dressed as the three Wise

Men, three protestors carried gifts for the Archbishop of condoms, birth control pills, and an abortion device (*Washington Blade*, 5 January 1990). Most Catholics who have access to accurate information about AIDS know that condoms can save lives; those endangered by the ignorant authoritarianism of the Archbishop are poor, minority Catholics, many of whom are Hispanics who speak no English.

In addition to the successes of radical activist gays, those in mainstream leadership positions have increased their visibility and power as a result of the AIDS epidemic. The director of the major gay lobby, the Human Rights Campaign Fund, believes that the political system has opened up to gay organizations (Miller 1989: 295). Politicians who could ignore gay issues in the past cannot ignore the public health issue of AIDS, and they need the cooperation and expertise of gay organizations. Dead and dying men pushed gay life into the center of national political consciousness more dramatically than the living could have done.

The impact of AIDS can also be considered in a psychological context. The former AIDS coordinator for the San Francisco Community College District, Mary Redick, believes that when people hear a friend or a co-worker has AIDS they become so preoccupied by the thought of death that they cannot acknowledge that the person may live. Seeing him or her as certain to die is a subtle form of discrimination. Revealing a diagnosis of AIDS is another kind of coming out for gay men, who risk rejection by their honesty. By creating an association between sex and danger, AIDS has encouraged a new introspection among gay men. The party atmosphere of the 1970s when sexual possibilities seemed limitless came to an end. Settling down in couples became more common. For many urban gay men life by the mid-1980s was a succession of funerals, a stark experience usually reserved for the old. They were forced to think of the meaning of life; some re-examined their values and choices. A man interviewed for the book *In Search of Gay America* planned to expand his business and make money but after two close friends died he decided to lead a more relaxed life (Miller 1989: 139).

Grief took up a very large place in the lives of gay men. Leon McKusick, a psychologist, researcher, and person with AIDS, gave the opening speech at the Sixth International Conference on AIDS in San Francisco in June 1990. "I contend that a large part of the anger of AIDS activists, that loud screaming and yelling outside, is grief," he said, adding that the resentment many scientists and doctors expressed towards activists is repressed grief (*Bay Guardian*, 27 June 1990: 16).

The most moving collective expression of grief is the immense AIDS quilt created by the Names Project of San Francisco. Colored cloth panels sewn together and variously decorated by lesbians and gay men were displayed in several cities. Each square represents one person who died of AIDS. The memorial demonstrates in a concrete way the grim death toll and preserves a sense of the individuality of those who died.

AIDS evokes anger as well as grief—anger that men are cut down in their prime, anger that no cure can be found more than ten years after the first cases were identified, anger that the procedures for testing new drugs are slow and hampered by red tape, anger at the loss of life partners and friends, anger that AIDS education efforts have been blocked or delayed by homophobic politicians, and anger that sex acts, which should be safe and life-enhancing, can result not only in death but in stigmatized death.

AIDS has raised legal and ethical questions: for example, discrimination against people with AIDS or those who are HIV positive; confidentiality; and the use of state power to limit the spread of AIDS.[5] Widespread discrimination has occurred in the US in employment and housing. Some insurance companies have canceled coverage of people with AIDS or capped payments soon after beginning them, and other companies have denied health care coverage to single men if they live in neighborhoods considered gay. Just as unethical is the decision by certain insurance companies not to insure artists, musicians, dancers, actors, and even workers at museums and galleries because of a fear that people in these professions have a high incidence of AIDS, or to raise their premiums by as much as 400 percent. In California, it is illegal for an insurance company to request an AIDS test before issuing a policy.

Two questions concerning confidentiality are (1) should names of people with AIDS or those who are HIV positive be reported to public health officials and (2) should sexual partners of those infected be informed? In either case, the right to privacy clashes with the public health mandate to prevent the spread of disease. Having been harmed often in the past by government intrusion into their lives, gay people harbor intense suspicion of public officials and do not want them to have lists of their names. Although contact tracing is usual for the control of sexually transmitted diseases, it poses problems for gay people because they are discriminated against and because there is no sure way to maintain the confidentiality of their medical records. On the other hand, unsuspecting sexual contacts of the infected have a right to know they are at risk, for example female partners of bisexual men.

How far should the state go to limit AIDS? The Department of Defense policy is that HIV-infected personnel must inform partners of their condition or face charges ranging from disobeying orders to assault or attempted murder, a coercive and unenforceable policy. The Cuban government plans to test the entire population for AIDS. Everyone who tests positive is placed in a quarantine center surrounded by a barbed-wire wall outside of Havana.[6]

Other ethical questions arising from AIDS are whether doctors or hospitals can refuse to treat AIDS patients (currently a high proportion do refuse) and whether euthanasia is appropriate for terminal AIDS patients. Should health care workers, especially doctors, be required to take AIDS tests? Should those who are HIV infected be barred from certain jobs? In January 1991, responding to pressure from AIDS activists and doctors, the Department of Health and Human Services proposed to strike HIV infection from the list of diseases for which a person can be kept out of the US. But before the new regulation was to take place in June 1991, the Bush administration changed its mind, reportedly after receiving angry letters from conservatives (*San Francisco Chronicle,* 25 May 1991: A1).

The special plight of minority people with AIDS raises ethical questions about unequal access to health care and even to information about AIDS, most of which is published only in English. White gay men can find out about AIDS from gay newspapers, clubs, and bars, sources not available to heterosexual minorities. The media have focused on AIDS when it strikes children and white gay men. Even though the media have stereotyped men with AIDS as promiscuous, while in fact many are in long-term partnerships, they have provided them with AIDS information. Not many Americans realize that 25 percent of the people with AIDS are Black. According to the book *Our Lives in the Balance: U.S. Women of Color and the AIDS Epidemic,* 52 percent of US women with AIDS are Black, and 20 percent are Latina.[7] In addition, women of color have played an important role as caregivers to people with AIDS.

The stigma attached to AIDS is especially severe for minorities because homosexuality itself tends to be severely stigmatized in their communities. Thus some of those who engage in homosexual acts may define themselves as heterosexual. In many Asian communities homosexuality is thought to result from "bad blood" and to be not only an affliction but a source of shame for the family. It is equated with effeminacy. Influenced by Roman Catholicism, many Hispanics condemn homosexuality. Although freedom of sexual expression tends to be more valued in the Black community than in the Asian American or Hispanic communities, fear of racial genocide leads Blacks to emphasize reproduction and consequently Black Gay men may seem a threat to their survival. When coming out causes members of minorities to be forced out of their communities, they lose their main support against racism, and they may feel unwelcome in the white gay community. Thus isolation is a greater problem for minority people with AIDS than for whites.

Finally, the impact of AIDS may be seen in a broader cultural context. Susan Sontag observes that in this society we get messages saying consume, grow, do what you want, amuse yourself. The economic system encourages us to defy limits. Capitalist ideology "makes us all into connoisseurs of liberty, of the indefinite expansion of possibility." Sex becomes a consumer option, an exercise in pushing back limits. From this perspective, recreational, risk-free sex is not just a practice of gay men, but an integral part of the culture of capitalism. But AIDS put an end to risk-free sex and substituted new messages of restraint and limitation.[8]

AIDS had the potentional to destroy the gay liberation movement.

It overwhelmed the gay community by exhausting and frightening its members, using up its resources, and giving its enemies a powerful new tool for stirring up hatred. Before he became director of Shanti in San Francisco, Eric Rofes feared that most gay men would die, those remaining would be forced back into the closet, no young people would want to come out, lesbians and gay men would be split into two camps, and the HIV positive would be shunned by those free of the virus.[9] None of this happened, but it was a possible scenario.

AIDS demonstrated the need for a gay movement: women and men lacking a political analysis of their oppression or lacking the examples of the anti-war movement, the civil rights movement, and women's liberation would not have been able to fight back against AIDS, against government indifference to their welfare, against all the bigots who welcomed the deaths of gay men. Changing sexual practices slowed the growth of the epidemic but, by 1993, a quarter of a million people in the US may have AIDS. In San Francisco alone, the total may be 25,000 by then (*San Francisco Examiner,* 17 January 1990: A5). By early 1991, 6,732 San Franciscans had died of AIDS. Over 1 million Americans will probably be infected by HIV and some estimates say 2 million. But numbers alone cannot give a true sense of the losses sustained by gay men and lesbians. Only art and literature can attempt to do that—*Ground Zero,* for example, an essay collection by Andrew Holleran; *Love Alone,* poems by Paul Monette; and Monette's *Borrowed Time: an AIDS Memoir.*[10] The human suffering and lasting damage caused by AIDS cannot be overestimated and the absence of a cure or a vaccine makes the present situation of many gay men bleak. But the movement survived. It had grown so rapidly in two decades and changed so many lives that even the spread of a usually fatal disease could not extinguish it.

8

CONCLUSION

Gay and lesbian liberation has come a long way since 1965 when ten people demonstrated for gay rights in front of the White House. When the movie *Anders als die Andern* (Different from the Others) was banned in Germany in 1920, difference meant outcast status. The same was true in 1957 when Allen Ginsberg's poem "Howl" was seized by San Francisco police. Homosexuality was equated with obscenity.

In the sixties, the spirit of defiant protest that united Blacks, opponents of the Viet Nam war and feminists also began to transform homosexuals from a people nearly universally pitied or condemned to a new political force. They adopted the name "gay" to show their self-acceptance and their group identity. In contrast to their past invisibility, they became openly gay in the 1970s. Their political and social organizations proliferated in the years after Stonewall, and their influence on American life increased. In 1969, not a single American city had a law protecting lesbians and gay men from discrimination; today eighty-one cities have gay rights laws. In 1969, forty-eight states had sodomy laws. Today they exist in twenty-five states (*Gay in America* 1989: 4). The number of people who believe homosexual acts should be illegal fell from 60 percent in 1970 to 36 percent in 1989 (*Washington Blade,* 27 October 1989: 23). In 1969, fewer than twenty gay newspapers and magazines were published, while today there are more than 300. Only a few hundred books on homosexuality were in print in 1969, and now the number is more than 9,000 (*Gay in America:* 4). These books helped to transform the concept of homosexuality from a behavior to an identity. Similar practices could not have united people as disparate as those who love their own sex, but common identity was a powerful unifying force.

Secondly, the authority of doctors, religious leaders, the courts, and the police to define homosexuality as an inferior way of being was almost completely overthrown in less than two decades. In place of the negative images of themselves that had existed for centuries, sometimes used to justify attempts to exterminate them, homosexuals created positive images, insisting on their own authority to interpret their experience. Finally, the sense of a common identity and anger at oppressive treatment led them to see themselves as a minority.

In the 1990s, gay and lesbian liberation has a strong impact on the dominant culture. City, state, and national lawmakers no longer ignore the gay community. Mainstream newspapers occasionally run stories about its issues. A new sophistication and honesty about sex exists today as a result of gay liberation. The arts have benefited greatly from the creative energy of people who no longer conceal their true identities. Intellectual life is richer because knowledge can be re-examined in the light of new understandings of sexual identity. Now that campus gay groups are common, the diversity of the student population is more accurately reflected. Neighborhoods are strengthened by lesbians and gay men living singly, in couples, or in families. Films

and television programs are more interesting if they tentatively acknowledge the existence of lesbians and gay men.

The year 1990 brought so many victories and signs of encouraging
developments for gay liberation that it seemed to mark a turning point
for the movement. Gay rights bills passed in communities where they
would not have had a chance of being enacted ten years earlier, in San
Diego and Pittsburgh, for example. The Hate Crimes Statistics Act
included lesbians and gay men, an official recognition of their minority
status. Congress revoked anti-gay immigration laws. On December
10, 1990, the San Francisco Board of Supervisors became the first
governmental body to call for legalization of gay marriages. General
Motors sent its executives a memo forbidding homophobic slurs. Gay
Pride parades in some cities were the largest ever held. Wichita and
Boise held their first Gay Pride celebrations (Boise was the scene of an
anti-homosexual witchhunt in the 1950s). Thousands attended the Gay
Games in Vancouver. The Soviet Union's first gay group, "Friends
in Moscow," was formed. The editors of the Harvard Law Review
published *Sexual Orientation and the Law,* a subject which did not
interest students at prestigious law schools in the past. An Episcopal
bishop in New Jersey ordained an openly gay man, and a lesbian couple
became pastors of a San Francisco Lutheran church. Reform Judaism
accepted openly gay rabbis. The San Francisco school board approved
a counseling program for gay and lesbian students. *Time* magazine
published a long article and a full-page color photo of gay writer
Edmund White (30 July 1990: 58–60). On a single day, the *New York
Times* ran four articles and an editorial on gay issues (2 March 1990).
Gay people were more visible than ever before.

Speaking to a crowd of 300,000 on Gay Freedom Day in San
Francisco, June 24, 1990, activist Eric Rofes likened the gay community to a phoenix rising from its ashes. No longer "shellshocked by
the horror of AIDS," lesbians and gay men, he said, are recapturing
the 1970s' spirit of gay liberation. Rofes pointed to victories that could
not have happened in the 1980s: passage of the Hate Crimes Act;
acceptance of gay men and lesbians as Big Brothers and Big Sisters in
Washington DC; and the defeat of Jesse Helms' amendment to stop

federal funding of AIDS education after the measure had passed for five years. He also noted that thousands of lesbians were organizing for a national conference in Atlanta in April 1991.

In the 1970s when Allan Berube began his research on lesbians and gay men in World War II, the only people who were interested in this topic were other gay men and lesbians. But when his book *Coming Out Under Fire* was published in 1990, it was reviewed by the *New York Times*. In 1978, *Word is Out,* a documentary about gay people by Peter Adair and Rob Epstein, was very well received in the gay community but shown in only a few theaters, whereas in 1985 Epstein won an Academy Award for his documentary on Harvey Milk. When Minnie Bruce Pratt began publishing poetry in the 1970s her audience was other lesbian feminists. In 1990, she won a $20,000 grant from the National Endowment for the Arts. These examples show that homosexuality has been demystified by gay liberation and that the work of lesbian and gay male writers and artists is finding a broader audience than would have been possible a decade ago.

Despite these signs of progress, gay liberation has a long way to go before all forms of discrimination end and gay and lesbian relationships are fully accepted. People are imprisoned for homosexuality in other countries, for example. In the United States, although homosexuality is increasingly viewed as a sexual orientation rather than an illness or a sign of arrested development, social disapproval remains strong. Some of the marchers in the Boise Gay Pride parade wore paper bags over their heads to hide their identities. America does not have a federal law protecting the civil rights of lesbians and gay men, and the 1986 Supreme Court decision *Bowers v. Hardwick* which upheld sodomy laws stands as a powerful reminder of their second class status. Furthermore, all mainstream institutions promote heterosexuality and thereby interfere with the development of homosexuality. Even when overt prejudice disappears it may be replaced by more subtle bias. A news magazine recently referred to the AIDS lobby, for example, as the "AIDS political machine." This language is inaccurate: a machine is made up of paid professionals working within a patronage system for their own advancement. The AIDS lobby is a grassroots volunteer effort with a humanitarian purpose. The pejorative label "machine" shows that gay people are still perceived as outsiders.

In the past twenty years, centuries-old prejudice against homosexual behavior has been challenged but not eradicated. The Roman emperor Justinian blamed homosexuals for famines, plagues, and earthquakes, and in October 1989 fundamentalist preachers blamed the San Francisco earthquake on the city's gay residents. The religious view that homosexuals are sick or sinful would be equally laughable if fundamentalists were not trying to impose their values on others. Gay men and lesbians must therefore continue to defend their rights. More than most citizens they have a stake in church state separation.

A hopeful sign for gay and lesbian liberation in the 1990s is that two of the three homophobic institutions described in Chapter 1, Roman Catholicism and fundamentalist religion, are weaker than they were in the 1980s. And even though hopes that the end of the cold war would cut defense spending and curb the influence of the military were short lived, anti-gay military policies, attacked only by gay people in the 1980s, are now under fire from liberals in Congress and university faculties. The American Catholic Church, torn by dissent, spent several million dollars in 1990 on a public relations campaign attempting to get Catholics to agree with its stand on abortion. Forty-six of its own theologians accurately branded Church teaching on homosexuality "abusive authoritarianism" (Adam 1987: 136). Pro-abortion forces are gaining strength despite opposition from Catholics and fundamentalists. If religious groups cannot force women to bear unwanted children, they may try all the harder to promote their anti-gay policies, in order to demonstrate their power. But they are slowly losing the battle between sexual freedom and repression.

The year 1990 gave a bittersweet victory to gay men and lesbians. In an October speech to law students, former Supreme Court Justice Lewis Powell, who cast the deciding fifth vote in *Bowers* v. *Hardwick,* acknowledged that he had made a mistake. He now believes the privacy rights of homosexuals are constitutionally protected. But he declared that the case was not important. Knowing that *Bowers* v. *Hardwick* has been used against them since 1986, gay people would never label it unimportant. Powell's opinion of the law changed, but he had no change of heart. He is no more able to identify with gay citizens than he was in 1986. Victory for gay and lesbian liberation will come when most heterosexuals regard homosexuals as fully human, a change that will not automatically result from legal reform.

What constitutes "success" for the gay movement? Laws affirming the basic citizenship rights of lesbians and gay men and an end to discriminatory practices, or a more fundamental change in heterosexual domination? Some gay people will be satisfied by the former, but many others believe their movement must restructure society.

Students who understand why gay liberation is important for gay people sometimes ask why heterosexuals should support it. A society which represses gay sex is not a healthy society for heterosexuals, either. They are better off when tolerant views of sexual difference prevail. Secondly, without the perceptions of gay and lesbian liberation, heterosexuals overlook a whole range of human experience and thus limit their world view. The contributions gay and lesbian citizens can make to America, in their private lives and as workers, will be greater if they are not psychologically burdened and physically threatened by anti-gay bigotry. Furthermore, the enemies of gay people are also the enemies of Blacks, Jews, and women who favor abortion. The religious right threatens First Amendment freedoms, a concern of many people besides those who are gay. Finally, when heterosexuals understand that gay and lesbian issues, far from being peripheral or trivial, are central issues in the last decade of the century, they are liberated from the misconception that only they lead significant lives.

This book has focused on the strengths and achievements of gay and lesbian liberation but the movement has limitations as well. As in other social change movements, its adherents sometimes get so caught up in power struggles and internal debates that the common goal is lost sight of. Disagreements exist between women and men in the gay community, for example, and between radicals and reformers. The interests of one segment of the community may be very different from the interests of another. Gentrification of urban neighborhoods benefits white gay men, for example, and harms gay people of color. Perhaps the most serious limitation of gay and lesbian liberation is that sexual identity, which has so far proven to be a sufficient basis for sustaining a mass movement, may over time be insufficient. For many, sexual identity is as central to self-definition as race, ethnicity, or sex. But it may lose this character. Thirty years from now, will being gay be as important as being Black, Jewish, or female are certain to be? Will decreased opposition to homosexuality lessen its significance? No historical parallels exist to shed light on these questions. If lesbians and gay men become much more assimilated into mainstream society than they are now, they may no longer be self-consciously gay. In that case, since a heightened awareness of being different is fundamental to motivating people to identify with gay liberation, the movement might not be able to survive. Or, from another perspective, it would have achieved its short-term goals—an end to all discrimination and complete acceptance of lesbians and gay men—if not its more ambitious aim of reordering society.

For the foreseeable future, however, gay people will remain an autonomous group with a keen sense of their social difference. Even if they want assimilation, which many do not, lingering prejudice in the dominant culture will make identification with the gay subculture inevitable. In America today it is possible for lesbians and gay men to organize their lives so that they interact with heterosexuals only at work and sometimes all their co-workers are gay, too. This life pattern was inconceivable before gay liberation. Even those who are less immersed in the gay world celebrate their sexuality in a way that was impossible before many thousands of people came out of the closet.

Whatever setbacks the gay movement experiences in the 1990s, the ideas of sexual freedom and self-determination will not die out. Just as the communist regimes of Eastern Europe failed to extinguish the idea of democracy, homophobia will not stop lesbians and gay men from expressing who they are. Homophobia may throw up temporary roadblocks, but for every lesbian mother who loses a child custody case, for every gay man expelled from the Marines, for every college student driven from a dorm by anti-gay harassment, for every person with AIDS punished by the health care system or the insurance industry, there will be a hundred more, or a thousand more, to carry on the fight.

EPILOGUE

From the vantage point of late 1991, the assertion in the last chapter that the year 1990 marked a turning point for gay and lesbian liberation seems too optimistic. To be sure, progress continued. Amnesty International finally agreed to consider people imprisoned for homosexuality to be political prisoners, for example, and more campus ROTC programs came under attack because the official anti-gay policy of the military conflicted with campus non-discrimination codes. With the help of gay and lesbian voters, a liberal Republican became governor of Massachusetts. In Russia, the fledgling gay movement played a role in toppling the coup leaders, who had issued veiled threats against it.

Gay men and lesbians saw that the first copies of Yeltsin's statement defying the coup were so badly printed as to be barely legible. Using a Mackintosh computer that had arrived in Moscow only two weeks earlier, the gift of U.S. gay activists, gay Russians printed and distributed thousands of copies of Yeltsin's words.

But the gay and lesbian liberation movement suffered a major setback a few months later, in October 1991, when California governor Pete Wilson vetoed the gay rights bill he had been expected to sign. Huge, spontaneous demonstrations in Los Angeles and San Francisco followed the veto. Gay men and lesbians were angry that the governor caved in to the far right. His defense was ludicrous: he did not wish to impose hardships on small businesses. Wilson could not have offered this argument to justify discrimination against any other class of people. And thousands of small business owners in the state are gay. The veto forcibly reminded lesbians and gay men of their second class status.

Another unwelcome reminder was media reaction to basketball star Magic Johnson's announcement in November 1991 that he has HIV. He was treated like a hero. His plight seemed to matter more to many Americans than the deaths of thousands of gay men. Tennis star Martina Navratilova accurately observed that if she had contracted HIV, media response would be "I had it coming" (Bay Area Reporter, 21 November 1991: 1). The eagerness of the President and the Vice President to express sympathy for Magic Johnson seemed hypocritical, given the emotional distance both had kept from gay men with AIDS and from the disease itself. A national survey reported that half of the doctors in the United States would not treat persons with AIDS if they had a choice, and a third see homosexuality as a threat to social institutions (San Francisco Chronicle, 27 November 1991: A1).

Two important legal decisions in December 1991 affected the lives of lesbians and gay men. A Minnesota appeals court granted Karen Thompson custody of her lover, Sharon Kowalski, severely injured in a 1983 car crash (The New York Times, 18 Dec. 1991: A 17). Years of homophobic legal decisions preceded the final victory, however. In a setback for the movement, a federal court judge ruled that the Navy could continue to discriminate against homosexuals in order to prevent the spread of AIDS (*San Francisco Chronicle*, 19 December 1991: A1). To reach this absurd decision, the judge had to assume that only males are homosexual and that AIDS is confined to the gay community, two demonstrably false notions.

Like other Americans, lesbians and gay men were harmed by the long recession. Those who are self employed or run small businesses were especially hard hit. If a depression comes, some gay people fear that scapegoats will be necessary and that they will be targeted.

On the other hand, the everyday grassroots work of gay liberation was not greatly affected by the California veto, doctors' homophobia, the bigotry of federal judges, or the downward spiral of the economy. Chapters of the militant group Queer Nation were formed in big cities and on college campuses, even at small, rural colleges such as Grinnell in Iowa. The National Gay and Lesbian Task Force's leadership conference in 1991 was attended by activists from forty one states, Central America, England, and Russia.

Gay liberation has been characterized by both the rapid rise and fall of groups and organizations and the longevity of others. Queer Nation's San Francisco chapter, for example, disbanded at the end of 1991 because of internal disagreements. But a sign of the strength of the movement is that some of its institutions such as community centers and bookstores celebrated their twentieth anniversary in 1991.

Margaret Cruikshank
San Francisco
January 1992

NOTES

CHAPTER 1
INTRODUCTION

1. This information is taken from the *Encyclopedia of Homosexuality*, 2 vols (New York: Garland, 1989), cited hereafter in the text—Krafft-Ebing, p. 668; Ellis, p. 353; Carpenter, p. 200. The Carpenter quote about homosexuals in the vanguard is cited by Barbara Fassler in "Theories of Homosexuality as Sources of Bloomsbury's Androgyny," *Signs* 5 (1979), p. 249. For Havelock Ellis on lesbianism see Lillian Faderman, *Surpassing the Love of Men* (New York: Morrow, 1981), pp. 241–5, and Carroll Smith-Rosenberg's essay in M. Duberman *et al.* (eds.), *Hidden from History*. (New York: New American Library 1989), p. 270.

2. See the bibliography entries for Faderman, Smith-Rosenberg, and Vicinus.

3. Paul Fussell, *The Great War and Modern Memory* (Oxford: Oxford University Press, 1977); Allan Berube, *Coming out under Fire* (New York: Free Press, 1990); "Coming Out Under Fire: an Interview with Historian Allan Berube on Gays and Lesbians in World War II," *San Francisco Bay Times* (April 1990), pp. 4, 6.

4. Amy Kautzman, "Coming Out in the Navy," *Hurricane Alice* (Winter 1988), p. 7.

5. Interview with Rosemary Denman in Neil Miller, *In Search of Gay America* (New York: Atlantic Monthly Press 1989), p. 224. Subsequent references to this book will be made in the text.

6. John McNeill, *The Church and the Homosexual* (Boston: Beacon Press, 1976).

7. Pat O'Donnell, "Dream Journey to Myself," in Rosemary Curb and Nancy Manahan (eds.), *Lesbian Nuns: Breaking Silence* (Tallahassee, FL: Naiad Press, 1985).

8. Sexual abuse of children, especially boys, is an explosive issue for the Catholic Church. In the past there was often a cover-up: priests who abused children were transferred to another part of the country where they resumed parish work and unfortunately found new victims. Church lawyers have warned bishops that legal claims arising from sexual misconduct cases may cost the Church $1 billion in the 1990s. See the *Los Angeles Times*, 3 August 1990, p. A1.

9. This hypocrisy is well documented in Brian McNaught's book *On Being Gay. Thoughts on Family, Faith, and Love* (New York: St Martin's Press, 1988), pp. 150–4.

10. Joyce Murdoch, "Gay Youths' Deadly Despair," *Washington Post,* 24 October 1988, p. A1. See also Eric Rofes, *I Thought People Like That Killed Themselves* (San Francisco: Grey Fox Press, 1983).

CHAPTER 2
GAY AND LESBIAN LIBERATION AS A SEXUAL FREEDOM MOVEMENT

1. Lee Ellis and M. Ashley Ames, "Neurohormonal Functioning and Sexual Orientation: A Theory of Homosexuality–Heterosexuality," *Psychological Bulletin* 101 (1987), p. 250. The problem with attempts to find a biological cause for homosexuality is that they reduce it to a physical entity.

2. Both sides of this debate have been labeled by social constructionists. See the *Encyclopedia of Homosexuality,* 2 vols (New York: Garland, 1990) p. 1208. Social constructionists base their ideas on the writings of Michel Foucault, especially the first volume of his *History of Sexuality* (New York: Random House, 1978).

3. Alan Bray, *Homosexuality in Renaissance England* (London: Gay Men's Press, 1982).

4. Wayne Dynes, "Wrestling with the Social Boa Constructor," *Out in Academia* (Multicultural Lesbian and Gay Studies, University of California, Berkeley) 2 (Spring 1988), p. 21. Dynes believes that the failure of psychiatry and therapy to change sexual orientation refutes social construction.

5. Judy Grahn, *Another Mother Tongue* (Boston: Beacon Press, 1984).

6. Sarah Franklin and Jackie Stacey, "Dyke-tactics for Difficult Times," Christian McEwen and Sue O'Sullivan (eds.), in *Out the Other Side. Contemporary Lesbian Writing.* (Freedom, CA: Crossing Press, 1989), p. 229.

7. This summary of the main points of K. J. Dover's *Greek Homosexuality* is given by David M. Halperin in *One Hundred Years of Homosexuality* (New York: Routledge, 1990), p. 5. See also "Homosexuality: a Cultural Construct," Chapter 2 of Halperin's book.

8. Charles Silverstein, *Man to Man: Gay Male Couples in America* (New York: Quill: 1982), p. 155.

9. Rik Isensee, *Love Between Men* (Englewood Cliffs, NJ: Prentice Hall, 1990).

10. Mohr believes that gay men and lesbians are regarded as lesser moral beings.

11. Celeste West, *Lesbian Love Advisor* (Pittsburgh, PA: Cleis Press, 1989).

12. Keith Vacha (ed.), *Quiet Fire* (Freedom, CA: Crossing Press, 1985); Marcy Adelman (ed.), *Long Time Passing* (Boston: Alyson, 1986).

13. Pepper Schwarz and Philip Blumstein, *American Couples* (New York: Pocket Books, 1985).

14. Only seven years later, Radclyffe Hall's novel *The Well of Loneliness* told the English-speaking world that lesbians exist.

15. Geoffrey Giles, *Homosexuality and the Nazis* (in progress).

16. Edmund White, *The Beautiful Room is Empty* (New York: Knopf, 1988).

17. Lani Kaahumanu and Lorraine Hutchins (eds), *Bi Any Other Name: Bisexual People Speak Out* (Boston: Alyson, 1990).

18. Peter Ackroyd, *Dressing Up* (London: Thames & Hudson, 1979), p. 104. See also Will Roscoe, "Making History: the Challenge of Gay and Lesbian Studies." *Journal of Homosexuality* 15 (3/4) (1988), pp. 26–9.

19. Ackroyd, *Dressing Up,* 133.

20. Patrick White, *The Twyborn Affair* (Harmondsworth, Middx: Penguin, 1981).

21. See Harriet Whitehead, "The Bow and the Burden Strap: a New Look at Institutionalized Homosexuality in Native North America," in Sherry B. Ortner and Harriet Whitehead (eds), *Sexual Meanings: the Cultural Construction of Gender and Sexuality* (Cambridge: Cambridge University Press, 1981); Jonathan Katz, *Gay American History* (New York: Thomas Y. Crowell, 1976), Chapter 4; and the *Encyclopedia of Homosexuality,* pp. 127 and 1218.

22. Walter Williams, *The Spirit and the Flesh: Sexual Diversity in American Indian Culture* (Boston: Beacon Press, 1986).

23. Will Roscoe, *The Zuni Man Woman* (Albuquerque, N.M.: University of New Mexico Press, 1992).

24. Margaret Cruikshank (ed.), *The Lesbian Path* (San Francisco: Grey Fox, 1985); Julia Penelope & Susan J. Wolfe (eds.) *The Coming Out Stories* (Freedom, CA: Crossing Press, 1990).

25. See "Why Sex is Private," a section of Richard Mohr's *Gays/Justice* (New York: Columbia University Press, 1988), pp. 94–126.

26. For example, *Lesbian Love Stories,* edited by Irene Zahava (Freedom, CA: Crossing Press, 1989).

27. Tee Corinne, *Yantras of Women Love* (Tallahassee, FL: Naiad Press, 1982); *Dreams of the Woman who Loved Sex* (Austin: Banned Books, 1987); *Intricate Passions: a Collection of Erotic Short Fiction* (Austin: Banned Books, 1989).

CHAPTER 3
GAY AND LESBIAN LIBERATION AS A POLITICAL MOVEMENT

1. This is the perspective of Australian gay writer Dennis Altman in "My America and Yours: a Letter to U.S. Activists," *Outlook* 8 (Spring 1990), p. 64.

2. For a more detailed description of the politics of gay liberation see Barry Adam, *The Rise of a Gay and Lesbian Liberation Movement* (Boston: G. K. Hall, 1987) and John D'Emilio, *Sexual Politics, Sexual Communities* (Chicago: University of Chicago Press, 1983).

3. A collection of essays and speeches, *Lesbians in Germany from the 1890's to the 1920's,* edited by Lillian Faderman and Brigitte Eriksson (Tallahassee, FL: Naiad Press, 1990), documents this subculture as does *Hindsight* (London: Quartet Books, 1982), the autobiography of Charlotte Wolff, a doctor who moved to England to escape the Nazis. Christopher Isherwood wrote about homosexual life in Berlin in the 1930s in *Christopher and His Kind* (New York: Farrar, Straus, Giroux, 1976). He described, for example, the destruction of Hirschfeld's Institute.

4. After the war, Holland became a place where homosexuals could meet openly and today it remains one of the countries most hospitable to them. Amsterdam is an international center of gay culture.

5. Esther Newton, "The Mythic Mannish Lesbian," in M. Duberman *et al.* (eds.), *Hidden from History* (New York: New American Library, 1989), p. 283.

6. See Barbara Fassler's "Theories of Homosexuality as Sources of Bloomsbury's Androgyny," *Signs* 5 (1979), pp. 237–51.

7. The source for most of the following account of the homophile movement is John D'Emilio's *Sexual Politics, Sexual Communities*.

8. Del Martin and Phyllis Lyon, "Reminiscences of Two Female Homophiles," in Ginny Vida (ed.), *Our Right to Love* (Englewood Cliffs, NJ: Prentice Hall, 1978). The work of two other pioneers of gay rights, Frank Kameny in Washington DC and Barbara Gittings in Philadelphia, is described by D'Emilio, *Sexual Politics, Sexual Communities*.

9. Conversation with Eric Rofes, July 5, 1990, San Francisco. Currently the director of the Shanti Project in San Francisco, Rofes earlier wrote for the influential paper *Gay Community News* in Boston and headed the Gay Community Center in Los Angeles. Conversation with Sharon Raphael, April 5, 1990, San Francisco. A founder of the National Association of Lesbian and Gay Gerontologists, Raphael is professor of sociology at California State University, Dominguez Hills.

10. See John D'Emilio's essay "Gay Politics and Community in San Francisco since World War II," in M. Duberman *et al.* (eds), *Hidden from History* (New York: New American Library, 1989).

11. Among the legal organizations dedicated to gay rights are the National Gay Rights Advocates and the National Center for Lesbians Rights in San Francisco, Lambda Legal Defense and Education Fund in New York, and Gay and Lesbian Advocates and Defenders in Boston.

12. Jeanne Jullion, *Long Way Home* (Pittsburgh, PA: Cleis Press, 1985).

13. The myth of lesbian evil is so pervasive that Lillian Faderman devotes a chapter of *Surpassing the Love of Men* (New York: Morrow, 1981) to it. She focuses on French literature.

14. Karen Thompson, *Why Can't Sharon Kowalski Come Home* (San Francisco: Spinsters Ink, 1988).

15. John D'Emilio, "Capitalism and Gay Identity," in Ann Snitow and Christine Stansell (eds.) *Powers of Desire. The Politics of Sexuality* (New York: Monthly Review Press, 1983), p. 110.

CHAPTER 4
GAY AND LESBIAN LIBERATION AS A MOVEMENT OF IDEAS

1. For a theoretical discussion of homophobia see Eve Kosofsky Sedgwick's *Epistemology of the Closet* (Berkeley, CA: University of California Press, 1990).

2. "Taking the Home out of Homophobia," a Dialogue between Jewelle Gomez and Barbara Smith, *Outlook,* No. 8 (Spring 1990), pp. 32–7.

3. *Censorship and Self-Censorship: Anti-Feminist Harassment in the Academy,* edited by Greta Gaard (New York: A Modern Language Association, forthcoming).

4. Barbara Ponse, *Identities in the Lesbian World* (Westport, CT: Greenwood Press, 1978).

5. Phyllis Robinson, *Willa: the Life of Willa Cather* (New York: Henry Holt, 1984); Sharon O'Brien, *Willa Cather: the Emerging Voice* (Oxford: Oxford University Press, 1986); Victoria Glendinning, *Vita: a Biography of Vita Sackville-West* (New York: Morrow, 1985); Michael Holroyd, *Lytton Strachey* (Harmondsworth, Middx: Penguin, 1987).

6. J. Siegel and C. Taeuber, "Demographic Perspectives on the Long-Lived Society," in Alan Pifer & Lydia Bronte, *Our Aging Society, Paradox and Promise* (New York: Norton, 1986).

7. Adrienne Rich, "Compulsory Heterosexuality and Lesbian Existence," *Signs* 5 (1980), p. 658. In this essay Rich identifies some of the elements of compulsory heterosexuality: "the female wage scale, the enforcement of middle-class women's 'leisure,' the glamorization of so-called sexual liberation, the withholding of education from women [and] the imagery of 'high art' and popular culture" (p. 659).

8. I take this phrase from John D'Emilio who used it to describe gay historical studies. See "Not a Simple Matter: Gay History and Gay Historians," *Journal of American History* 76 (2) (1989), pp. 435–42.

9. Will Roscoe, "Making History: The Challenge of Gay and Lesbian Studies," *Journal of Homosexuality* 15 (314) (1988), p. 19. Roscoe proposes six dimensions for the multidisciplinary field of gay and lesbian studies: sexuality, subjectivity and identity, gender, social roles, economic roles, and spirituality. For another extensive discussion see Richard Mohr's "Gay Studies as Moral Vision," *Educational Theory* 39 (Spring 1989), pp. 121–32. Mohr believes women's studies should be a model for gay studies.

10. Susan Krieger, *The Mirror Dance* (Philadelphia, PA: Temple University Press, 1983).

11. See my text *Lesbian Studies* (Old Westbury, NY: The Feminist Press, 1982).

12. Susan Ware (ed.), *Modern American Women. A Documentary History* (Chicago: Dorsey Press, 1989); Ann Garry and Marilyn Pearsall (eds.), *Women, Knowledge, and Reality: Explorations in Feminist Philosophy* (Boston: Unwin Hyman, 1989).

13. Dennis Altman, "My America-and Yours—a Letter to U.S. Activists," *Outlook,* No. 8 (Spring 1990), p. 65.

14. John Preston (ed.), *Personal Dispatches: Writers Confront AIDS* (New York: St Martin's Press, 1989); Dennis Altman, *AIDS in the Mind of America* (New York: Doubleday, 1987).

15. Clare Potter, *Index to Lesbian Periodicals* (Tallahassee, FL: Naiad Press, 19?6); Barbara Grier, *The Lesbian in Literature* (Tallahassee, FL: Naiad Press, 1981; J.R. Roberts, *Black Lesbian Bibliography* (Tallahassee, FL: Naiad Press, 1981).

16. Mike Hippler, *Matlovich* (Boston: Alyson, 1988); Paula Gunn Allen, "Lesbians in American Indian Cultures," in M. Duberman *et al.* (eds.), *Hidden from History* (New York: New American Library, 1989); James G. Wolf (ed.), *Gay Priests* (New York: Harper & Row, 1989); Rosemary Curb and Nancy Manahan (eds.), *Lesbian Nuns: Breaking Silence* (Tallahassee, FL: Naiad Press, 1985).

17. Other important works are David M. Halperin's *One Hundred Years of Homosexuality* (New York: Routledge, 1990); *Independent Women: Work and Community for Single Women, 1850–1920,* by Martha Vicinus (Chicago: Univ. of Chicago Press, 1985); and Lillian Faderman's book on twentieth-century lesbian life, *Odd Girls and Twilight Lovers* (New York: Columbia University Press, 1991).

18. In addition to work with explicitly lesbian content, lesbian scholars have produced some of the best work on women generally: for example, Estelle Freedman's study of women's prison reform, *Her Sister's Keeper* (Ann Arbor, MI: University of Michigan, 1981); the anthology on incest *Voices in the Night,* edited by Toni McNaron and Yarrow Morgan (Pittsburgh, PA: Cleis Press, 1982); Pauline Bart's *Stopping Rape: Women Who Did* (New York: Macmillan, 1982); and the powerful analysis of ageism *Look Me in the Eye* by Barbara Macdonald and Cynthia Rich (San Francisco: Spinsters Ink, 1984).

19. Richard Hall, "Gay Fiction Comes Home," *New York Times Book Review,* 19 June 1988, p. 1.

20. Lois Helmbold, introduction to *A Lesbian Photo Album, Lives of Seven Lesbian Feminists* by Cathy Cade (Oakland, CA: Waterwomen Books, 1987), p. 13.

CHAPTER 5
GAY CULTURE AND COMMUNITY

1. See Eric Garber's article "A Spectacle in Color: the Lesbian and Gay Subculture of Jazz Age Harlem," in M. Duberman *et al.* (eds), *Hidden from History* (New York: New American Library, 1989). The World War II gay subculture is documented in Allan Berube's *Coming Out Under Fire* (New York: Free Press, 1990).

2. Ellen Klages, "When the Bar was the Only Place in Town," *Unity and More in '84* (program of the San Francisco Lesbian and Gay Freedom Day), p. 39. In 1974, when I went to a lesbian bar in Minneapolis, the wholesome atmosphere reminded me of the girl scout camp where I had been a counselor. In fact, on my first night in the bar, several women I knew from the camp greeted me.

3. Susan Sontag, "Notes on Camp," in *Against Interpretation* (New York: Farrar, Straus, Giroux, 1966), p. 279.

4. Conversation with Jack Collins, February 10, 1991, San Francisco. See also Jeffrey

Escoffier, "Sexual Revolution and the Politics of Gay Identity," *Socialist Review,* Nos 81 and 82 (October 1985), p. 140.

5. Topics of a few of these slideshows are Passing Women, Allan Berube; Paris lesbians, Karla Jay; World War II, Allan Berube; and the berdache, Will Roscoe. See the article by the San Francisco Gay and Lesbian History Project, "She Even Chewed Tobacco: a Pictorial Narrative of Passing Women in America," in Duberman *et al., Hidden from History.*

6. Judy Grahn, *Another Mother Tongue* (Boston: Beacon Press, 1985); Arthur Evans, *Witchcraft and the Gay Counterculture* (Boston: Fag Rag, 1977); Mark Thompson, *Gay Spirit: Meaning and Myth* (New York: St Martin's Press, 1987).

7. Vito Russo, *The Celluloid Closet: Homosexuality in the Movies* (New York: Harper & Row, 1987).

8. Emmanuel Cooper, *The Sexual Perspective: Homosexuality and Art in the Last 100 Years in the West* (London: Routledge & Kegan Paul, 1986).

9. Art critic Ingrid Sischy wrote that, for some gay men, Mapplethorpe's work provided "the mirror they had been waiting for all their lives. And his attitude toward his material was also welcome. No apologies, no disguises, no theories: he just laid it all out." "White and Black," *The New Yorker,* 13 November 1989, p. 146. This article deals in part with the decision of the Corcoran gallery to cancel a Mapplethorpe show because of its explicit homosexual images.

10. Barbara Gittings is quoted in Jonathan Katz, *Gay American History,* (New York: Thomas Y. Crowell, 1976), p. 423.

11. Michael Denneny, "Gay Culture—The Present Moment," *The New York Native,* 25 June 1990, p. 22.

12. *Companeras,* edited by Juanita Ramos (New York: Latina Lesbian History Project, 1988); *Home Girls: a Black Feminist Anthology,* edited by Barbara Smith (Latham, NY: Kitchen Table Press, 1983); and *In the Life: a Black Gay Anthology,* edited by Joseph Beam (Boston: Alyson, 1986).

13. This information on the 1983 conference and the influence of the women's health movement comes from Mary Redick, anthropology department, City College of San Francisco.

14. Excerpt from Pat Parker, "Where Will You Be," in *Movement in Black* (Diana Press, 1978; reissued 1990, Ithaca, NY: Firebrand Books).

15. D. Merilee Clunis and G. Dorsey Green, *Lesbian Couples* (Seattle: Seal Press, 1988), p. 112.

16. Marcy Adelman (ed.), *Long Time Passing* (Boston: Alyson, 1986); Keith Vacha (ed.), *Quiet Fire. Memoirs of Older Gay Men* (Freedom, CA: Crossing Press, 1985).

17. John D'Emilio, "Gay Politics and Community in San Francisco since World War II," in M. Duberman *et al.* (eds.), *Hidden from History* (New York: New American Library, 1989), pp. 459–461.

18. Denyse Lockard, "The Lesbian Community: an Anthropological Approach," in Evelyn Blackwood (ed.), *The Many Faces of Homosexuality* (New York: Harrington Park Press, 1986), pp. 86–8.

CHAPTER 6
LESBIAN FEMINISM

1. Lois Helmbold, introduction to *A Lesbian Photo Album,* by Cathy Cade (Oakland, CA: Waterwomen Books, 1987), p. 15. This book gives mini-histories of seven lesbian feminists through photos from childhood, adolescence, and young adulthood. Subjects are working-class women, middle-class women, Blacks, Asian Americans, Hispanics, and Jewish women. They are pictured in a wide variety of settings: playing with children and pets, working, hiking, gardening, marching in demonstrations, reading poetry in public, building a house, dancing, cooking, clowning around, and swinging from a trapeze.

2. Audre Lorde, *Zami* (Freedom, CA: Crossing Press, 1982).

3. This information on the Daughters of Bilitis is taken from "Reminiscences of Two Female Homophiles," by Del Martin and Phyllis Lyon in Ginny Vida (ed.), *Our Right to Love* (Englewood Cliffs, NJ: Prentice Hall, 1978), pp. 124–8. See also "Lesbians and the Gay Movement," an article in the same book by Barbara Gittings and Kay Tobin, pp. 149–50. John D'Emilio discusses DOB throughout *Sexual Politics, Sexual Communities* (Chicago: University of Chicago Press, 1983), especially pp. 101–7. A video documentary on DOB, coordinated by Morgan Gwenwald, Sara Yager, and Manuela Soares, is interviewing members from the 1950s through the 1970s.

4. Virginia Woolf, *Letters*, Vol. 3, eds. Nigel Nicolson and Joanne Trautmann (New York: Harcourt Brace Jovanovich, 1980), p. 381.

5. Jill Johnston, *Lesbian Nation* (New York: Touchstone, 1973).

6. Cherrie Moraga and Gloria Anzaldúa (eds.), *This Bridge Called My Back: Writings by Radical Women of Color* (Persephone Press, 1981; reissued 1984, Latham, NY: Kitchen Table Press).

7. Evelyn Beck (ed.), *Nice Jewish Girls* (Boston: Beacon Press, 1989).

8. Arlene Stein, review of *The Social Construction of Lesbianism* by Celia Kitzinger (London: Sage, 1987), in *Coming Up!* (February 1988), p. 45. The elaboration of Stein's last point is my own.

9. Harriet Alpert (ed.), *We Are Everywhere: Writings by and about Lesbian Parents* (Freedom, CA: Crossing Press, 1988).

10. Elly Bulkin, Barbara Smith, and Minnie Bruce Pratt, *Yours in Struggle, Three Feminist Perspectives on Anti-Semitism and Racism* (Ithaca, NY: Firebrand Books, 1984).

11. For a separatist point of view see Jeffner Allen, *Lesbian Philosophy: Explorations* (1986) and Sarah Hoagland, *Lesbian Ethics* (1988), both published by the Institute for Lesbian Studies in Palo Alto; Sarah Hoagland and Julia Penelope (eds.), *For Lesbians Only. A Separatist Anthology* (London: Onlywomen Press, 1989); and Marilyn Frye, *The Politics of Reality* (Trumansburg, NY: Crossing Press, 1983). A section of Frye's book is reprinted in Ann Garry and Marilyn Pearsall (eds), *Women, Knowledge, and Reality. Explorations in Feminist Philosophy* (Boston: Unwin Hyman, 1989).

12. D. Merilee Clunis and G. Dorsey Green, *Lesbian Couples* (Seattle: Seal Press, 1988).

13. Joan E. Biren, *Eye to Eye* (Washington: Glad Hag, 1980).

14. Cathy Cade, *A Lesbian Photo Album* (Oakland, CA: Waterwomen Books, 1987).

CHAPTER 7
CONFLICTS AND DEBATES IN THE GAY AND LESBIAN LIBERATION MOVEMENT

1. Ruth Benedict, "Anthropology and the Abnormal," in Margaret Mead (ed.), *An Anthropologist at Work. Writings of Ruth Benedict* (Boston: Houghton Mifflin, 1959), p. 268. See "A Sister Reclaimed," Mildred Dickemann's review of *Ruth Benedict: Stranger in This Land* by Margaret M. Caffey, in *Society of Lesbian and Gay Anthropologists Newsletter* 12 (June 1990), pp. 5–9.

2. Jack Collins, "Letter from San Francisco," *European Gay Review* 2 (1989), p. 72.

3. Jim Foster, "Impact of the AIDS Epidemic on the Gay Political Agenda," in Inge B. Corless and Mary Pittman-Lindeman (eds.), *AIDS: Principles, Practices, Politics* (Washington: Hemisphere Publishing, 1988), p. 210.

4. *Ibid.*, p. 213.

5. Ronald Bayer and Larry Gostin, "Legal and Ethical Issues in AIDS," in M.S. Gottlieb (ed.), *Current Topics in AIDS,* (New York: John Wiley, 1989), pp. 263–86. See also Marcia Ann Gillespie, "HIV: the Global Crisis," *Ms 1,* No. 4 (January/ February 1991), pp. 16–22, and in the same issue Peg Byron, "HIV: the National Scandal," pp. 24–29.

6. Bayer and Gostin, "Legal and Ethical Issues in AIDS," pp. 280, 277.

7. Alma Crawford, *Our Lives in the Balance: U.S. Women of Color and the AIDS Epidemic* (Latham, NY: Kitchen Table Press, 1990).

8. Susan Sontag, *AIDS and its Metaphors* (New York: Farrar, Straus, Giroux, 1989), pp. 76–8.

9. Conversation with Eric Rofes, July 5, 1990, San Francisco.

10. Andrew Holleran, *Ground Zero* (New York: Morrow, 1988); Paul Monette, *Love Alone* (New York: St Martin's Press, 1988); Paul Monette, *Borrowed Time: an AIDS Memoir* (New York: Harcourt, Brace, 1988).

BIBLIOGRAPHY

Adam, Barry D. 1987. *The Rise of a Gay and Lesbian Liberation Movement*. Boston, MA: G. K. Hall.

Allen, Jeffner, ed. 1990. *Lesbian Philosophies and Culture*. Albany, NY: State University of New York Press.

Altman, Dennis. 1982. *The Homosexualization of America*. Boston, MA: Beacon Press.

Berube, Allen. 1990. *Coming Out Under Fire*. New York: Free Press.

Blackwood, Evelyn, ed. 1986. *The Many Faces of Homosexuality. Anthropological Approaches to Homosexual Behavior*. New York: Harrington Park Press.

Boswell, John. 1980. *Christianity, Social Tolerance and Homosexuality: Gay People in Western Europe from the Beginning of the Christian Era to the Fourteenth Century*. Chicago: University of Chicago Press.

Bronski, Michael. 1984. *Culture Clash: The Making of Gay Sensibility*. Boston, MA: South End Press.

Cooper, Emmanuel. 1986. *The Sexual Perspective. Homosexuality and Art in the Last 100 Years in the West*. London: Routledge & Kegan Paul.

Crompton, Louis. 1985. *Byron and Greek Love*. Berkeley, CA: University of California Press.

Crompton, Louis. 1980/81. "The Myth of Lesbian Impunity: Capital Laws from 1270–1791." *Journal of Homosexuality* 6:11–25.

Cruikshank, Margaret. 1982. *Lesbian Studies*. Old Westbury, NY: The Feminist Press.

D'Emilio, John. 1983a. "Capitalism and Gay Identity." In Ann Snitow and Christine Stansell, eds, *Powers of Desire: The Politics of Sexuality*. New York: Monthly Review Press.

D'Emilio, John. 1983b. *Sexual Politics, Sexual Communities. The Making of a Homosexual Minority in the United States, 1940–1970*. Chicago: University of Chicago Press.

D'Emilio, John and Estelle Freedman. 1988. *Intimate Matters. A History of Sexuality in America*. New York: Harper & Row.

Duberman, Martin, Martha Vicinus and George Chauncey, Jr, eds. 1989. *Hidden from History. Reclaiming the Gay and Lesbian Past*. New York: New American Library.

Encyclopedia of Homosexuality. 1990. 2 Vols. Wayne R. Dynes, ed. New York: Garland Publishing.

Epstein, Steven. 1987. "Gay Politics, Ethnic Identity: the Limits of Social Construc-tionism." *Socialist Review* 17, 9–54.

Faderman, Lillian. 1981. *Surpassing the Love of Men. Romantic Friendship and Love Between Women from the Renaissance to the Present*. New York: Morrow.

Faderman, Lillian. 1991. *Odd Girls and Twilight Lovers. A History of Lesbian Life in Twentieth Century America*. New York: Columbia University Press.

Fuss, Diana, ed. 1991. *Inside/Out. Lesbian Theories, Gay Theories*. New York: Routledge.

Gay in America. 1989. 16 part series. *San Francisco Examiner*, June 4–June 25.

"Gay Voices, Black America". 1991. *The Advocate*, February 12.

Hall, Richard. 1988. "Gay Fiction Comes Home." *New York Times Book Review*, June 19.

Halperin, David M. 1990. *One Hundred Years of Homosexuality*. New York: Routledge.

Harris, Bertha. 1973. "The More Profound Nationality of Their Lesbianism: Lesbian Society in Paris in the 1920's." In Phyllis Birkby, ed., *Amazon Expedition*. New York: Times Change Press.

Hasbany, Richard, ed. 1989. *Religion and Homosexuality*. New York: Harrington Park Press.

Hinsch, Bret. 1990. *Passions of the Cut Sleeve. The Male Homosexual Tradition in China*. Berkeley, CA: University of California Press.

Jay, Karla and Joanne Glasgow, eds. 1990. *Lesbian Texts and Contexts.* New York: New York University Press.

Johnson, Susan. 1990. *Staying Power. Long Term Lesbian Couples.* Tallahassee, FL: Naiad Press.

Katz, Jonathan. 1976. *Gay American History.* New York: Thomas Y. Crowell.

Keen, Lisa M. 1989. "Beyond Stonewall." Four part series. *Washington Blade,* October 6–27.

Kehoe, Monika, ed. 1986. *Historical, Literary and Erotic Aspects of Lesbianism.* New York: Haworth Press.

Kitzinger, Celia. 1987. *The Social Construction of Lesbianism.* London: Sage Publications.

Lambda Legal Defense and Education Fund. 1990. *Cooperating Attorney Update.* New York: Lambda.

Lee, John Allen, ed. 1990. *Gay Aging Studies and Gerontology.* Special issue, *Journal of Homosexuality* 20 (3/4).

Licata, Salvatore and Robert Petersen, eds. 1985. *The Gay Past. A Collection of Historical Essays.* New York: Harrington Park Press.

Lorde, Audre. 1980. "The Erotic as Power." In Laura Lederer, ed., *Take Back the Night. Women Against Pornography.* New York: Morrow.

Miller, Neil. 1989. *In Search of Gay America.* New York: Atlantic Monthly Press.

Mohr, Richard. 1988. *Gays/Justice. A Study of Ethics, Society, and Law.* New York: Columbia University Press.

Mohr, Richard. 1989. "Gay Studies as Moral Vision." *Educational Theory* 39 (Spring), 121–32.

Murray, Stephen O. 1984. *Social Theory, Homosexual Realities.* Gai Saber Monographs, No. 3. New York: Gay Academic Union.

Nestle, Joan. 1987. *A Restricted Country.* Ithaca, NY: Firebrand Books.

Newton, Esther. 1979. *Mother Camp. Female Impersonators in America.* Chicago: University of Chicago Press.

Pharr, Suzanne. 1988. *Homophobia: a Weapon of Sexism.* Little Rock: Chardon Press.

Preston, John, ed. (1989). *Personal Dispatches. Writers Confront AIDS.* New York: St Martin's.

Rich, Adrienne. 1983. "Compulsory Heterosexuality and Lesbian Existence." In Ann Snitow and Christine Stansell, eds., *Powers of Desire. The Politics of Sexuality.* New York: Monthly Review Press.

Roscoe, Will. 1988. "Making History: the Challenge of Gay and Lesbian Studies." *Journal of Homosexuality* 15 (3/4), 1–40.

Rule, Jane. 1975. *Lesbian Images.* New York: Doubleday.

Schmidt, Robert, MD and Joseph Catalano, eds. 1989. "AIDS and an Aging Society." Special issue of *Generations* 13 (4).

Sedgwick, Eve Kosofsky. 1990. *Epistomology of the Closet*. Berkeley, CA: University of California Press.

Shewey, Don, ed. 1989. *Out Front. Contemporary Gay and Lesbian Plays*. New York: Weidenfeld & Nicolson.

Smith-Rosenberg, Carroll. 1975. "The Female World of Love and Ritual: Relations between Women in Nineteenth-Century America." *Signs* 1(1), 19–27.

Vicinus, Martha. 1985. *Independent Women: Work and Community for Single Women, 1850–1920*. Chicago: University of Chicago Press.

Vida, Ginny. 1992. *Our Right to Love. A Lesbian Resource Book*. Englewood Cliffs, NJ: Prentice Hall; 1st ed 1978.

Weeks, Jeffrey. 1981. *Sex, Politics, and Society. The Regulation of Sexuality since 1800*. London: Longman.

Zimmerman, Bonnie. 1990. *The Safe Sea of Women. Lesbian Fiction 1969–1989*. Boston, MA: Beacon Press.

INDEX